Two and Eight

The School for the Child from Two to Eight

By

ILSE FOREST

Associate Professor of Education

Bryn Mawr College

GINN AND COMPANY

BOSTON · NEW YORK · CHICAGO · LONDON · ATLANTA
DALLAS · COLUMBUS · SAN FRANCISCO

The Athenæum Press

GINN AND COMPANY · PRO-
PRIETORS · BOSTON · U.S.A.

PREFACE

The content of this book was gathered and organized in connection with a course entitled "Kindergarten-Primary Education," given by the writer for several summer sessions of the Connecticut State Teachers' College held at Yale University.

The book itself and the course out of which it has grown are intended, first of all, as an introduction to the study of lower-school methods and curricula for students of early education. Judging by the summer-school enrollment, some of these students are already kindergarten and primary teachers; others are prospective teachers.

A second group of people who have found the course useful and may find the book equally so are supervisors of lower-school work who desire more information about the activity curriculum and who are interested in studying the means through which nursery school, kindergarten, and primary work may be more completely integrated.

The writer hopes that the book may serve a still larger group, including students of general education, and perhaps also the increasing number of parents who are taking an active interest in school affairs.

Current movements in psychology and widespread social reorganization are constantly adding to the interest and the challenge of lower-school teaching. The day when a kindergarten or primary teacher was selected purely because of her motherly qualities and her placid disposition has passed. There is now enough involved in the profession of lower-school teaching to challenge the most intelligent of highly trained specialists, in addition to the perennial satisfaction of working with little children and observing the rapidly changing pageant of growth during these early years.

So far as possible this book presents the many-sided character of education in the lower school, indicating the various movements which are influencing it and the very different ways in which gifted teachers may make individual contributions to the field. Many practical discussions and illustrations are included, which have grown out of the writer's contacts with her adult students and her own experiences as lower-school teacher and supervisor.

For several units of work described in Chapter VI, for continued encouragement and many helpful suggestions, the author is indebted to Anna McManus, training teacher in the Roger Sherman School, one of the training centers of the New Haven Normal School. Helen Armstrong of the Haverford Friends School, Haverford, Pennsylvania, contributed the unit on airplanes, appearing in Chapter VI; Helen Shanley and Marion Goode of the Abraham Lincoln School, New Haven, the "Library Project," used in Chapter XI. Dr. Lester K. Ade, principal of the New Haven State Normal School, courteously gave permission for the use of the pictures and descriptive material taken from the Roger Sherman School, appearing in Chapter VI. For the pictures appearing in Chapter VIII the author wishes to express her thanks to the Department of Industrial Arts of the Philadelphia public schools.

The writer wishes to express her grateful appreciation of the courtesy accorded by the several publishers who have permitted the use of copyrighted material: to the Bureau of Publications, Teachers College, Columbia University, for permission to use the tables from C. H. Mann's study "How Schools Use their Time," appearing in Chapter VII; to Greenberg, publisher, for permission to use the timetables from Caroline Pratt's *Before Books* and *Experimental Practice in the City and Country School*, appearing in the same chapter; to the Lincoln School of Teachers College for the table taken from Lula Wright's book *A First Grade at Work*; to the Barnes Foundation for permission to quote from the symposium *Art and Education*, by Dewey and others, the matter appearing in Chapter IX; to Charles Scribner's Sons for the privilege of quoting from the Introduction to *A Conduct Curriculum for the Kindergarten and First Grade*, by Patty S. Hill and others, and from *First Experiences with Literature*, by Alice Dalgliesh, the matter appearing on pages 177 and 178; to the Macmillan Company for permission to include the matter from *Interest and Ability in Reading*, by Arthur I. Gates, appearing in Chapter XI; to the Macmillan Company and to the author, Dr. Arnold Gesell, for permission to reproduce from *Infancy and Human Growth* the developmental schedule appearing on page 248.

For reading the manuscript of Chapter XIV and making many valuable suggestions thanks are due to Dr. Esther Katz Rosen, of Philadelphia. For the preparation of the index the writer is indebted to her aunt, Elizabeth Greanellé; for the typing and general organization of the manuscript, to her mother, Helene R. G. Bosch.

ILSE FOREST

CONTENTS

THE SCHOOL FOR THE CHILD
FROM TWO TO EIGHT

CHAPTER I

KINDERGARTENS OLD AND NEW

Kindergartens found their way into the American public school as early as 1873, when, under the direction of William T. Harris, United States Commissioner of Education, Miss Susan Blow opened one in a St. Louis school. A few years later, at the Philadelphia Exposition, there was a demonstration of kindergarten work which brought it to the attention of the American people. After that kindergartens increased very rapidly. They were introduced into settlements and day nurseries and were organized privately for the benefit of the children of the rich. Gradually but surely public-school systems began to take the responsibility for kindergarten education, and the private enterprises became less numerous and less important.

The American kindergarten enjoyed the great advantage of starting under the aegis of an unusually fine and cultivated group of people. Dr. Harris was a scholar, and Miss Blow a very brilliant woman. They were both members of the Concord school of philosophical thought, and they believed sincerely in the value of kindergarten education because they held the philosophy of Friedrich Froebel, its German founder, in great esteem. Mrs. Horace Mann and her sister, Miss Elizabeth Peabody, also were members of the Concord school, and they too worked for the development of Froebel's educational theories. Miss Peabody had founded in the city of Boston, in 1860, the first kindergarten for English-speaking children in America. This pioneer kindergarten was under private auspices.

Intelligence and a certain scholarly interest were required to understand the basic principles of Froebel's philosophy of education. Therefore in the early days of kindergarten training there were attracted to the profession young women of culture and ability whose work and whose devotion to their ideals were a great credit to the teaching profession. Unfortunately the interest in Froebel's mystical theories and the preoccupation with these, rather than with the study of children, made these early kindergartners blind to the many absurdities and deficiencies inherent in Froebel's ideas. For absurdities and deficiencies there were, despite the fact that Froebel was perhaps the first educator to appreciate the value of play for its own sake and to state clearly that the self-activity of the child was the ideal method of learning.

Miss Blow, who was a German scholar, devoted much of her life to the study of Froebel's theories and to the development of a kindergarten program based on these theories. This program — the "Blow Program," as it was called — quite generally determined the procedure in the kindergartens in the East for a period of about twenty years. It was organized around the mother-play sequence of Froebel, and it prescribed the way in which the Froebelian play materials, the "gifts" and "occupations," were to be used. The games, too, were planned in a definite order. Thus Froebel's theories, often, as he originally stated them, very remote from the practical needs and interests of children, became yet more remote and far more rigidly organized in the hands of the first generation of American kindergartners. Preoccupied as they were with his mystical philosophy, his American interpreters lost sight of the delightful play spirit which lent both charm and practical value to Froebel's own educational work.

An adequate discussion of the educational philosophy of Froebel is beyond the compass of this brief chapter. Froebel himself gives the clearest presentation of it in his really important book *The Education of Man.* He was a Hegelian; but he was further influenced by some of the minor philosophers of his time, and his personal bias was decidedly mystical. He believed that "in all things there lives and reigns an eternal law. This law is Unity; this Unity is God."[1] He believed also that all growth and development take place according to one law, beginning with unity, proceeding through diversity, and ending by a return to unity. In the course of this process opposites are evolved, and these opposites are then reconciled or "mediated" through a series of orderly steps. The child, Froebel thought, has within him at birth a presentiment of the universal laws of life. Innate ideas of great truths are, he believed, slumbering in the soul. The awakening process, in the course of which the child becomes aware of the laws of his nature and of the world, takes place as he learns the significance of certain symbols which express these laws. The mother play, the gifts, and the occupations were intended for use as symbols, to interpret the world to the child, to awaken his slumbering presentiments of the law of unity and diversity.

Now the mother-play sequence actually represents a series of simple, spontaneous games which mothers play with their babies. Froebel gathered them together by the very sensible method of journeying about the German countryside and watching mothers and babies. But the charming simplicity of these natural games was quite spoiled in the kindergarten by a forced attempt to see in these finger plays symbols of universal laws. Moreover, plays and games which were delightful for real babies became rather silly when they were used with children four and five years old, most of whom are quite beyond the finger-play stage. Where the Blow program was the order of the day each mother play was the center of the kindergarten's activity for about one week. In the autumn one began with "The Play with the Limbs," pushing with the hands and kicking in time with the music of the game. There followed in succession the "Falling, Falling" (difficult to dramatize in kindergarten, for it meant the game of letting the baby fall a few inches and then catching him in his mother's arms), "All's Gone," "The Weather Vane," "Pat-a-cake," and all the others. "Pat-a-cake" was stressed at Thanksgiving, because it was supposed to symbolize co-operation in the production of the world's goods.

Frobel's insistence on the law of development through the reconciliation of opposites is well illustrated in his series of building gifts.

The gifts are a series of permanent play materials intended to give the child familiarity with the geometric forms and their derivation and, by the use of these as symbols, to help him realize universal truths. The first gift is a ball, symbol of unity and completeness, with which the child was encouraged to play so that through it he might apprehend the unity of the world. It was presented to him on a string, and he was directed to play with it in such a way that the directions "up and down," "side to side," "back and forth," and "round and round" became clear to him. In Miss Blow's program for the kindergarten year, which dominated the work for twenty years or more, four-year-old children were expected to follow passively the direction of a kindergartner in going through all these motions with a crocheted ball attached to a string.

The second gift is a set of three blocks — ball, cylinder, and cube. These represent unity, in the form of the ball; diversity, in the cube with its six faces, twelve edges, and eight corners; and a mediating form between the two, in the cylinder. They also represent rest, in the cube; motion, in the ball; and a combination of rest and motion in the cylinder, with its one curved surface. The second-gift blocks were provided with small dowel sticks fitting into holes made in the blocks themselves. The sticks could be inserted, and the blocks twirled to illustrate to the three-year-olds and four-year-olds the apparent changes in form of the cube and the cylinder with motion.

The third gift is a two-inch wooden cube divided into eight one-inch cubes. In the traditional kindergarten this was

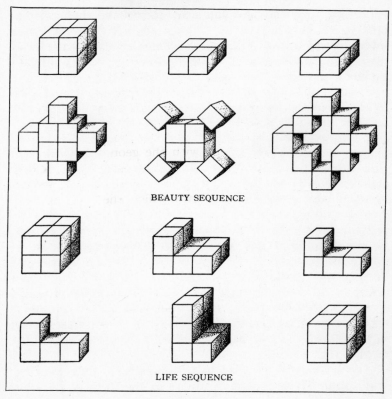

BEAUTY SEQUENCE

LIFE SEQUENCE

Third Gift

presented in a box and very carefully opened so that the
child might first see a complete cube, then divide it into equal
parts, and then recombine the parts to form the original
unity. The normal impulse to knock the blocks down and
build with them was curbed; and the child was made to
build in unison with other children, following the teacher's
direction until a complete sequence (or series) of forms had
been achieved in an orderly fashion. These sequences were
of two sorts: beauty sequences, or geometric patterns; and
life sequences, or the orderly transformation of the original

cube into a "bed," two small "beds," two "chairs," and so on. At the very end the children were allowed to "invent" in comparative freedom for perhaps five minutes, but any disorderly tumbling about of the blocks was frowned upon.

The fourth gift also is made from a two-inch wooden cube, and is cut into eight rectangular parallelepipeds, or "bricks." The fifth and sixth gifts are cut from three-inch cubes, and include a greater variety of parts than the third and fourth, but all the building gifts were presented to the child in the same stereotyped fashion. True, the good kindergartner was supposed to derive the forms and patterns through "suggestion" from the children, but these suggestions were rarely effective without much prompting.

The remaining gifts are designed to acquaint the child with surfaces — rectangular, circular, triangular; with lines — curved and straight; and with the properties of the point, which was usually represented by lentils. All were developed in sequences; all designed to illustrate the law of development through the mediation or reconciliation of opposites.

The occupations are a series of handwork activities: pricking, to help the child combine points into designs; the sewing of straight lines, slanting lines, circles, squares, triangles, and the derivation of designs from these; weaving, to teach the child how to derive a surface; interlacing and intertwining; and various sorts of construction work. All were used according to rule, with a little encouragement for very restricted "invention"; most were far too exacting from the point of view of eyestrain and muscle strain; none were planned to help the child's play life in any special way.

Not even the games of the traditional kindergarten escaped symbolic interpretation: the circle games, the "Knights," "Pigeon House," "Bird's Nest," and the "Garden Bed," were all dramatized for their symbolic value. Toys and playthings other than the gifts and occupations were tolerated for use before the kindergarten day began and by some of the freer spirits during the recess period, but were definitely frowned upon by Miss Blow.

Such was the prevailing theory of the kindergarten for the first thirty-five years or so of its development in this country. Yet it was often the one bright spot in an otherwise dingy settlement, and many a kindergarten teacher showed imagination as well as devotion in transforming an abandoned church basement into a presentable classroom. In many a forbidding public-school edifice the kindergarten was a refreshing spot where grade teachers surreptitiously stole in to get new ideas for mounting pictures, and primary-grade children returned for pleasant visits long after their own kindergarten days.

Among the various kindergarten training schools preparing young teachers there soon appeared many shades of difference in their manner of interpreting kindergarten theory. Strongest in their adherence to the whole of Froebel's philosophy as Dr. Harris, Miss Blow, and other American idealists had translated and developed it were the training schools at Pratt Institute in Brooklyn, the Froebel League of New York City, and the Elizabeth Harrison Training School in Chicago. Simpler in theory and much more spontaneous in method was the work of Maria Kraus-Boelte in New York City and of the Wheelock Training School, Boston. The professional standards of the teachers and students in these schools were very high; devotion to the cause of kindergarten education amounted to little less than a religion in some cases. On the whole an admirable group of women controlled the progress of the movement.

The reaction against the traditional system began in Louisville, Kentucky, in the work of Miss Anna Bryan and her gifted student, Miss Patty Hill. Very early in the days of the Louisville training school, children were allowed to play imaginatively with the gifts, making paper dolls to fit the beds made with the third and fourth gifts, and generally considering the gift blocks as toys rather than a sacrosanct collection of symbols. These innovations would have been frowned upon by the conservatives had they known about them; but Louisville was a little outside the beaten path of kindergarten development, and the result was that this experimentation went on quietly for several years without attracting much comment. Then it attracted significant comment from Dr. John Dewey, who became acquainted with Miss Bryan and her kindergarten theories in Chicago and who saw in this more freely organized class for little children a concrete illustration of some of his educational principles. During his years at Chicago Dr. Dewey watched the development of the work in Louisville with interest, and his suggestions inspired more and more experimentation. The kindergarten in Louisville became the mecca of those who would study innovations in kindergarten procedure, and all too soon it was regarded by the conservative group as a genuine danger point which threatened the values inherent in the pure Froebelian methods. A really bitter controversy went on for more than ten years; the records of the meetings of the International Kindergarten Union for the years 1892 to 1905 give one a clear picture of what the struggle was. The conservative group believed that their cause must be defended at all costs; the radicals, under the leadership of Miss Hill and Miss Alice Temple of Chicago, believed that changes were necessary and inevitable. The progressive group had at least one asset against which no opposition could prevail: from the beginning they had allied themselves with the projects of the leaders in the new movement for child study and child hygiene. G. Stanley Hall and William H. Burnham were the teachers of the new group of kindergartners, and this alliance with the scientific movement in education made the radical group invincible. It also led to changes in the methods and materials of kindergarten education far more radical than the radicals themselves had considered at the beginning.

The traditional kindergarten had been conspicuously lax in the attention given to the physical needs of the child. A teacher working in a settlement who paid too much attention to the health and nutrition of her kindergarten children was adversely criticized. The conservatives thought physical care was distinctly not her job. On the other hand, the new group emphasized the health of the child and saw the possibilities of the kindergarten as a health measure and safeguard. The very materials of the traditional kindergarten violated the laws of hygiene. No one could keep crocheted gift balls clean (they were laundered once a year or so, with doubtful results). The elaborate moves required in the building-gift work, and the fine co-ordination demanded by occupations, were responsible for nervousness and tremors which the orthodox group refused to admit but which the progressive group soon noticed, once Dr. Hall directed their attention toward studying children rather than exclusively revering Froebel.

Through their sincere co-operation with the movement for child study and hygiene, the progressive group effectively broke the barrier which had made of the kindergarten an institution set apart. The desire to subject Froebelian theories and methods to the impartial scrutiny of modern science forever dissipated the air of mystery which had surrounded kindergarten teachings in the earlier days. The interest expressed by progressive kindergartners was fully reciprocated by the child-study experts, who found in freely organized groups of children four and five years old a laboratory for psychological study which was invaluable. The closest sort of co-operation between the two groups was made possible with the development of departments of kindergarten education at Columbia and The University of Chicago. In 1904 Miss Hill was called to Teachers College, Columbia, as a lecturer. In 1910 she was made head of the kindergarten department. At Chicago the work of Miss Alice Temple created another center for the advanced study of the problems of early childhood.

Meanwhile a new movement in early education made itself felt in America. Maria Montessori, a physician in a psychiatric clinic in Rome, worked for many years on the development of a set of sense-training equipment for use in the teaching of mental defectives. Later she conceived the idea of using these materials in the education of young normal children. The municipal government of Rome made it possible for Madame Montessori to put her plans into effect by inviting her to open a school for young children in a model tenement block which had just been erected. She called her project a *casa dei bambini* (babies' house), and her purpose in the *casa* was to create for the young children of working mothers a wholesome environment which should serve as a demonstration of proper methods of child care. She introduced the sense-training materials in much the same way as the early kindergartens used Froebelian gifts and occupations. However, there was one important difference from the Froebelians in her method: instead of placing the responsibility for directing the work upon a teacher, the material itself was supposed to be self-corrective. Each child was permitted to choose what material he preferred to work with, but he must work with it in such a way that he correctly performed the task set by the material. For instance, one unit of the didactic apparatus is the "Montessori tower," a set of nine graduated cubes which the child is expected to pile correctly, with the largest at the bottom and the smallest at the top. He is not permitted to vary this performance in any way; for example, he may not turn his tower into a train and push it about the floor. Should he do so, the tower is removed, and he is directed to select another plaything.

One of the most interesting activities in the *casa dei bambini* was the preparation and serving of the midday meal. In this the children participated with great joy to themselves and great appreciation on the part of visitors. The picturesqueness of the Montessori school and Madame Montessori's own charming personality were very impressive, and soon a *casa dei bambini* for the children of the rich was opened in Rome. The idea spread to England, where Montessori schools became very popular, and also to America, where they were critically examined.

Madame Montessori lectured in America in 1913 and 1914,

illustrating her descriptions by moving pictures of the children at work and play in her schools. Interest was aroused, and Montessori schools were opened under private auspices, both settlement schools and private schools. But the idea never took very firm root in American educational thought because of the progress which had already been made here in the study of children and the development of a consistent educational psychology. Madame Montessori's educational work was in many ways delightful and successful, but her philosophy and psychology have never stood the test of frank scientific criticism. Her theory of sense-training is based upon a discarded psychological doctrine, the so-called "faculty psychology," and her very slight provision for dramatic play and imaginative work also seems a shortcoming from our American point of view.

Yet her work has not been without its effect upon the development of the modern kindergarten. The importance of letting little children participate in the practical work of the school was impressed upon kindergartners, and the Montessori emphasis upon a passive, quiet teacher was a good corrective for the average overstimulating kindergarten director. Sensory games came into new vogue, and in many places some parts of the "didactic apparatus," as Madame Montessori designated the sense-training materials, were introduced for use with the youngest kindergarten children.

The popularity of the newer and freer kindergarten work grew by leaps and bounds between 1912 and 1922. This was especially true in the Middle West, where the Froebelian tradition had never been firmly entrenched and where certain German immigrants had early established some very simple kindergartens for German-speaking children. These were probably much more like Froebel's own group than like the very formal groups sponsored by Miss Blow and the Concord school.

The spread of the progressive-kindergarten idea created new problems in the training of teachers, especially the training of teachers in service. The new kindergartens were gradually equipped with more toys to stimulate vigorous large-muscle activity and promote dramatic play. They were also equipped with materials from which the child might construct things which would really help him in his play: with roving for making rugs and hammocks, with clay in generous amounts for modeling doll dishes, with wood for the construction of doll furniture and other toys. Large floor blocks replaced the tiny ones of the Froebelian gifts. Few teachers at first knew how to use these new materials effectively. To many of the lazy-minded it all looked easy. Holding children to a set of formal gift and occupation lessons required force of character and some teaching skill; letting them play with dolls and doll dishes required little planning and, it was thought, less control. In a certain Eastern city in the year 1918, after a lecture in the course of which there had been shown pictures of the activities in the Horace Mann Kindergarten, a young teacher remarked: "Well, that settles it. I'll order washtubs for doll clothes on the next requisition, and stop working so hard."

Certainly many kindergartens went through a period of confusion and readjustment. The Froebelian kindergartner had to know certain things rather definitely when she was given her diploma: to wit, Froebel's educational theory and the proper way to use his games, gifts, and occupations. The young progressive kindergartner escaped the discipline of this older training and often, as a result, lacked clear-cut ideas and the requisite technique to accomplish *something* with a group of small children. Her problem was much more difficult than that of a teacher trained in the old school; and yet many people, sometimes even the teacher herself, thought it was easier.

A general clarification of the aims of the kindergarten and a great improvement in method have been achieved in the last ten or fifteen years through the gradual unification of the kindergarten and first grade. Under the old regime the kindergarten teacher thought herself a woman set apart, with a vision impossible to share with her colleagues in the first, second, and third primary grades. Often she openly said how much she disliked letting her children go on into the grades. The inference was that when they did go into the grades they would no longer be understood and no longer educated according to truly ideal principles. The first-grade teacher reciprocated by commenting none too gently on the fact that kindergarten children were difficult to manage when they reached first grade, more difficult than children who entered directly from home at the age of six.

Gradually but very steadily this division has been wearing away. It became less pronounced once kindergarten teachers grew to be really critical of their own methods and attentively studious of children. Study soon showed that the kindergarten child and the first-grade child are so nearly related in the span of development that it is senseless to make much distinction between them. Then came the mental-testing movement, which proved that in actual mental age there was great overlapping between kindergarten and first-grade children. Why, then, should reading be forbidden the one and forced upon the other? Accordingly, "connecting classes" were formed, in which older kindergarten children were taught reading. Sometimes the first-grade teacher went into the kindergarten room to do this teaching; sometimes the children were sent to her. In other cases the kindergarten teacher prepared herself for the teaching of reading and took care of the group without help from the first grade.

Then, too, the kindergarten activities began to be extended upward into the first grade. If the child of five gets great joy and benefit from project work and the free use of industrial-arts material, why not the first-grade child of six? One barrier after another was broken down, until in many schools there has been achieved a rather complete unification between kindergarten and grade work.

Of course this process began with the first informal visits of first-grade teachers to kindergarten rooms to get ideas on a few subjects; but it was furthered with great vigor by the general movement for progressive education, by the development of educational tests and measures, and by the gradual evolution of the philosophy of the progressive school under the guidance of such leaders as Dr. Dewey and Dr. Kilpatrick. Rigid division among parts of the school process is impossible according to this new philosophy, which takes as its basic principle the essentially unitary character of the growth process, and ideally admits no gaps between the educational policies of the kindergarten, the grades, the secondary school, and the college.

In the spread of modern educational philosophy and the gradual growth of understanding between kindergarten and grade teachers, organized associations of kindergartners have played no small part. The strong professional interest and pride characteristic of the first kindergarten group in America led to the early development of professional organizations. In 1884 the Froebel Institute met at Madison, Wisconsin, in connection with the annual gathering of the National Education Association. As a result of this meeting there was formed the Department of Kindergarten Education of the National Education Association. At the meetings of this association Miss Hill and Miss Anna Bryan read their first telling papers in criticism of the traditional Froebelian methods. In 1892 was organized the International Kindergarten Union, which, as its title implies, included within its membership kindergarten workers the world over. The work of this organization in furthering the development of early education in this country has been characterized throughout by clarity of vision, integrity of purpose, and breadth of outlook. Through its meetings and publications both conservatives and progressives found a hearing in the days when the radicals were contending for their own. Again through its meetings the contact of the kindergarten group with specialists in other fields, such as child psychology, physical hygiene, and primary education, was continually encouraged and strengthened. In 1925 the I.K.U. first published its own periodical, *Childhood Education*. From the first this periodical has presented a wide range of well-selected material designed to bring the worker with kindergarten children into real sympathy with the nursery and primary teacher; above all, the magazine has been directed toward giving the teacher of young children sound scientific information about psychology, nutrition, and other aspects of child welfare. For the first five issues the magazine was exclusively the publication of the I.K.U. The sixth volume was published with the co-operation of the National Council of Primary Education and the National Association for Nursery Education. In 1929 the I.K.U. convention undertook a serious reorganization of its purposes and activities, and emerged from this reorganization with a new name and an admittedly wider purpose. It became the Association for Childhood Education, the A.C.E.; and the magazine *Childhood Education* became the publication of this reorganized I.K.U. Volumes VII and VIII of *Childhood Education* accordingly were published by the A.C.E. in co-operation with the National Council of Primary Education and the National Association for Nursery Education. Then the Primary Council decided to merge its identity with the A.C.E., with the result that in 1933 there appeared the periodical *Childhood Education*, published by the A.C.E. So the I.K.U. resigned its name and, as it were, its privacy, to become the foundation of a new and broader organization, designed to include within its activities all efforts to educate and care for children of preschool and early school years. In so doing, it would seem to have fulfilled the vision of its early leaders, who hoped that it would be a worthy exponent of the best and finest in early education as they then saw it. Some of these leaders are now active in the new organization; others have passed on and given place to a group of younger members to many of whom the Froebelian theory is but a tradition, trained, as they have been, in the more scientific modern training schools. These share with their older colleagues the vision of a better educational opportunity for early childhood years. Where once this better educational opportunity meant intensive education along Froebelian lines, today it means a wider and wider application of the best in scientific thought to the care and education of little children.

Speaking in 1916, Miss Hill mentioned "three distinct stages of the kindergartens of yesterday." The first of these was the naïve stage, in which the kindergarten was simply the concrete expression of Froebel's educational ideals. The second period, according to Miss Hill, was a period of arrested development: "the kindergarten fell in love with itself," and kindergartners as a whole formed an exclusive, self-satisfied, rather intolerant group. The third period was torn by the strife of the opposing factions, conservative and radical. The fourth period represents the kindergarten's coming of age, with many of its leaders "ready to forswear both the name and the system, when better ones are found." This readiness was put to the test in the reorganization of the I.K.U. In all probability it will be put to further tests in the years to come.

The work of the newer, freer type of kindergarten must be judged according to a less definite set of standards than those which were once set for the Froebelian school. Results are in some ways more intangible, because they must be considered in terms of the actual growth of the children rather than in terms of so much of the Blow program successfully completed. The new methods leave much wider scope for the originality of the teacher, but perhaps also wider latitude for careless and unintelligent work. One of the very pressing problems of kindergarten work today is the development of adequate systems of recording progress — adequate, and at the same time concise enough to allow them to be kept faithfully without adding too much to the detail of the kindergarten teacher's work. The projects and units of work which have replaced the old gift sequences need to be described objectively, so that methods and outcomes may be evaluated fairly. The growth of each child in specific social habits also should be recorded.

The Froebelian kindergarten was developed through the blind faith of a group of individuals in one philosophy, consistent but rather fantastic. The new kindergarten has been evolved with respect to the demands of modern educational psychology. The older kindergarten was a highly specialized activity with no relation, either theoretical or practical, to the work of the primary grades. The new kindergarten is an integral part of a modern primary school, closely related in all its work to the activities of the primary grades. The early kindergartners were conscious of belonging to a special clique; the modern kindergartner is a member of a school staff, with a particular piece of work to do. Where children once sat at squared-surfaced tables and followed the minute directions of a teacher, they now move about freely from sand table to workbench and from block-building to a vigorous turn on the swing. Where once they played elaborate ring games, they now move rhythmically and freely to the accompaniment of good music. Instead of spending a year at work and play unrelated to either their own spontaneous interests or the work of the primary grades, they now have the experience of a preprimary year of wholesome group play leading directly into the work of the first grade. But the activities in the new kindergarten exact more of the teacher rather than less in comparison with the demands of the old.

BIBLIOGRAPHY

BLOW, SUSAN, "Kindergarten Education," in *Monographs on Education in the United States*, edited by Nicholas Murray Butler. J. B. Lyon Co., Albany, N. Y., 1900.

A brief but thorough exposition of kindergarten theory as it developed in this country under the early leaders of the movement. The "conservative" point of view concisely explained.

Childhood Education, Vols. I–IX. Published by the Association for Childhood Education, Washington, D. C., 1925–1933.

A thoughtful study of the files of this periodical gives the reader an interesting and significant picture of recent and current trends in kindergarten education.

DAVIS, MARY DABNEY. General Practice in Kindergarten Education in the United States. National Education Association, Washington, D. C., 1925.

A comprehensive study of kindergarten practice made in co-operation with the Research Committee of the Department of Kindergarten Education of the National Education Association.

DAVIS, MARY DABNEY. Kindergarten-Primary Education, *United States Office of Education Bulletin No. 30*, 1930.

Contains valuable information in statistical form.

DAVIS, M. D., and KEESECKER, W. W. State Legislation Relating to Kindergartens in Effect 1931, *United States Office of Education Pamphlet No. 30*, 1932.

Deutsches Archiv für Jugendwohlfahrt, Vol. III. Taschenbuch für Kindergärtnerinnen und Hortnerinnen. Berlin, 1931.

FOREST, ILSE. "Preschool Education," in the Encyclopaedia of the Social Sciences, Vol. XII.

A convenient summary, including both kindergarten and nursery-school developments.

FOREST, ILSE. Preschool Education, a Historical and Critical Study, pp. 154–190. Macmillan, New York, 1927.

A brief historical sketch of the Froebelian kindergarten and the Montessori school.

FROEBEL, FRIEDRICH. Education by Development (translated by J. Jarvis). Appleton, New York, 1902.

An elaboration of Froebel's basic principles of education.

FROEBEL, FRIEDRICH. Education of Man (translated by Hailmann). Appleton, New York, 1892.

Froebel's most significant work.

FROEBEL, FRIEDRICH. Letters on the Kindergarten (translated by Michaelis and Moore). Bardeen, Syracuse, New York, 1896.

A simple and conversational treatment of Froebel's educational views.

FROEBEL, FRIEDRICH. Mottoes and Commentaries of Friedrich Froebel's Mother-Play (translated by H. R. Eliot). Appleton, New York, 1908.

The complete mother-play sequence as taught in the earlier kindergarten training schools and outlined in the Blow program.

FROEBEL, FRIEDRICH. Pedagogics of the Kindergarten (translated by J. Jarvis). Appleton, New York, 1895.

An elaboration of Froebel's ideas about the gifts and occupations.

HARRISON, ELIZABETH. The Montessori Method and the Kindergarten, *United States Bureau of Education Bulletin No. 28*, 1914.

A criticism of Madame Montessori from the Froebelian point of view.

HILL, PATTY S. "Changes in Curriculum and Method in Kindergarten Education," *Childhood Education* (November, 1925), Vol. II, pp. 99–106.

A paper read before the Department of Kindergarten Education of the National Education Association, Indianapolis, June 29, 1925.

HILL, PATTY S. (Ed.). A Conduct Curriculum for the Kindergarten and First Grade. Scribner, New York, 1924.

> A thorough analysis of modern kindergarten procedure in terms of educational principles, objectives, activities, and outcomes. The introduction gives an interesting account of how the conduct curriculum was formulated.

HILL, PATTY S. (Ed.). "Experimental Studies in Kindergarten Theory and Practice," *Teachers College Record* (January, 1914), Vol. XV, No. 1.

> Contains articles by John Dewey, Meredith Smith, Grace L. Brown, Julia Wade Abbot, Luella Palmer.

HILL, PATTY S. "Kindergartens of Yesterday and Tomorrow," *Kindergarten-Primary Magazine* (September, 1916), Vol. XXIX, pp. 4–6.

> Quoted in this chapter.

International Kindergarten Union, Committee of Nineteen: The Kindergarten. Houghton Mifflin, Boston, 1913.

> Three reports on theory and practice representing the conservative, radical, and radical-conservative viewpoints, by Susan Blow, Nina Vandewalker, and Lucy Wheelock.

International Kindergarten Union, Committee of Nineteen: Pioneers of the Kindergarten in America. Century, New York, 1924.

KILPATRICK, WILLIAM H. Froebel's Kindergarten Principles critically Examined. Macmillan, New York, 1916.

> A thorough criticism of the Froebelian kindergarten from the point of view of American educational theory.

KILPATRICK, WILLIAM H. The Montessori System Examined. Houghton Mifflin, Boston, 1914.

> The ideas of Madame Montessori are keenly analyzed and criticized in the light of American educational psychology.

KLEIN, FÉLIX. Mon Filleul au "Jardin d'Enfants." Libraire Armand Colin, Paris, 1920.

> A description of the methods used in French kindergartens, including a discussion of Froebel's gifts and occupations.

LOCHHEAD, JEWELL. The Education of Young Children in England, Teachers College Contributions to Education, No. 521. Columbia University, 1932.

> Discusses the relation of kindergarten methods to the infant school.

MONTESSORI, MARIA. The Montessori Method (3d ed., translated by Anna George). Stokes, New York, 1912.

> Madame Montessori's description of her theory and method.

MUDGETT, MILDRED D. European Schools for Preschool Children. Educational Office, American Association of University Women, Washington, D.C., 1927.

National Society for the Scientific Study of Education, Sixth Yearbook, Part II (University of Chicago Press, 1907): "The Kindergarten and its Relation to Elementary Education."

Contains discussions by Ada V. S. Harris, E. A. Kirkpatrick, Maria Kraus-Boelte, Patty S. Hill, Harriette Melissa Mills, Nina Vandewalker.

National Society for the Scientific Study of Education, Seventh Yearbook, Part II (University of Chicago Press, 1908): "The Co-ordination of Kindergarten and Elementary School."

A supplement to the Sixth Yearbook, Part II. Contains articles by B. C. Gregory, Jennie B. Merrill, Bertha Payne, Margaret Giddings. Emphasizes "the practical problem of how to co-ordinate the work of kindergarten and first grade," in contrast to the more theoretical discussion in the Sixth Yearbook.

National Society for the Scientific Study of Education, Twenty-eighth Yearbook, Part I (Public School Publishing Company, Bloomington, Illinois, 1929): Chapter IX, "The Kindergarten in Relation to Preschool and Parental Education."

PARKER, S. C., and TEMPLE, ALICE. Unified Kindergarten and First-Grade Teaching. Ginn, Boston, 1925.

Chapter II gives a history of unification.

SIMONIC, ANTON. Kindergartenpädagogik. Hölder-Pichler-Tempsky, Vienna, 1931.

A comprehensive handbook for kindergarten-training students, including every phase of child care from physical hygiene to kindergarten methods and materials.

VANDEWALKER, NINA. The Kindergarten in American Education. Macmillan, New York, 1908.

An interesting historical account.

White House Conference on Child Health and Protection, Section III, B, Nursery Education: "Education and Training." Appleton-Century, New York, 1931.

Interesting data on privately run kindergartens.

CHAPTER II

THE CHANGING PRIMARY SCHOOL

The kindergarten owed its growth and development to the interest in humanitarian movements which was characteristic of the nineteenth century. Froebel developed his plan for the education of little children at a time when, in both Europe and America, society as a whole was thinking increasingly in terms of the right of all individuals, whether young or old or weak or strong, to opportunity for self-development. The primary school, on the other hand, arose as a practical means of solving an inescapable social problem. In order to preserve the spiritual heritage of the race, it was necessary that the young generation learn to read and write. Reading and writing were special skills which could not well be acquired through the incidental learning which went on in the home and the primitive community. They had to be taught; and when community life had developed to the point where its adult members generally had no leisure to teach, schools were organized to carry out this function.

Jean Jacques Rousseau, champion of youth in a world of men which he considered utterly corrupt, spoke of reading as "the scourge of infancy." Such through the centuries reading undoubtedly was, between the ignorance and stupidity of teachers and the vast amount of symbolic learning the young child must achieve in acquiring the ability to read. There is little in symbolic learning *per se* which appeals immediately to the young child's interest, and only rarely in the world's history do we find adults genuinely concerned for the child's happiness in his work. In the schools of ancient Athens children indeed learned to read as joyously as they learned to sing and play, and this was true whenever and wherever schools tried to return to the Athenian aim of education. The will to develop a beautiful soul within a beautiful body always makes for wholesome living and learning. But this ancient ideal was not compatible with early Christian teaching, with its emphasis on original corruption and the need of salvation. So for centuries most of what was happy and spontaneous in early childhood education was lost.

In the drab history of elementary teaching during the Middle Ages, the Renaissance, and the early modern period, there are, it is true, a few colorful pages. Such, for instance, is the story of the Palace School of Mantua, conducted by a great teacher, Vittorino da Feltre, in the early years of the fifteenth century. His work influenced a few other teachers to work joyously with children; but the net result was not very great and benefited mostly the little sons and daughters of the rich. One can therefore sympathize with Rousseau's assertion and appreciate some of the circumstances which made primary education a misery to most children. To begin with, from its earliest history the school became a special institution, apart from the life of the community, where special skills were learned. When boys and girls came into the schoolroom they left their real interests behind them, for their real life was not there. With few exceptions this was no less true of the children educated by tutors in wealthy homes than it was of those less fortunately placed in society. Comparatively few of them could have experienced much that was really thrilling in their school tasks. Those to whom school work was vital were probably those whose intelligence ratings, did we but know them, would have placed them in the genius group. Then, too, only a few really great teachers understood anything of what we today call child psychology or educational psychology. The child was looked upon as a baby adult, and treated accordingly. He was expected to respond as an adult does to a teaching situation.

These things were universally true of primary education until Rousseau's day and for a long time after his life and work. Only for the last century has the question of method received serious attention. The interest in finding better ways of teaching has been the joint product of the humanitarian outlook and the interest in the problem of mass education which became prominent with the development of the great national school systems.

Until the end of the eighteenth century universal education was an ideal held only by a few enlightened individuals. Martin Luther, in a famous letter to "The Mayors and Aldermen of all the Cities of Germany on behalf of Christian Schools," had urged the provision of elementary education for all the citizens of a Christian state. Centuries before Luther's time Charlemagne, in his famous Capitularies, had commanded the establishment of schools throughout the Holy Roman Empire and had, through his *missi dominici* (messengers of the lord or king) provided a crude sort of supervision; but both in practice and in prevailing theory education was provided for a selected group only until the beginning of the last century. Then Germany and France, having developed strong national consciousness, set to work to develop strong national school systems which should in their turn create national unity through a common education. In Great Britain the idea of a national school system developed more slowly. Government interest in education was expressed through large subsidies to religious societies already engaged in educational work, rather than through the rapid development of national schools. But here too the principle of universal, free primary education gained ground rapidly with the passing of the years.

Simultaneously with the development of plans for national education in France and Germany, the attention of political and social leaders was arrested by the work of a Swiss teacher, Johann Heinrich Pestalozzi, whose interest in the learning of young children led him to analyze minutely the process by which he thought such learning took place. As a result of his work and his observations, Pestalozzi concluded that exclusively literary training was not appropriate for the young child; that he learned better through the exercise of his senses in the apprehension and study of objects. Pestalozzi accordingly developed a practical method of object teaching which was first introduced into the new German national schools and later into the primary schools of France. In England a very formal version of object teaching was introduced into the infant schools, whence it finally reached the schools of the United States.

Another contribution to the theory and practice of education was made in the early decades of the nineteenth century by the philosopher-psychologist Johann Friedrich Herbart, who was born in 1776 and died in 1841, having devoted his life to the study of education. Unlike Pestalozzi, who had read and studied very few books, Herbart was a scholar, with a broad outlook upon the problems of social living and education and a deep faith in the value of studying history and literature. Herbart thought that the intellectual life develops through what he called "cycles of thought." A cycle begins in the observation and apprehension of natural objects and proceeds thence to a study of the history and literary activity of men, from which is derived an ideal of character expressing itself in subsequent conduct. Herbart believed that the "social studies" — history and literature — should be the core of the curriculum. He analyzed the learning process carefully, stating that every lesson involves a number of distinct steps. These steps he defined as follows: (1) preparation, or the awakening of interest in the mind of the learner by bringing to his consciousness ideas already acquired which relate to the new matter to be learned; (2) presentation, or the clear-cut introduction of the new material to be mastered; (3) development, or the relating of the new material to many other relevant ideas; (4) generalization, or the deduction by the learner of a principle which he has not before apprehended. Herbart used the term "apperceptive mass" to describe the existing content of the learner's mind, a content which is modified by every new learning and which, on its part, lends color and context to that which is newly learned.

Herbart's views were of great influence in Germany. His followers, Ziller and Rein, modified his theory of concentration upon history and literature as "core subjects" into a theory of correlation, and developed it further in terms of the so-called "culture-epoch" theory. According to this theory each individual recapitulates in his own life the evolution of the race : he is first savage, then barbarous, then semicivilized, then civilized in the ancient manner, then medieval, and finally a modern. A course of study in history based upon the culture-epoch idea later became quite popular in American schools.

Very far-reaching in its effect upon primary-school teaching was Herbart's analysis of the steps in the teaching and learning process. It led to a great preoccupation with "lesson plans," which were required in many schools for each subject taught in the school day, even formal lessons in writing. These plans sometimes loomed larger in the minds of teachers and supervisors than the actual teaching itself. Thus the work of Pestalozzi and Herbart affected both the theory and the actual practice of education in this country.

The institutional background of our American schools is naturally to be found in the schools of Europe. By 1750 there were three distinct attitudes toward the question of elementary education evident in the American colonies. First, there was the compulsory-maintenance attitude, characteristic of New England. As early as 1642 the Massachusetts Bay Colony passed a law requiring all communities of fifty families to maintain a primary school, where reading, writing, and arithmetic might be taught to all children. In the Middle Atlantic colonies the prevailing form of primary education was the charity school, modeled on the charity schools maintained by religious bodies in Great Britain. In the South the pauper school was typical. Naturally attendance at pauper schools was a stigma upon the children educated in them. The spirit motivating the founding of such schools was a self-righteous one : Christian communities must educate the children of the indigent poor, else these children would be a disgrace and perhaps a menace to the prosperous and the self-respecting.

The Constitution is silent on the subject of education; but the battle for free schools was won in America by the middle of the last century, since all states then in the Union had subscribed to the idea of public, state-supported, undenominational schools which children of the rich and children of the poor might attend together. The social attitude responsible for such schools was very different from that which dominated the primary schools of Europe. Until the World War the primary school in European countries was a class school maintained by the state or by a religious organization for the education of the children of the lower classes. The children of the rich generally received their education in the home, from tutors and governesses, until the age of nine or ten. Then they entered the secondary schools: the German Gymnasium, the French lycée, the English "public schools" —Eton, Rugby, Winchester, St. Paul's. If by any chance the children who started out in elementary schools could eventually afford secondary education, it was necessary for them to *transfer* to the secondary school by the age of nine or ten. The primary school led on only to a higher primary school and to technical and vocational training. The end of the European primary school is to prepare the children of the working classes to earn an honest living. The American primary school, on the contrary, is simply one step of a ladder leading from the kindergarten to the university.

The teaching in American primary schools during the nineteenth century was not unlike that in the lower schools abroad. We had our Pestalozzian object teaching, imported from England by Mr. Edward A. Sheldon, Principal of the Normal School at Oswego, New York. The progressive spirits in American education organized a Herbartian Society in 1892. The society published the *Herbartian Yearbook*, now appearing as the *Yearbook of the National Society for the Scientific Study of Education*. Of the prominent Herbartians, Dr. Charles McMurry, Dr. Charles de Garmo, and Dr. Frank

McMurry published textbooks on educational methods which were of the greatest importance in shaping classroom procedure in the succeeding decades. Thus the principles of Herbart were incorporated into the American philosophy of education.

One member of the American Herbartian Society was Dr. John Dewey. Dr. Dewey was not content with a mere adaptation of Herbartian ideas to American school needs: he envisioned a change of method which would be much more fundamental than conformity to Herbart's analysis of the lesson situation or the organization of a correlated course of study. Dr. Dewey saw the school as a place where children should not only read history and literature but also live normal, rounded lives, learning ethical discrimination and developing the ability to manage social situations in the course of their school experience. This meant a very different estimate of the teacher's place than that inherent in Herbartian theory, and a completely new interpretation of school discipline. In his experimental school in Chicago Dr. Dewey put his theories to the test. As was mentioned in the previous chapter, he found in the progressive kindergarten much that was in harmony with his point of view.

Many interesting changes and modifications in the American primary school have come about during the present century through the following principal causes: (1) the gradual spread of Dr. Dewey's educational theories, which led to the organization of laboratory and demonstration schools, gradually also affecting the practice of public-school systems; (2) the movement for mental and educational measurement, which challenged the primary school to a revision of its methods and standards; (3) the movement for mental hygiene, which made the individual child and his response to the school situation a matter of new concern to the teacher and administrative officer; (4) the increasing willingness of legislative bodies to vote school funds for the provision of well-paid teachers, adequate buildings, and suitable equipment for primary schools.

Abroad the changes in school organization, curricula, and methods during the years following 1914 have been vivid and dramatic in Germany and Russia and significant, although less kaleidoscopic, in England, France, and Italy. To a degree not approximated in the United States, these changes have reflected profound social upheavals and reorganizations. A discussion of early education abroad is beyond the scope of this book, but for those readers who are interested in the subject a few important references are included in the bibliography accompanying this chapter.[1]

In the United States the influences mentioned above all helped to raise lower-school teaching from a ladylike occupation to a profession. They account, too, for the enormous increase in the university study of education and for the establishment in many university centers of strong elementary, primary, and kindergarten departments. In their turn the university departments have affected school practice to no insignificant extent. Graduates in education have taken back with them into the field the ideas gleaned in their lectures and classes. In the Middle West and the Far West great changes have resulted in public-school practice. In the East long-established traditions are less easily modified; but even in the East university-trained administrators and teachers are beginning to attempt significant changes in curriculum and classroom method.

As a result of the increasing interest in educational theory and method a need for laboratories where innovations could be developed and tested soon became apparent. Practice schools, or schools where teachers in training might take their first tryout in the classroom, had been established as early as the middle of the nineteenth century. But the experimental, or laboratory, school is something very different from a practice school. In the laboratory situation highly trained teachers attempt, under fairly ideal conditions, to work out new principles and methods of teaching. The

---

[1] A very interesting item about education in Italy is that in 1930 Premier Mussolini recalled Madame Montessori to work in the schools of Rome.

Lincoln School of Teachers College, Columbia, the Walden School, the City and Country School of New York, and the Community School of St. Louis are engaged in such experiment. Some of the excellent country day schools also might be called experimental.

Somewhat different from the laboratory school is the demonstration school, which, as its name implies, exists to demonstrate good teaching by methods already proved good. Such schools are a part of every large public system; the Horace Mann School of Teachers College and some of the training schools in connection with modern normal schools and state teachers' colleges exist for this purpose. Provision for observation, participation, and well-supervised practice by advanced student teachers is made in most of these schools.

At no point in the school systems are changes more rapid and radical than in the primary grades. Experimentation in these grades seems much less hazardous, because the moment when the child must achieve the formal standards imposed by the college or by society at large seems a long way off. In progressive systems the organization of the very lowest grades is quite informal, and the unification of these grades with the kindergarten is fairly complete. Where school budgets have permitted the change, movable furniture has replaced screwed-down desks and seats. New materials, especially for work in the industrial arts, have found their way to requisition lists. The intention behind these changes is the setting of a situation in the public primary school which shall make possible a wide latitude in individual choice and a truly democratic atmosphere. Many times school authorities and teachers themselves have failed to understand that changed furniture and equipment cannot of themselves achieve the desirable results: that a movable teacher is actually more important than movable furniture, an original teacher more essential than a wide selection of plastic materials. However, these measures have gradually borne in upon school boards the wholesome belief that a laborer is worthy of his tools; that neither a teacher nor anyone else gets very far with the task of making bricks without straw.

The movement for objective measurement has exerted a profound influence upon the work of the lower school. As was mentioned in Chapter I, measurement soon demonstrated that there was a great amount of overlapping in mental age as between kindergarten and first-grade children, and of course this was true also as between children in the upper primary grades. In addition, measurement has served as a much-needed check upon the progress of lower-school children in learning the skills of reading, writing, and number. It often reveals unsuspected weaknesses in teaching and has helped to do away with much waste effort.

However, objective measurement has been subjected to much wholesome criticism by protagonists of the "child-centered school." The group of progressive teachers and administrators who were deeply interested in purposeful activity as a means of character growth and educational progress soon pointed out that the mental and educational tester tested a very narrow range of abilities when he confined himself to the skills and the content of a formal course of study. Such testing, the progressives held, would encourage teachers and children to exert their efforts toward very narrow ends, that is, toward achievement in the school subjects rather than toward real growth in character.

Psychologists who are interested in the lower school have sought to meet these objections by strenuous efforts to devise methods of testing the more intangible and more important results of education — the growth of the child in desirable social attitudes and habits. In 1922 Dr. Agnes Rogers published *A Tentative Inventory of Habits of Children Six Years of Age*. Subsequently numerous other investigators went to work on inventories and rating scales designed to estimate the standing and the progress of children in the acquisition of desirable character traits. Of course many of these efforts are still in a crude, preliminary stage of development; for it will always be easier to measure progress in narrow skills than to measure ability to get on in a group, fertility of suggestion, breadth of outlook, and the other vitally important outcomes of education. Meanwhile, if inventories of habits and rating scales do no more than force teachers and parents to *consider* the results of education in terms of character growth as well as in terms of subject-matter achievement, such instruments, crude though they may be, serve a most important purpose.

An interesting result of the psychological study of learning problems in the lower grades has been the publication of many excellent reading methods, following each other from the press in rapid succession, any one of several of them a safe guide for beginning teachers of primary reading. The drab primers and readers of a generation ago have been replaced by really delightful books planned according to definite psychological principles. Drill work in number has been subjected to the same rigid scrutiny, with excellent results in terms of increased efficiency. Spelling and writing have come in for their share of revision, and the general effect of the measurement movement has been to make beginning teaching in every field a much more definite and exact procedure.

The effect upon the lower school of the movement for mental hygiene has been less exactly definable than that of mental measurement, but it is, nevertheless, very far-reaching. As early as 1890 G. Stanley Hall began his investigations of the effect of early school life upon the mental health of the child. His efforts were strengthened by the work of William H. Burnham, but it was not until the general enthusiasm for the subject which followed the World War that a concentrated movement began for better mental hygiene in the schools. The effect of the movement appears in the provision for more conferences between home and school, for more readily accessible psychiatric advice, for the training of teachers in child psychology, and for a more flexible organization of school work so that the happiness and success of the individual child may receive more attention. These provisions are made in varying degrees in different communities; but even where organized measures have not been initiated, a new attitude has percolated into the classroom, so that even the more hidebound and conservative of the teaching profession take some responsibility for the emotional life of their pupils. The progressive school, by its very organization, took more thought for the happiness of individuals than did the more conservative school; and as once it took the lead in the introduction of democratic classroom organization, so it has again led the way in its study of the emotional adjustment of its pupils.

The movement for mental hygiene has been an important factor in the education of the public to the need for providing suitable buildings and equipment for primary schools. The happiness and wholesome freedom of the young school child are certainly promoted through the provision for shops and laboratories and enough plastic material to encourage creative work. Before the depression great progress had been made in providing for children those material surroundings which promote happiness and health. There was a growing tendency to spend school funds as generously upon the younger child as upon his high-school brother and sister. The effect of the depression has been to curtail expenditure for buildings and equipment, as well as to increase the size of classes and to eliminate some of the school's activities which could not be shown to have an immediate utilitarian value.

One of the ways in which the primary school in recent years has enlarged and enriched its provision for the welfare and education of children has been through the development of a variety of activities in place of a continued concentration upon a very few. The interesting possibilities of arts and crafts, taught with the aim of giving children insight into the processes involved in providing food, clothing, and shelter, were explored by the late Dr. Frederick Gordon Bonser and other leading educators. Intelligent and original teachers of young children have come to use the field of the industrial arts as one of the most promising means of enriching and expanding the lower-school curriculum. The aim of this work is not to teach technique, but rather to develop appreciation through achieving some understanding of the processes involved in preparing food, weaving fabrics, building with wood and with concrete. In many schools the industrial arts became the core of the primary classroom's activities. A great deal of expensive material was used for this work; perhaps the curtailment of funds because of the depression will lead to a wholesome revaluation and the elimination of avoidable waste.

One can but hope that restricted funds will not permanently cripple the work of the new primary school. By 1929 this school had begun to shake off the ancient stigma of being an institution apart from the life of the community; it had begun to take an interest in the whole growth of the child — not merely, as of old, in his acquisition of the arts of reading, writing, and arithmetic. The varied interests of child life had found a place within its walls. A restriction of its activities now would perhaps be more deleterious to child welfare than were its limitations of fifty years ago. In the nineteenth-century American home, especially in the comfortable middle-class home, the child could learn many things about the conduct of human life and the provision for its necessities. All sorts of handicrafts were still carried on in the home; he could assist in the preparation and preservation of foodstuffs; often he enjoyed all the varied experiences of farm life. The joys as well as the difficulties of outdoor life were known to him: he could explore the woods and fields, finding in them numerous delights and enjoying without effort the varying beauties of the seasons. Today the child of the same social status lives in a small apartment. Much of his food is purchased in cans and prepared on a gas range; of handicraft he sees little or nothing, for clothing and household requisites are cheaply supplied by factories. There is no one at home who has time to explain the processes of production to him, if, indeed, any of the adults in his family know anything about these processes themselves.

There is no attic in which he may ransack trunks and enjoy the fun of dressing up. What he sees of natural beauty he sees, as in a kaleidescope, through the windows of a car, on family picnicking expeditions. These trips are excellent in themselves, but they do not take the place of rambling through the woods and fields on one's own private explorations.

Today the school must substitute for the home through providing analogous experiences as best it may and through interpreting to the child the varied impressions which pour in upon him on every side. This it cannot do if each teacher is expected to handle forty-five or fifty young children, and if equipment and supplies are clipped to suit the demands of the penurious taxpayer who knows nothing about the real problems of the school and who fatuously believes that what was good enough for him is good enough for his children and grandchildren.

One of the interesting issues of modern education is the enduring effort of lower schools to shake off the historic domination of the college and the university. The primary school of nineteenth-century America won its place as a first step of a ladder leading to the university and the professional school. This was a great victory ; but in achieving the proud position of a bottom rung, the lower school found itself forced to arrange its work so that its continuity with later rungs might be unbroken. This led to an unfortunate emphasis on preparation for later school work and tended to make the best good of individual children subordinate to a preparatory aim. Gradually but surely the primary school has escaped from this domination, partly through its own experimentations and partly because the American philosophy of education has tended to become more and more democratic. A growing democracy has made of the high school a school for all adolescents, not a strictly college-preparatory institution for a very few. This radical change is effectively breaking up the old domination of education from the top down. On the whole, modern changes have come from the bottom up, and the lower school is coming into its own.

Preparation, in the sense of definitely fitting a child for the next grade, is losing its prestige as an educational aim. We now think that a child is best prepared for the future by living fully and contentedly in the present.

In the development of the modern primary school private institutions have played a not inconsiderable part. These private progressive schools have been patronized by people who understood the newer educational philosophy and wanted their children educated according to the newer ideas. Their pioneer work has been of great service to the necessarily more conservative public schools; they have been most generous in welcoming observers, and their publications have been of value to teachers throughout the country. Through the Progressive Education Association their strengths and their weaknesses are openly and very helpfully discussed by their directors and faculties for the benefit of all those interested in educational experiment.

In summary, the primary school has an ancient tradition as a place where children attain the rudiments of literary education. It has been greatly broadened in its scope, its methods have been improved, and its atmosphere has been revolutionized in the direction of child freedom and child activity. These changes have been wrought through the progress of educational psychology, the growth of the humanitarian attitude, and the coming of a democratic philosophy of education. This school today serves a different purpose in the lives of children from what it did fifty and seventy-five years ago, and it is to be hoped that no economic exigencies can effect a really permanent setback to its progress. At the same time its methods and curriculum, which will be discussed more fully in later chapters, are being subjected to a scrutiny which is probably wholly desirable.

The primary school has been affected by the philosophy and the methods of the kindergarten, as well as by the broader social and educational changes which we have discussed. Both the kindergarten and the primary grades at the present time are facing new problems of integration and new modifications of outlook because of the development of the nursery school, the latest educational venture in the interest of early childhood. Like the primary school and the kindergarten, this new departure was stimulated at one stage of its development by humanitarian interests; but more distinctly than in the case of either of the older institutions its purposes and methods are the outcome of modern scientific research.

BIBLIOGRAPHY

ALEXANDER, THOMAS, and PARKER, BERYL. The New Education in the German Republic. John Day, New York, 1929.

> A very interesting account of postwar education. Chapter XVII, on the "Curricula of Elementary and Secondary Schools," is probably most significant for the general reader.

BIRCHENOUGH, CHARLES. History of Elementary Education in England and Wales. W. B. Clive, London, 1920.

> Gives a very interesting account of the early philanthropic schools and describes the slow steps toward a national school system which culminated in the Fisher Act of 1918.

BREED, FREDERICK S. "What is Progressive Education?" *Elementary School Journal* (October, 1933), Vol. XXXIV, No. 2, pp. 111–117.

> A telling criticism of the more radical social theories held by certain leaders in progressive education.

CALDWELL, OTIS W., and COURTIS, S. A. Then and Now in Education. World Book, Yonkers, N. Y., 1924.

COBB, STANWOOD. The New Leaven. John Day, New York, 1928.

> A popular discussion of progressive education, interesting to teachers as well as to parents and the intelligent public. The last three chapters concern secondary and higher education.

DE GARMO, CHARLES. Herbart and the Herbartians. Scribner, New York, 1896.

> A study of Herbart's educational theory, with special emphasis upon method and the theory of concentration.

DEMIASHKEVICH, MICHAEL J. The Activity School. Copyright by the author, New York, 1926.

> A study of postwar tendencies in educational method in western Europe. On the whole, an adverse criticism of the European activity school. Chapter I, "New and Old in the Philosophy of Educational Method."

DEWEY, JOHN. The Educational Situation, Part I, "The Elementary School." University of Chicago Press, 1902.

Dr. Dewey's exposition of the problems of the American elementary school at the beginning of this century.

DUGGAN, STEPHEN P. A Student's Textbook in the History of Education, revised edition. Appleton, New York, 1927.

Chapter XIV gives an excellent concise account of Pestalozzi and Herbart.

Encyclopædia of Education, edited by Paul Monroe. Macmillan, New York, 1912.

Articles on Pestalozzi and Herbart.

HERBART, JOHANN FRIEDRICH. Science of Education, translated by H. M. Felkin and E. Felkin. Heath's Pedagogical Library. Heath, Boston, 1895.

A very important educational classic difficult to read and interpret without some previous reading in philosophy.

KANDEL, I. "Education and Social Disorder," Teachers College Record (February, 1933), Vol. XXXIV, No. 5, pp. 359–367.

A rather serious indictment of the American progressive school.

KANDEL, I. "The New School," Teachers College Record (March, 1932), Vol. XXXIII, pp. 505–514.

A criticism of the American progressive-school theory.

KELLERMAN, FRITZ. The Effect of the World War upon European Education. Harvard University Press, Cambridge, 1928.

A convenient summary, with brief references of interest to students of early education.

MCMURRY, CHARLES A. Course of Study in the Eight Grades, Vol. I, Grades I to IV. Macmillan, New York, 1906.

A splendid illustration of an early attempt to organize and systematize the course of study by recognizing that "all studies reach back with living roots . . . into a few great social ideas and institutions."

MCMURRY, CHARLES A. Elements of General Method. Fifth edition. Public School Publishing Company, Bloomington, Illinois, 1897.

Based on principles of Herbart. First copyrighted in 1893. Of great interest and significance for the student of lower-school methods as developed in this country.

MARSHAK, ILIA IAKOVLEVICH. New Russia's Primer, translated by G. P. Counts and N. P. Lodge. Houghton Mifflin, Boston, 1931.

An excellent illustration of propaganda through the lower schools.

MEAD, CYRUS DE WITT. The Transitional Public School. Macmillan, New York, 1934.

"An attempt to reconcile and harmonize and mediate the subject-matter-centered public school and the child-centered experimental school." A timely and valuable discussion.

MOORE, ANNIE E. The Primary School. Houghton Mifflin, Boston, 1925.

> The first five chapters give a good contrast between the old primary school and the new.

NAUMBURG, MARGARET. The Child and the World. Harcourt, New York, 1928.

PESTALOZZI, JOHANN HEINRICH. How Gertrude Teaches her Children, translated by Holland and Turner. Syracuse, New York, 1898.

> An educational classic which should be read by all serious students of early education.

PINKEVITCH, A. P. The New Education in the Soviet Republic, translated by Nucia Perlmutter. John Day, New York, 1929.

REISNER, EDWARD H. Nationalism and Education since 1789, Part IV. Macmillan, New York, 1922.

> A discussion of the development of our school systems, especially valuable for those interested in the evolution of methods of administration and supervision. References to the lower school scattered throughout.

REISNER, EDWARD H. The Evolution of the Common School. Macmillan, New York, 1930.

> A scholarly account which begins with "the vernacular schools in mediaeval towns," and closes with "the common schools and the future of world society."

REISNER, EDWARD H. "What is Progressive Education?" *Teachers College Record* (December, 1933), Vol. XXXV, No. 3, pp. 192–201.

> A sane and helpful article setting forth the underlying assumptions which are common to all truly progressive education, regardless of the slight shades of difference between different schools and leaders.

RUGG, HAROLD O. A Century of Curriculum Construction in American Schools. Twenty-sixth Yearbook of the National Society for the Study of Education, Part I. Public School Publishing Company, Bloomington, Illinois, 1927.

RUGG, HAROLD O., and SHUMAKER, ANN. The Child-Centered School. World Book Company, Yonkers, N. Y., 1928.

> Describes the philosophy and procedure of a progressive school.

SHERMAN, RITA. A Mother's Letters to a Schoolmaster. Knopf, New York, 1923.

WASHBURNE, CARLETON, and STEARNS, MYRON. Better Schools. John Day, New York, 1928.

> A discussion of the new education, intended for the parent and unspecialized teacher. The book discusses how certain communities have secured better schools.

WOODY, THOMAS. Historical Sketch of Activism. Thirty-third Yearbook of the National Society for the Study of Education, Part II. Chapter II, pp. 9–43, "The Activity Movement." Bloomington, Illinois, 1934.

> A very interesting historical account of the development of activity schools from ancient times to the twentieth century.

CHAPTER III

THE NURSERY SCHOOL

Schools for young children of working mothers were first organized by philanthropic people in England and on the Continent of Europe during the first decade of the nineteenth century. These philanthropists saw how great was the need to help large numbers of children who were suffering neglect and abuse as a result of the new industrial conditions, which had taken their mothers and their older brothers and sisters out of the home to work in mills and factories. At New Lanark, Scotland, Robert Owen, the owner of a large cotton mill, and on the Continent a Lutheran pastor, Jean Frédéric Oberlin, conceived the idea of establishing infant schools which should provide physical care and training in desirable social habits for the runabout babies of the working classes.

Owen was a socialist who believed that the career of a man, his success or his ultimate failure, depended not upon his original nature but upon the environment in which society placed him. The school which Owen started at New Lanark was designed to provide "a rational training for infants from one to six years of age." The discipline of the school was reasonable and kindly, music and singing were among its most important activities, and the children were given plenty of opportunity for play. As the venture was most successful, philanthropic people all over England became interested in it, and other infant schools were soon established. Unfortunately Owen's vision of early education was not fully shared by his followers. The playful atmosphere which he considered so important and the kindly discipline in which he believed were not always found in the schools modeled on Owen's New Lanark venture; indeed, the English infant school became a very formal institution, permitting the children little or no freedom and having as its chief aim early training in social conformity and early drill in the three R's. As the movement progressed, and the Home and Colonial Infant School Society was established, Pestalozzian object teaching of the most formal sort was introduced. Later certain kindergarten methods also were adopted, these too being bereft of all spontaneity.

The work of Oberlin in France was followed by the establishment in several of the larger French cities of *salles d'asiles*, which, like the English infant school, were designed to care for the young children of working mothers. Groups of philanthropic women and, above all, a wealthy lawyer named Cochin worked vigorously in support of the movement. Cochin's educational ideas were very modern; in fact, he went so far as to say that *salles d'asiles* were needed for the children of the rich as well as for the children of the poor, since rich children were ruined by spoiling in their own homes. In 1833 these institutions were made part of the French national school system, and in 1848 their name was changed to *écoles maternelles*, because it was thought that they should properly be regarded as *educational*, rather than philanthropic, institutions. Although these schools were probably formal enough in comparison with a modern kindergarten, from the descriptions which are available they seem to have been much more childish and spontaneous in their atmosphere than the later British infant schools.

Infant schools were established in certain cities of Italy in the third decade of the century, and in Germany and Belgium too institutions were established to care for the children of the poor. In Germany they were called *Kleinkinderbewahranstalten* and were concerned almost entirely with the physical care and protection from injury of small children whose mothers were at work. In Belgium similar schools were known as *écoles gardiennes*.

The nineteenth-century infant schools, as it were, set a

The Nurse's Inspection

precedent for the modern nursery-school movement, which
began in England about 1908 with the work of Miss Rachel
McMillan and her sister, Miss Margaret McMillan.) In the
early years of the present century the intelligent British public was aroused on behalf of the poor physical status of many
school children. The provision of school medical inspection
was urged, and soon after this inspection was begun it became apparent that many of the physical defects discovered
had originated long before the child came to school. The
long-established infant schools seemed to the modern medical
authorities and social workers very deficient in the physical
care which they provided for the children. Accordingly the
Misses McMillan determined to organize a nursery school
in which the runabout babies of working mothers could get
adequate physical care and through which both mothers and
babies might be trained in good hygienic habits.

War conditions added fresh incentive to the English
nursery-school movement. The children of the many women
munition workers needed care and shelter such as the nursery
school provided. In addition to this new reason for providing

physical care, the need for mental hygiene became very clearly apparent. The new data gathered in war hospitals concerning neuroses and psychoses demonstrated the fact that in many cases mental and emotional abnormalities can be traced to early childhood experiences and to a lack of good mental hygiene in home and school. The mental adjustment of the children accordingly came to assume great importance among the aims of nursery schools.

In 1918 the famous Fisher Act permitted the establishment of nursery schools as part of the British national school system. The spread of such schools was checked by the postwar economic depression; nevertheless the principle had been adopted that the child of runabout age is a proper object for the use of public-school funds.

On the whole the English nursery-school movement has been concerned with helping the children of the underprivileged groups. Since 1918 only a few schools have been established for the children of the rich. As Miss McMillan has expressed it, the purpose of the nursery school is to provide for the children of the poor really adequate *nurseries* such as more fortunate children enjoy in their own homes.

Teachers in English nursery schools are required to have had some hospital experience as a part of their training, for the provision of excellent physical care remains a most important part of the school's program. It is recognized also that workers with groups of small children must know how to provide suitable occupations and play materials, because there must always be things to do when the children are not occupied with eating or sleeping or other matters related to their physical welfare. The English nursery school, then, like the early infant school of Robert Owen, has been organized to do away with some of the most serious inequalities of opportunity as between the children of the rich and the children of the less privileged social groups. As in the early nineteenth century Owen tried to give the children in his infant school the best training of which he knew, so in the modern nursery school the effort is to give children the best

" That's Mine!"

hygienic care which is possible in the light of present scientific knowledge. This greater scientific knowledge in the possession of its leaders is the great difference between the modern nursery school and Owen's ideal infant school. The nursery school differs from the later formal infant school much more radically. The formal infant school neglected physical care and substituted a repressive, formal school procedure for the atmosphere of a nursery.

In the United States the nursery-school movement originated from a variety of social interests and purposes, and therefore its development has proceeded along several different lines. As we look back over the history of the American nursery school the following types, each with its special purposes and organization, are clearly distinguishable : (1) the research-center nursery school ; (2) the co-operative nursery school ; (3) the private-school nursery group ; (4) the philanthropic nursery school ; (5) the nursery school conducted as part of a teacher-training program ; (6) the Federal Emergency Relief nursery school, which at this writing has been in progress only a few months, and the effects of which upon nursery-school work as a whole cannot yet be fairly estimated.

The research-center nursery schools were organized first at certain of the large universities, where research workers in the fields of psychology, psychiatry, medicine, and nutrition needed the opportunity of observing normal children. The growing emphasis upon prevention in the field of medicine was one of the important factors in stimulating interest in observing the normal in child development rather than exclusively the pathological. Psychologists too had become convinced that the study of young children would provide the best key to problems of adolescent and adult adjustment, first, because many nervous and mental difficulties begin in early childhood; second, because young children are so naïve that their reactions may be more readily observed; and third, because in early childhood corrective measures can be introduced with much better chance of realizing good results and much better ease of recording progress than in the case of older patients. It was very soon apparent that in any group of so-called normal children selected at random there would be plenty of opportunity to study the beginnings of emotional maladjustment; for "normal" is a relative term, and the perfectly normal child is far to seek, if not nonexistent. Above all, certain psychologists, notably Dr. Gesell of Yale University, were interested in clearing up just this very concept of normality and in deciding, on the basis of observing many young children, just what constitutes normal or average social, emotional, physical, and intellectual attainment at different age levels.

At first it was thought that the groups gathered together for observation could be conducted very informally, and that no specially trained teacher was necessary; but fairly soon it was discovered that this was a mistake. Someone capable of setting up a good play environment, someone skilled in managing young children, was needed to take care of these groups if they were to be really good laboratories for specialists. The children themselves must be assured the best of opportunities for growth if fair and valid research studies were to be made. Accordingly, several of the research-center nursery schools, with the assistance of funds from the Laura Spelman Rockefeller Foundation, developed into very elaborately equipped schools indeed. Skilled leadership was provided; buildings and playgrounds were carefully planned; and every facility for the preparation of meals and for caring for the children's rest hour was made available, together with the best of play equipment. These schools, of which the nursery schools at the universities of Iowa and Minnesota, at Columbia University, and the Institute of Human Relations at Yale are examples, remain the most elaborate set-ups in the country, with the exception of a private nursery school or two. In this group too should be included the nursery school of the Merrill-Palmer School in Detroit, Michigan. Although this school was originally endowed under the will of Mrs. Merrill-Palmer, who was interested in the education of girls for motherhood and homemaking, it speedily developed into a research center where graduate students may engage in advanced study, receiving credit for their work from accredited colleges and universities. At the same time the aim of the founder is being realized also, since parent education is an important part of the school's work and since training in nursery-school teaching is offered.

In contrast with the elaborately equipped schools just described, stand the very simple set-ups provided by small groups of parents who wished to provide co-operative nursery schools for their children. One of the most interesting of these was organized in Berkeley, California, and is described in full by Katherine Taylor in one of the references given in the bibliography for this chapter. The co-operative nursery school received a good deal of impetus during the World War, when, in some cases for the first time, many young mothers with professional training or business experience wished to undertake remunerative work outside the home. Unwilling to leave their children to the care of such nursemaids as their budgets would permit, some of these mothers determined to pool their resources and try to care for their children as a group. In several instances the first plan was to have the different mothers take turns in managing the children. But these ventures did not enjoy unqualified success; a trained person, it soon became apparent, was needed to manage eight or nine babies. Therefore in almost every case a specialist was eventually called in to take charge of the group with the assistance of the co-operating mothers — a kindergartner, or a Montessori teacher, or a trained nurse. A little co-operative venture of this sort was the seed from which grew the nursery school of the City and Country School in New York City, finally conducted by the Bureau of Educational Experiments under the direction of the late Harriet Johnson.

Since nursery schools have become popular among intelligent groups of parents, and since they have gained the sanction of most pediatricians, private schools have opened nursery groups for young children. These schools are found in many cities and suburban districts; the nursery school of the Dalton School, New York City, may be cited as a private-school nursery which is very completely equipped.

Serving the same type of people who patronize the private schools are a growing number of nursery schools and so-called "preschool play groups" conducted by private individuals, with greater or less or no special training, in their own homes. Some of these schools, among which the Berkeley Nursery School of Haverford happens to be best-known to the writer, represent really fine educational standards and are of the greatest benefit to a whole community. Other private ventures are less desirable, either because the people conducting them have inadequate background and training or because the housing and equipment provided for the group are inadequate. In judging such undertakings the same standards which would be applicable to a nursery group in a real school situation should be applied: Is the director capable? Does being a member of such a group really promote the child's physical well-being? Is he making desirable

Simple Equipment

social adjustments? Is there provision for intellectual development? for vigorous outdoor play? for music and the beginnings of fine and industrial art? Elaborate equipment is not necessary; the director need not be a finished musician; she need not have the equivalent of a Ph.D. in psychology; but provision for the child's ordinary needs of growth must be evident, and the director must be possessed of the personality requirements, including intelligence and teaching skill, which are expected of a regular school's staff if the little independent venture is to be educationally sound.

The philanthropic nursery school is to be found in many of our well-equipped nurseries and settlements. The nursery-school worker in a day nursery is on duty all day or at least for a greater part of the day, including the children's midday meal and the resting hour. Consequently the educational work with the children can be carried on consistently throughout the greater part of their waking hours, instead of for just three hours or so as has been the case when kindergarten teachers were employed.

Early in the development of the American nursery-school movement it became evident that trained persons were needed to carry on nursery-school work. The question of what training would be most desirable and what should be the standards required of nursery teachers was the subject of animated debate between 1926 and 1928. At this time too the National Association for Nursery Education was organized, and the problem of the preparation of teachers received much thought and attention from the members of this new association. The question was especially interesting because several different fields were represented in the first professional group who engaged in nursery-school work. There were, first of all, the people with a great deal of psychological training, who were interested in research with nursery-school children. This group has continued to exert leadership, and many fine contributions to our knowledge of child development have been made as a result of its activities. The publications released through the institutes of child development at the universities of California, Minnesota, and Iowa, the Child Development Abstracts published by Teachers College, Columbia University, and numerous publications in other centers represent the thought and labor of the many fine psychologists who have devoted their energy to the preschool field.

Within the group interested in the new nursery-school movement were also a number of persons whose training and experience qualified them for leadership in the general field of early education, a leadership to be exerted less through publication of scientific studies than through administrative work or the direct teaching of young children. Dr. Patty Smith Hill was a leader among this contingent. Her enthusiasm for nursery education had led her to follow the accounts of the work done by our government nurseries for the children of munition workers during the war and also moved her to investigate the first records which were published here of the nursery school in England. Through Miss Hill's influence Miss Grace Owen, a prominent English nursery-school worker, was brought over to lecture at Teachers College, Columbia University, in the summer of 1921;

and in the spring of 1922 Miss Hill arranged to have an English nursery-school teacher come and conduct a demonstration in the Manhattanville Day Nursery of New York City.

Other nursery-school teachers had been brought from England to work in the Merrill-Palmer School, and through them the American venture was brought into close contact with the English movement, with its well-organized plans, its technically trained nursery workers, and its fine provision for physical care and hygiene.

In New England Dr. Abigail Adams Eliot, whose previous professional training had been that of a social worker, was a pioneer in nursery-school education. From the first, Dr. Eliot had been interested in the training of nursery-school teachers. The center for preschool education which she organized at the Ruggles Street Nursery in Boston is now known as the Nursery Training School of Boston.

The late Dr. Bird T. Baldwin, as a part of the work in child development and parent education which he directed under the Laura Spelman Rockefeller Fund in the state of Iowa, organized a demonstration for teachers in training at the State Teachers College of Cedar Falls, Iowa. The present writer was in charge of this work during the fall, winter, and spring terms of 1926–1927. The original purpose of the work was to bring all the students in the college who were on the kindergarten-primary curriculum into contact with the nursery-school children, and eventually to give a few chosen individuals real training through participation. About seventy students were enrolled each term for the course in child development, which required systematic observation in the nursery school.

Still another important group of nursery-school leaders has been drawn from the departments of home economics in colleges and universities. A very fine nursery school has been conducted for the last ten years or so in the College of Home Economics at Cornell University, where students may study child development in connection with their home-economics

Does he Want to Help?

training in child care, where other advanced students may conduct psychological research, and where a limited number may be given the opportunity to observe and participate to the point where they are trained for actual nursery-school work. At Ames, Iowa, as well as in several other home-economics centers, the nursery school has an important place, and the Merrill-Palmer School was originally endowed as an institution for training in homemaking.

It is probably because of the diversity of training and consequent breadth of outlook represented by the leaders in the National Association for Nursery Education that formulations of a dogmatic sort about training requirements for nursery-school teaching have not been made. In practice, however, a bulletin of the United States Office of Education shows that persons selected for nursery-school positions in 1928 were usually highly trained. Of 331 nursery-school directors reporting to the Office in 1931, 132 held bachelors' degrees, 75 masters' degrees, and 6 had the degree of Ph.D. This situation with regard to the preparation of nursery-school teachers is rather different from the one in England, where nursery-school training is about equivalent to our typical normal-training courses for kindergarten and primary teachers. The explanation of this difference probably lies in the fact that the American nursery-school director is supposed to be a qualified leader of parents as well as a teacher of young children. It must be remembered too that in the greater number of cases the American nursery worker has been expected to deal with parents who were intelligent and well-read beyond the average of the unselected population. Good academic preparation was therefore imperative for successful leadership.

The recent establishment of nursery schools as a part of the Federal Emergency Relief Administration's plan for the relief of unemployed teachers has brought sharply to the foreground the question of what constitutes minimum training for nursery-school teaching. Teachers in the emergency schools are supposed to have been already prepared for kindergarten or primary work, and in addition are given four weeks or so of intensive training through observation and classes at various child-development centers. They are then expected to conduct all-day nursery schools, with only a limited amount of trained supervision. These qualifications present a striking contrast to those which heretofore have been regarded as essential. It must be borne in mind, however, that these are literally *emergency* schools, designed to relieve the present situation for both teachers and children.

Before the recent developments under the FERA, there were very few nursery schools existing as part of public-school organizations. Only twelve such schools were reported to the United States Office of Education in 1931–1932. This small number, and the fact that there are not more nursery schools in philanthropic institutions, are accounted for by the very high cost of providing nursery-school education or, at least, of providing nursery education according to the standards set by the research centers. The FERA activities are forcing administrators, teachers, and nursery-school specialists to reconsider the whole matter of standards from a somewhat different angle.

In December, 1933, the sum of $2,000,000 a month was set aside by the Relief Administration to be used for " unemployed teachers and those qualified to teach." As one feature of this relief, the organization of nursery schools for children two years of age to the age of school entrance was recommended. The April report of the Administration records the fact that until that time thirty-one states had availed themselves of the right to establish nursery schools under the Federal grant, that 61,000 children had been enrolled in these schools, and that 4000 hitherto unemployed teachers or persons qualified to teach had been given employment as emergency nursery-school workers. In addition to the purpose of giving relief to unemployed members of the teaching profession, these schools are "designed to promote the physical and mental well-being of children of unemployed parents."

The emergency nursery schools, then, have been established in public-school systems in those states which have availed themselves of the privilege of establishing them, and in those districts where school administrators were able and willing to house them and administer them as part of the public-school organization. Under such circumstances the housing is difficult to provide and can rarely be ideal, the funds available for equipment are very small, and the problems arising in connection with supervision and administration are numerous and difficult. Yet the project is full of vitality and is arousing a great deal of interest. Smaller considerations about nursery-school management, staffing, and equipment are swept aside; and every effort is being made to work out a plan which shall have educational value for the young children of unemployed parents and which shall at the same time be sufficiently simple and economical to permit of operation under the FERA plan. The Administration has published a brochure giving the minimum standards which must be met if a school is to be carried on by means of FERA funds, and requires that the work in each state be supervised by adequately trained persons.

A Very Good Time

A demonstration nursery school, run under conditions very like those encountered by teachers in the emergency schools, was conducted in the summer session of the Connecticut State Teachers College in 1934. The school was housed in one of the new public-school buildings in New Haven, the kindergarten and first-grade room being assigned for the use of the group. In addition, outdoor play space was provided by a rather large grassy plot in front of the building. A well-equipped home-economics laboratory in the basement provided good facilities for preparing the noonday meal, but this room was unfortunately directly under the kindergarten room, with the stairs at the opposite end of the building. The lavatory facilities were below standard, as only one toilet bowl and one washbowl were available for the children.

The equipment of the regular kindergarten was at the disposal of the nursery school. The kindergarten slide, while rather high for nursery-school children, was very much enjoyed, as well as a rocking boat, which unluckily required a great deal of adult supervision because it had been designed for older children and was consequently rather dangerous. The sand table was opened a few times during the session, but it did not provide very successfully for activities because it was much too high for two-year-old children. The kindergarten tables and chairs were used for the luncheon period and for the occasions when quiet group work was carried on.

The dollhouse equipment of the regular kindergarten was supplemented with a number of borrowed playthings, and proved extremely popular with the children. Easels were used and painting was begun on one or two rainy mornings, and floor blocks were chosen occasionally by a few of the older children. Trucks and wagons borrowed from other nursery schools were exceedingly popular. Of outdoor equipment there was none except packing cases and boards which were kindly donated. A rather precarious swing, requiring constant watching by an adult, was made by passing a piece of iron tubing through two discarded gymnasium standards and suspending a board from it by means of a strong rope.

The nursery-school staff consisted of a director, who was also an instructor in the summer school in charge of two adult classes, and three assistants.[1] These assistants had all had a full-year course in child psychology (and in one case in education) at Bryn Mawr College, and they had observed in nursery schools. For the first two weeks no kitchen help was available except some voluntary assistance from the summer-school students. Thereafter a kitchen helper was provided through the FERA employment office. A member of the State Department of Home Economics supervised the serving of the meals.

Twenty-two children were admitted to the school, ranging in age from twenty months to three years eight months. Because of ill health two were excluded by the physician after the first week, and two were withdrawn by their parents. The average daily attendance for the first two weeks

[1] E. Louise Davis, Lydia C. Hemphill, and Louise C. Turner.

was seventeen; for the last three weeks, fifteen. The nursery school began at eight in the morning and closed officially at three in the afternoon. The day's schedule follows:

8–8.30	Children arrived, were given a glass of water, and played indoors.
8.30	Picture books were taken out or an informal music period was arranged.
9.15–9.30	Fruit juice was served. Toilet.
9.30–11	Free play out of doors.
11–11.30	Washing for dinner.
11.30–11.45	Rest before dinner.
11.45	Dinner.
12.15	Toilet. Rest on cots.
12.30–2.30	Nap.

The school was in session for only twenty-five mornings, and therefore little could be expected in the way of progress on the part of individual children. All the director hoped was that members of the summer-school class in nursery education would gain something from seeing what is involved in getting even the simplest all-day nursery school under way. The members of the class were given the greatest possible freedom to observe (using a rather imperfect one-way screen to provide a crude observation corner). They were also encouraged to participate in the work of the nursery school under the direction of the instructor, both for their own benefit and because additional help was often sorely needed.

The weaknesses of the whole demonstration were many, yet at the end of the session the notes of adult observers who were members of the nursery-education class showed real progress on the part of most of the children.

J. R., the oldest in the group, was very intelligent, an only child, and very much spoiled. He cried a great deal, wanted to go home, and was generally unhappy for the first three weeks. At first he would not lie down on his cot without a real battle. By the end of the session he was sleeping an average of an hour or so each day and playing happily

Dinnertime

with a group of children most of the time. Through an oral hygienist who visited the school, his mother learned that J. had two badly decayed teeth. She also discovered that he could be admitted to a four-year-old kindergarten group in October by getting a special permit to send him to a school in an adjoining district. This was important, because J. R. needed kindergarten experience very much.

V. N., also one of the older children, was very antisocial and constantly suspicious of adults at the beginning of the session. During the last two weeks he was playing happily with a group of four or five older children, settling his differences through discussion more frequently than through pounding with fists.

L. N., the two-year-old brother of V. N., was bewildered and cried a great deal during the first two weeks. No intelligible word did he speak during these weeks. He seemed very insensitive to the people about him and was noticeably rough in his treatment of less robust children. By the end of the session a friendly smile was characteristic of him, and he was beginning to articulate a few words.

A. T., aged two and a half, appeared undernourished and in generally poor physical condition when admitted to the nursery school. He cried most of the first day, and when he finally desisted from crying he walked about with his head hanging and a most lugubrious expression on his face. He did not even attempt to feed himself the first few days, expressing timidity, repression, and unhappiness in his very posture. By the end of the session his expression had brightened noticeably; he frequently joined other children in their play, and he went stamping gaily out from the rest room to meet his older brother or sister in the afternoon, laughing happily and demanding that his hair be carefully combed before he started home.

Some progress could be recorded for practically every child. The group as a whole improved a great deal in behavior at table and in settling down for the afternoon nap. Almost all the children ate with their fingers when they came; practically everyone was manipulating a spoon quite successfully at the end of the session.

The greatest gain, however, was in co-operative group play. For the first two weeks there was almost no group play — at the most two children who knew each other outside of school would get together. If two children wanted the same plaything, they fought about it or cried or went to an adult for help. Of conversation between the children there was virtually none.

The following conversation is illustrative of the co-operative play during the last two weeks:

CHILD A. [Playing with the boxes out of doors] We need another box.
CHILD B. What for?
CHILD A. To make the door.
CHILD C. He's got one.
CHILD B. He won't give it.
CHILD D. Go and ask him.

Making a "Store"

The instructor in music at the summer session was interested in work with nursery-school children. Under her direction members of the class in music education came up and played to the children on the piano and the violin. The spontaneous responses of the children were pronounced and interesting. One child always ran to the rocking boat, rocking back and forth in time to the music. Other children played with wooden clappers and cymbals, maintaining remarkably good rhythm. All the children in the group showed some interest in music.

One parents' meeting was held in the third week of the school. It was attended also by some of the students in the nursery-education class. The parents were quite enthusiastic about the school and much more intelligent about its educational purpose than the nursery-school staff had expected them to be. Their questions about the school's habit-training program were especially intelligent, and their comments on their own children were interesting and helpful.

From all the foregoing discussion it is evident that the American nursery school has developed very differently from

the English institution with its simply defined purposes.
The American school serves the purposes of research, parent
education, and the assistance of parents who are too much
occupied with professional work or with business to devote
full time to their children. The nursery school also provides
extra educational opportunity for children attending private
schools; it helps philanthropic institutions for children to
carry on their educational work in a better way; it serves
as a demonstration and laboratory for teachers and parents;
and, finally, in its emergency form the nursery school is finding its place as a part of public-school organizations.

Yet with all this variety of organization and interest, certain clear-cut and important purposes characterize all good
nursery schools. In every school the first consideration is
the provision of the best possible environment for the particular group of children served in that particular situation,
be it a private-school group, a child-development laboratory,
or an emergency nursery. In every school, too, contact with
the parents is essential. Some nursery schools can offer
parents the services of trained psychologists; others can
command only the friendly and intelligent interest of teachers who bring to each individual case the benefit of having
had experience with many other children and who are presumably reading and thinking about child development more
constantly than parents can find time or inclination to do.
No matter what the school's particular *raison d'être*, a sincere
and honest effort to do the most that one can with the
children and to be as helpful as possible to their parents
should be the aims of the nursery-school worker.

From this brief description it is evident that the procedure in the nursery school itself, regardless of its particular
purpose, is extremely simple. All the efforts of the teachers
are directed toward having the children do in the best possible way the very same things they would do in a good
home nursery. But in the nursery school these things are
done in company with other children, under the friendly
supervision of an interested adult, and are free from all the

unnecessary restrictions which have to be imposed in a home. A home has to be organized for people of all ages, whereas the nursery school is planned for the convenience of the baby himself. A typical day in a nursery school will be more fully described in another chapter; but, to an extent which may make the teacher of older children wonder why it is called a school at all, the time is taken up in taking care of the child's physical needs, in teaching him to be as independent as possible of adults in caring for his own needs, and in giving him the opportunity to learn how to play in a group situation.

The greater number of schools have a session long enough to permit the serving of the midday meal at school, and a large number also include a long nap in their daily program. Some schools, however (among which are many independent groups having no school connection), have only a half-day session. These short sessions serve the purpose of providing the child with the opportunity for group play, but can deal only indirectly with problems of eating and sleeping.

The nursery school represents an extension of the kindergarten downward to include younger children than those heretofore in the organized activities of the school. It also represents the extension of the day-nursery idea to include the children of professional parents and other socially privileged groups. This extension of nursery-school facilities to all economic and social levels is made in the belief that it is good for many children, and good for their families, to remove the toddler from the home environment during a part of the day. In this way the baby acquires interests of his own and a healthy independence of mother or nurse. At the same time the home is relieved of the strain of providing all day long safe and adequate facilities for the toddler's endless tour of investigation of people and things. This is especially helpful in these days of apartment-house living, where many very good homes can provide little nursery space and no opportunity for free play out of doors.

Eventually the nursery school, like other educational innovations, will probably find its way into a permanent place in our American public-school systems. The emergency nursery schools, temporary though they may be, are a move in this direction; upon the reception which these emergency schools earn for themselves from public-school administrators the future of the nursery school as a public institution depends in no small measure. But before the nursery school can become a permanent part of our educational system a great deal of thought and effort must be expended in the direction of integrating nursery-school curriculum and method with the work of the kindergarten and the primary school.

BIBLIOGRAPHY

BALDWIN, B. T., and STECHER, LORLE. The Psychology of the Preschool Child. Appleton, New York, 1925.

A description of the work in the preschool laboratories at Iowa City. The book is a standard reference for the earlier scientific work in the preschool field. It includes a good historical summary of preschool education.

BLATZ, W. E., and BOTT, H. Parents and the Preschool Child. Morrow, New York, 1929.

A very helpful book on parental education in relation to the nursery school.

CHRISTIANSEN, HELEN. "An All-Day Nursery School Set-Up," *Childhood Education* (April, 1934), Vol. X, No. 7, pp. 356–360.

DAVIS, MARY DABNEY. Emergency Nursery Schools, *Childhood Education Bulletin* (January, 1934), Vol. X, No. 4, pp. 201–202, 207.

A brief statement of the general principles of the FERA nursery schools.

DAVIS, MARY DABNEY. Nursery Schools, Their Development and Current Practices in the United States, *United States Office of Education Bulletin No. 9*, 1932.

A convenient statistical summary.

FOREST, ILSE. Preschool Education. Macmillan, New York, 1927.

Especially Chapter VIII.

FOREST, ILSE. "Preschool Education," in the Encyclopaedia of the Social Sciences, Vol. XII. Macmillan, New York, 1934.

FOSTER, J. C., and MATTSON, M. L. Nursery School Procedure. Appleton, New York, 1929.

A nontechnical discussion of the actual running of a nursery school. Indispensable for nursery-school teachers.

GESELL, ARNOLD. Guidance of Mental Growth in Infant and Child. Macmillan, New York, 1930.

> The first part gives the reader an excellent orientation with respect to the modern point of view in early education.

GESELL, ARNOLD. The Preschool Child from the Standpoint of Public Hygiene and Education. Houghton Mifflin, Boston, 1923.

> One of the first comprehensive discussions of preschool hygiene and education; of the greatest interest for students of the subject.

GREENWOOD, BARBARA, WADDELL, CHARLES W., SCANTLEBURY, EVA, and others. A Six-Year Experiment with a Nursery School. University of California at Los Angeles, 1931.

> Full description and record blanks, pp. 149–175.

HILL, PATTY S., and LANGDON, GRACE. Nursery School Procedures at Teachers College. Reprinted from the *Revue Internationale de l'Enfant* (May, 1930), Vol. IX, No. 53. Save the Children International Union, Geneva. 10 pages.

> A simple narrative account.

JOHNSON, HARRIET M. Children in the Nursery School. John Day, New York, 1928.

> A charming account of the nursery school, with a detailed description of the nursery-school environment. An indispensable reference book for teachers of young children.

KAWIN, ETHEL, and HOEFER, CAROLYN. A Comparative Study of a Nursery School versus a Non-Nursery-School Group. University of Chicago Press, 1931.

> In seven months the nursery school does not produce measurable effects on the mental and physical status of children two and three years old.

LANGDON, GRACE. Home Guidance for Young Children. John Day, New York, 1931.

> An excellent handbook for the parents and teachers of young children.

LOCHHEAD, JEWELL. The Education of Young Children in England. Teachers College, Columbia University, New York, 1932.

> As the name implies, this study describes and evaluates the English institutions and methods for early education. The nursery school, the infant school, and the kindergarten are included.

McCARTHY, DOROTHEA. "The Nursery School and the Social Development of the Child," *Journal of Home Economics* (January, 1933), Vol. XXV, pp. 13–18.

> A review of studies on the effect of the nursery school on social growth.

McMILLAN, MARGARET. The Nursery School. Dent, London, 1919.

> A description of the school organized by Miss McMillan and her sister in London.

National Society for the Scientific Study of Education, Twenty-eighth Yearbook, Part I (Public School Publishing Company, Bloomington, Illinois, 1929): "Preschool and Parental Education."

Chapter II, "History of the Movement in Preschool and Parental Education"; Chapter VIII, "Nursery Schools"; Chapter XIII, "The Professional Training of Nursery-School Teachers."

OWEN, GRACE. Nursery School Education. Dutton, New York, 1920.

A symposium edited by Miss Owen, on the theory and practice of the English nursery school.

PINKEVITCH, A. P. The New Education in the Soviet Republic, translated by N. Perlmutter. Williams and Norgate, New York, 1929.

Chapter V: an interesting account of the place of the nursery school in the educational system of Soviet Russia.

RAND, W., SWEENEY, M. E., and VINCENT, E. L. Growth and Development of the Young Child. Saunders, Philadelphia, 1931.

Gives an excellent and not too technical account of the child's physical development from conception to the end of the preschool period, stressing the unitary character of growth despite its varying aspects.

RAYMOND, E. MAE. A Score Card for the Guidance of Nursery School Teachers. M. A. thesis, Teachers College, Columbia University, 1931. 44 pages with bibliography.

Includes instructions for making a diary record for evaluation, a formula for competency scores, and items relating to teachers' equipment, curriculum standards, plant, room.

SALMON, BAIRD, and HINDSHAW, WINIFRED. Infant Schools. Longmans, London, 1904.

Interesting for students of the history of early education.

SCHAEFER, MARIE. "Social Development in the Nursery School," Childhood Education (April, 1934), Vol. X, No. 7, pp. 352–355.

SHINN, ALIDA VISSHER. "Visiting the Homes of Nursery School Children," Childhood Education (February, 1934), Vol. X, No. 5, pp. 240–246.

STRANG, RUTH. An Introduction to Child Study. Macmillan, New York, 1931.

An excellent discussion of the preschool child from the psychological point of view.

STURT, MARY. The Education of Children under Seven, Part I. Kegan Paul, Trench, Trübner and Company, London, 1932.

An interesting discussion from the British point of view.

TAYLOR, KATHARINE WHITESIDE. The Children's Community, Berkeley, California. American Association of University Women, 1634 Northwest I Street, Washington, D.C., 1931.

Describes a co-operative nursery-school venture.

United States Federal Emergency Relief Administration, Monthly Report, December 1 to December 31, 1933; April 1–30, 1934.

VAN ALSTYNE, DOROTHY. The Environment of Three-Year-Old Children. Teachers College, Columbia University, New York, 1929.

> Relationship between various environmental factors and results of tests.

VAN ALSTYNE, DOROTHY. Play Behavior and Choice of Play Materials of Preschool Children, pp. 93 ff. Behavior Research Fund co-operating with the Garden Apartments and Franklin Public School Nurseries. University of Chicago Press, 1922.

> Undertakes to discuss what difference can be observed in uses of play materials by children two, three, four, or five years old in nursery-school and kindergarten free-play situations. Interesting conclusions.

White House Conference on Child Health and Protection, Section III, B, Nursery Education: "Education and Training." Committee of the Infant and Preschool Child. Appleton-Century, New York, 1931.

CHAPTER IV

INTEGRATING THE WORK OF THE LOWER SCHOOL

The integrating of nursery-school, kindergarten, and primary-school activities is one of the most challenging and interesting of present-day educational problems. Gradually the kindergarten has been assimilated into the general plan of the progressive school; gradually its philosophy and method have found their way upward into the primary grades. In this process of integration the first grade has been the midpoint. Through the persistent efforts of forward-looking kindergarten and first-grade teachers, the planning of the work in the two school groups they represent is approaching a satisfactory unification. The first grade and the second have always stood in a rather close relationship one with the other; therefore once the first grade and the kindergarten had made steps toward mutual understanding and integration, it was quite natural to include the second grade and even the third in the program. In the kindergarten and first three grades of progressive schools it is not unusual to find a curriculum organized entirely in terms of children's interests and play needs. With the fourth school year, unfortunately, there often comes a break. The pressure of upper-school demands makes itself felt, and the children pass from three or four years of informal play experience into the traditional routine of phonics, spelling, tables, and the forty-five combinations. This situation is not wholly desirable, and doubtless intelligent planning for the child from two to eight years will gradually eliminate it; for it must be borne in mind that though we are planning especially for the earliest school years, this period is not separate and distinct from the rest of the child's educational experience.

Though the primary years are the bottom rung of the ladder and must be protected from a too serious domination by the rungs higher up, they are still a part of the ladder and, as such, must adjust to the pattern of its whole structure. In this adjustment the claims of the youngest children must not be given a monopoly, but a fair share of consideration in the minds of curriculum makers. While we are here considering the special needs for integration of the earliest school years it must not be thought that the claims of the upper elementary and high schools can be ignored in our planning. The preschool and primary years should properly lead the child naturally and inevitably toward the work of the higher grades.

One of the undoubted services which the nursery school has already rendered education in general has been to compel the kindergarten — and, indeed, the early grades also — to reconsider objectives and activities. At first the situation between nursery school and kindergarten teachers was not unlike that between kindergarten and first-grade teachers a generation ago. The nursery-school teacher had a special technique; she was "scientifically" trained; she knew the needs — physical, mental, and emotional — of her young charges. The kindergarten teacher, trained in the use of techniques which to the nursery school seemed a little passé, was suspected by some of the younger generation in education of being a trifle sentimental. Songs, poems, and handwork, the nursery-school teacher thought, were not regarded by her colleague in the kindergarten as duly subordinate to the needs of the child's developing personality. The kindergarten seemed less "scientific" in its approach to educational questions.

On her own part the nursery-school teacher seemed to the experienced kindergarten worker a little short on the side of providing constructive activities and enriching the intellectual life of the young child. Given the fact that in the nursery school much of the day is properly consumed in attending to the well-ordered physical regime of the runabout baby, there were still gaps when activities in the way of stories, or expressive work, or music were indicated. Life in a group is not quite like life in a nursery at home, after all, and moments do come when the nursery group is at loose ends unless some activity is provided. With too little stimulation, and the unavoidable restrictions of a group situation, the nursery school palled for some of the brighter children. Then the nursery school proceeded to borrow from the progressive kindergarten many of its procedures and much of its material. Large crayons and vast sheets of Manila paper delighted nursery babies. Brushes and paints and easels were happy additions to the lives of the older nursery-school children. Sand, clay, and picture books possessed undoubted attractions. This borrowing could not go on without some reaction on the part of the kindergarten group. Nursery-school children went on to kindergarten at the age of four or five, definitely bored by some of the activities which would have been appropriate had they not already been explored in nursery schools. Kindergarten teachers complained that the nursery school had stolen their thunder. In private schools parents complained that their children went on for several years — on fairly high tuitions — doing a little more of the same thing. Some nursery-school teachers have been, and are, inclined to pass the matter off with a shrug and an injunction to the kindergartner to look to it herself. Such shifting of responsibility, however, cannot go on indefinitely, and the questions raised by teachers and parents alike about the future of group work in the preschool years are much too pertinent and fundamental to be ignored. The question of integrating the work of the preschool and primary years so that there may be progression and a continual broadening and deepening of experience rather than growing boredom on the part of the active child must be considered in terms of what the child at each age level is capable of doing happily and well. The conflicting claims of kindergarten, grades, and nursery school, as such, cannot be given serious attention.

In many progressive schools there has long been a practice of doing away with the idea of "grades" and substituting for them age groups. The "twos" and "threes," the "fives," "sixes," "sevens," and "eights," are all, supposedly, pursuing the interests proper to their ages and abilities, rather than the arbitrary courses of study arranged by grades. To this arrangement the objection may be raised that chronological age grouping does not make for homogeneity because of the considerable difference in mental age to be found in any group of children chronologically at the same level. This objection is thoroughly understood in progressive schools, and in practice is allowed for. Many of these schools employ staff psychologists who are qualified to advise in cases where the plan does not work out well. In extreme cases adjustments are made. A very mature seven-year-old might be placed with the "eights"; a very immature five-year-old, with the "fours." Such factors as physical growth and strength also are taken into account in placement. But, as a general measure, age grouping seems socially the most satisfactory and, educationally, the most desirable in situations where classes are small enough to permit the teacher to give children individual attention. This is not the place to consider the relative merits of homogeneous and heterogeneous grouping so far as mental age is concerned. The difficulties of handling a large heterogeneous group of young children are much too serious to minimize. The point of this discussion is rather to call attention to the fact that when one thinks of young children as "twos," "threes," "fours," "fives," and so on, rather than as nursery-school, kindergarten, and primary pupils, many of the artificial gaps and distinctions of the separate departments of the school naturally disappear. If age grouping itself is not feasible for big public-school classes, the attitude which is expressed in age grouping rather than grade grouping is nevertheless indispensable for an intelligent consideration of how to integrate the work of the lower school. The five year-old *qua* five-year-old is so like his six-year-old friend and his three-year-old or four-year-old brother that to plan for them in radically different departments seems utterly absurd; but at the same time he should not be repeating what he did when he was four, nor anticipating what he will be doing at six.

The fundamental questions at issue in integrating the work of the lower school are two: How can the school engage the child's time and attention most profitably at each age level? Of those things which it is profitable for him to do, which does he undertake with the greatest zest and interest at each age level? These questions should be considered, and tentatively answered, with reference to the materials to be introduced, the standards to be upheld, and the activities to be encouraged at each age level.

With regard to materials, the answers to these two main questions should be attempted through trying to reply to the following minor queries: Can these two-year-old and three-year-old children use this medium — crayons, clay, paint, or what not — effectively? Do they use it spontaneously, without having it forced upon them by the teacher or because there is nothing else to do? Will their use of this material now give them a facility which will enable them to use it better next year, or will they merely exhaust its possibilities for enjoyment without getting any real benefit if they use it now? Will the attempt to use this material meet with so little success that the children will be disinclined to use it later? These practical questions have until now received too little attention from intelligent teachers in our lower grades, kindergartens, and nursery schools. Through the observations and reports of teachers answers to these questions must be found, because only the teachers see the progress of individual and group work from day to day. A medium of expression, a toy, or a piece of apparatus for vigorous play is well chosen if the children show increasing pleasure in using it, and increasing control of it and of themselves in its use. It is inappropriate if used in an aimless fashion and finally either abandoned or boisterously abused.

Progress in drawing, in block-building, in singing, in any form of group play, depends in no small measure upon the teacher's skill in interpreting the child's purposes and in gradually raising his standards. But there is a vast difference between raising the child's own standards and imposing the adult's upon him. At three does the child comprehend what is meant by the remark "That is a fine, clear red. This green looks a bit muddy"? or "That is lovely color, John"? Does he know and care what is meant by the remark that his tower is so squarely built it will stand, while that house would fall over with one little knock? At what age can he understand the comment "That was a friendly thing to do"? Does he really perceive the horizon as we perceive it when he is seven or eight? Does it help his work in painting when we insist upon the way we see it, or does it hinder? These questions, too, need discussion by teachers of young children — by people who work every day with fives and sixes, with twos and threes. Thus may desirable integration gradually be effected.

If the child is first to attend nursery school, then kindergarten, then primary school, between the ages of two and seven, what is the best use to make of his time? If an intelligent four-year-old has attended nursery school for two years, and the nursery school was good enough to justify his attendance, he should be socially more capable and mature than a four-year-old who has not had this advantage. He should have learned certain ways of behaving in a group which it was once necessary to teach at the six-and-seven-year-old level. He has had some experience with plastic materials, probably he has played at block-building in a small co-operative group. Frankly he is, or should be, two or three jumps ahead of the child who appears at the door of the kindergarten at four or five to make his first entrance into a group. How shall we lead on our experienced four-year-old? How shall we enrich his experience so that life for the next three years won't be just a little more of the same thing?

Different people propose different answers to this question. One group, not without a show of justice, would like to solve the problem by pushing the formal work of the school downward. In order to get on in this perplexing world of ours, these people argue, one needs a great deal of education. Professional demands especially lengthen the years to be spent in formal study to a very long span. Art is long, and time is fleeting! Why not economize time by beginning the teaching of the fundamental skills at five instead of at six, in the case of the intellectually well-endowed child? Such a child, they say, after three years of preschool group life, is quite ready for new fields of endeavor; he will welcome new worlds to conquer.

To many experts in the field of early childhood education the objections to this proposal seem very serious and very fundamental. The five-year-old child has by no means exhausted the possibilities of construction, the beginnings of art and the industrial arts, music, and the enjoyment of nature-study explorations. His physical development still demands plenty of vigorous play involving the larger muscles, and much time spent out of doors. If he is to be socially happy and effective, the more experience he gets in playing with children of his own age the better. If he is encouraged to learn to read, and does so eagerly, he will tend to explore books to the exclusion, or at least the curtailment, of other equally valuable activities. Books encourage solitary activity and tempt the more introverted child away from group play. A really interesting and delightful person can do many things. Why not continue to stimulate the child to engage in varied activities instead of putting a premium on concentration upon one? Let the child continue to explore his environment, enrich his store of meanings, and increase his social sensitiveness and efficiency before you permit him to spend his energy on the acquisition of literary skills.

Another suggested solution is that the most capable children be allowed to skip a year of preschool work, going into a regular first grade at five. This, it is argued, keeps the preschool years free from the contamination of books and formal teaching. It makes it possible for the average child and the slow child to proceed peacefully in the enjoyment of their play life without being disturbed by finding some of their peers engaged in learning to read. They are thus protected from overstimulation, and the time of the bright child is not wasted.

"Skipping" at any age level has plenty of undesirable concomitants. Growth is a gradual, orderly process best furthered by gradual, orderly methods. Sudden jumps are not wise, because they are usually contemplated and made without consideration of the child's whole problem. Grades, for instance, organized to meet the needs of the average six-year-old or seven-year-old, are not planned to meet in the best possible way the physical and emotional requirements of the five-year-old.

However, the seriousness of not making some intelligent provision for the capable five-year-old child who went to nursery school at the age of two or thereabouts should not be overlooked. Several cases of this sort have recently come under the writer's observation. Jane, aged five and a half, is in the first grade of a progressive school where project work forms the main part of the curriculum. This is Jane's fourth year of group work. At two she was the most capable member of a nursery group made up of twos and threes. At three she was bossing the activities of the same group. At four she entered a class comparable with a kindergarten, where group projects, most of them initiated by the teacher, were the order of the day. Most of her schoolmates had not attended nursery school; the pace of the group was adapted to their needs, rather than to Jane's. At five Jane is thoroughly bored and blasé, disliking most of the school's activities. Much of her time is still spent in helping — much against the grain — the development of group projects.

In this case the child's preschool and first-grade activities show too much sameness and not enough real integration. What Jane has done each year was a little more of the same thing she did the year before. Intellectually extremely well endowed, she finds little challenge in the projects going on in her first-grade group. Because her efforts have never been seriously called upon, she has developed into a rather bossy, indolent young person whose adjustment to her present group is anything but desirable.

Such a sameness as that evident in Jane's case is not easy to avoid. Its avoidance requires ingenuity and resourcefulness in excess of that possessed by many teachers. The various fields of human knowledge must be canvassed to discover what they yield for the benefit of the youngest children. The enrichment of content at the preschool and primary level is absolutely essential.

Three hundred years ago Comenius bravely attempted to plan a rich curriculum for children between the ages of one and seven, in the little book which he called *The School of the Mother's Knee*. Today what he wrote seems quaint and charming, sometimes a little bizarre, often quite indefensible from the point of view of modern child psychology. But with no little insight and ingenuity Comenius drew upon the different school subjects, trying to show what they had to give to the child of preschool years. Geography, for instance, begins to enter the child's experience when he distinguishes his mother's breast from his other surroundings; it enters into his experience more fully as he successively investigates his nursery, the living room and kitchen, the garden, the community. At each step Comenius expected the mother to help him gain all that he could from each new venture.

Today the modern curriculum should be studied by teachers much as Comenius studied the problem. Language and literature; science; number; the fine arts and the industrial arts, — all these have a place in the child's experience, even in the nursery school. There should be definite progress and enrichment in each of these fields as the child grows older and as the horizon of his experience is extended.

At two and three the "work" in language is taken up: clarity of enunciation is encouraged, baby talk is gradually eliminated, and the vocabulary is increased so that the child may have a means of communicating his thoughts and impressions to adults and other children. Mother Goose rhymes, simple realistic stories of everyday life, very simple folk tales, are gradually acceptable for nursery-school use. Overstimulation should always be avoided; but what is done at four and five should show a progression beyond the first rhymes and stories of the nursery years. Too often, in preschool and primary groups, the prior experiences of the child are simply discounted by the teacher.

In elementary science and nature study there lies a vast field of interest for the child. Beginning with the care of pets and the investigation of the immediate environment, preschool and primary experience should include all manner of interesting explorations of natural surroundings. Collections — of leaves, of stones, of flowers — should be encouraged and respected. The possibilities of simple experiments in the physical sciences have only just begun to be tapped by teachers of young children. But the introduction of such experiences should not be a haphazard affair: it should be planned with reference to the changing needs and growing maturity of the child from year to year. Long before there is any thought of beginning formal work in number, the intelligent teacher should be helping the child to develop clear number concepts through various experiences. She should be alive to the chances of clearing up number concepts which occur in connection with almost every activity in which the group engages. This accumulation of rich and varied experience should be deliberately encouraged by the lower school from year to year.

The industrial arts are receiving much attention in lower-school work today. Probably more is being made of these possibilities with the youngest children than with any others. Yet even here sameness must be guarded against. When group projects are under way, children must be assured enough to do to make the work worth their while; otherwise they should be encouraged to go on with their individual plans. No child should be left standing about waiting to drive one nail as his contribution to a group piece of work. Some might argue that this arrangement teaches self-control; others say it puts a premium on the inefficient method of having too many hands available for too little work. The ability to work in groups develops slowly. The two-year-old works alone. Then he reaches the point where he likes to work *near* other children, even while he is still carrying out his own job by himself. Older children gradually organize small groups; then, larger ones. Left to themselves, they do not tend to have a fringe of helpers standing about. If the teacher wishes to stimulate group co-operation, she must provide natural conditions as sensible, at least, as those children provide for themselves.

A most important factor in the integration of the work of the lower school is the keeping of accurate and significant records, both of individual children and their growth and of the interesting, educative experiences provided through the guidance of the teacher. Such records will prevent the duplication of experiences, which leads to wasted effort on the teacher's part and boredom on the children's. If teachers of successive age groups can discuss these records among themselves, a progress in method should surely be achieved which will do much toward enriching the work of the pre-school and primary years.

The fundamental question in the integration of the work of the first school years is the achievement of a consistent philosophy, embracing within its scope the problems and questions which concern the nursery school, the kindergarten, and the primary grades. The implications of this philosophy should, ideally, be carried out with equal consistency in the cases of the two-year-old and the seven-year-old child.

The first step in the achievement of such a philosophy would necessarily be the breaking down of artificial barriers between nursery schools, kindergartens, and grades, a breaking down already virtually accomplished by the progressive schools which have done away with the grade system. Is there a place for a kindergarten as a separate institution in the new school's philosophy? Hardly. The kindergarten grew up as a special educational unit to do a particular piece of work according to a particular plan, in a day when a faulty educational psychology described the child of four or five as being in a vastly different stage of development from the child of six or seven. In good school systems it has gradually recognized its function as that of educating the child during a "preprimary" year. Even though it clings to its old name with sentimental fervor, the kindergarten is, properly, simply a five-year-old group carrying on interesting, planful work under the direction of a teacher. To cling to an old name which must always suggest an outworn tradition seems unintelligent and inappropriate. Willingly or no, in using this special name we suggest to the public mind an old division of policy and philosophy which the modern school has actually transcended.

Nursery schools, as we have said, are the product of modern scientific research in the field of child welfare. Their name suggests the consistency of their theory with the best modern thought. A nursery school has no ulterior motive beyond being the best possible kind of nursery. Unlike the infant school and the kindergarten, it does not attempt to force any formal teaching procedure upon the child or even to anticipate the curriculum of the old formal primary school. Whatever may be its faults and weaknesses in practice, the nursery school in theory is committed to the task of doing the best possible for the individual child's growth at each moment in his career.

Whether or not the name "nursery school" be destined to survive, the consistent philosophy which that name implies should distinguish not only our group work with children two and three years old, but our work with sixes and sevens and eights as well. This does not mean that the informality of the nursery school should be indefinitely prolonged, nor that teaching of formal skills should be deferred beyond all reason. What is natural, right, and proper for the two-year-old differs from what is best for the older child. With the passing of the years the child develops to the place where he appreciates the need for the tools which formal teaching places in his hands. He grows increasingly conventional; he is ready and eager to try to approximate conventional standards. By the time he is mentally six he normally not only does not resist learning to read, but actually desires to do so. If there is some resistance to hard work at the beginning, in the normal healthy child the sense of power which a mastery of reading gives him soon overcomes the resistance. An insistence that the nursery school is an example to the rest of the school in its honesty of approach to educational problems does not imply a recommendation that freedom from conventional requirements should be prolonged beyond a sensible time. It is probably as natural for the six-year-old to work at reading as it is for the three-year-old to play with toys most of the day. The point at issue is not how long the school can maintain the informality of a nursery school, but how consistently it can bring itself to do what is best for the child at each age level. It should also be added that the nursery school takes due account of individual differences, modifying its procedure as much as possible to meet the individual child's need. The same respect for individual differences should govern the work in the higher-age groups, but the older child's real wish to achieve conventional standards should not be overlooked in an unintelligent effort to cater to the individual.

One of the most radical and, undoubtedly, one of the most worthy efforts of the modern school to depart from the older tradition is found in the attempt to make school life a part of real life, to break down the old barrier which the school's walls formed between the interests of the community and the interests of the scholar. The success which one school achieved in this direction is nicely expressed in the comment of a ten-year-old pupil, who remarked at the luncheon table: "I like the W— school. It is just like living." No greater compliment could be paid to a school. But in this wholly laudable attempt to give reality and vitality to school experience, the selective function of organized education must not be forgotten. Schools developed, in the first place, to do better than the home or the general community could something which needed to be done for the young generation. The reason for their continued existence is that they can do certain important things better than home and other institutions. A well-trained teaching personnel, adequate professional leadership of faculties, provision for buildings and equipment, theoretically make it possible for every school, from the nursery group to the university, to select and perform adequately certain functions which the home and the community are not equipped to carry on. The school is a supplement, of a very important sort, to home and community education. As such it should not duplicate what is being done for the child elsewhere unless such duplication gives real reinforcement. In the nursery school the more closely certain aspects of the home situation are approached the better ; the school is simply a large group home where benefits are shared and expert guidance is provided. But as the child passes on through four-year-old and five-year-old and six-year-old groups, his interests and abilities demand more and more a kind of environment and guidance not represented by the home. In one sense home and school become more and more different, and properly so. Recognizing how vast are the needs of the child today for education and guidance in many different directions, it would be reprehensible to duplicate effort and otherwise waste energy by failing to select with great care those activities and experiences which are most needed and which can be best provided by the school. The adults of any generation are all of them more or less responsible for selecting what the young generation shall be taught, but the school as a highly specialized agency is particularly responsible for choosing and encouraging at each age level those experiences which are most valuable for the individual and significant for the social group. When the school extends its interests downward to include the earliest years, as an institution it becomes responsible for exercising its selective responsibility here just as conscientiously as at the higher-age levels.

Herein lies the real problem of integrating the work of the lower school: in selecting for the child of two, three, four, five, or six years those activities which are the most valuable and the most interesting for him to carry on in the school group at each age level. Neither early school groups among themselves nor the school and the home should wastefully duplicate effort; reinforcement rather than duplication, and enrichment rather than repetition, are the ends to be desired throughout the child's school progress.

BIBLIOGRAPHY

BAIN, WINIFRED E. An Analytical Study of Teaching in Nursery School, Kindergarten, and First Grade. Teachers College, Columbia University, New York, 1928.

"A scaled analysis of specific observable teaching acts typical of procedures in the nursery school, kindergarten, and first grade." When used by raters it brings out certain strong and weak points in teaching procedure in each.

California Curriculum Commission. Teachers' Guide to Child Development. Manual for Kindergarten and Primary Teachers. California State Printing Office, Sacramento, 1930.

CARR, W. G. "Status of the Kindergarten," *Childhood Education* (March–April, 1934), Vol. X, pp. 283–285, 374–376.

The place of the kindergarten in the school system.

CLOUSER, LUCY W., and MILLIKAN, CHLOE E. Kindergarten-Primary Activities Based on Community Life. Macmillan, New York, 1929.

The units described show definite integration and progression as between kindergarten and Grades I, II, III.

HILL, PATTY S. (Ed.). A Conduct Curriculum for the Kindergarten and First Grade. Scribner, New York, 1927.

The integration of kindergarten and first grade in terms of objectives, clearly presented.

ISAACS, SUSAN. The Children We Teach. University of London Press, London, 1932.

The individual differences of children in mental development at any given chronological age, studied with special reference to the child from seven to eleven.

LANE, ROBERT H.   A Teacher's Guide Book to the Activity Program. Macmillan, New York, 1932.

> Discusses the theory of the "life-centered" school, describes units of work, and evaluates procedure.

LANGDON, GRACE.   Similarities and Differences in Teaching in Nursery School, Kindergarten, and First Grade. John Day, New York, 1933.

Lincoln School Staff. Curriculum Making in an Elementary School, Chapters I–V. Ginn, Boston, 1927.

> A discussion of curriculum making and the standards for selecting units of work in the various grades.

MCLAUGHLIN, KATHARINE.   "Selected References on Kindergarten-Primary Education," *Elementary School Journal* (April, 1934), Vol. XXXIII, No. 8.

> A list of publications appearing from January 1, 1933, to January 1, 1934. In general, studies in the field of special subject matter or in that of preschool work have been excluded unless they give major emphasis to kindergarten-primary problems.

MILLER, M., and WILSON, M. B.   "Integration of Kindergarten and First-Grade Work," *Childhood Education* (October, 1933), Vol. X, pp. 33–37.

> A description of a concrete plan for integration, accompanied by a bibliography.

National College of Education.   Curriculum Records of an Elementary School, by members of the staff of the National College of Education, Evanston, Illinois, 1932.

> A complete presentation of curriculum planning in a fully staffed progressive school. Very helpful as an example of a well-integrated program.

PARKER, S. C., and TEMPLE, ALICE.   Unified Kindergarten and First-Grade Teaching. Ginn, Boston, 1925.

> For the integration of a lower-school program read especially Chapters I–VI.

REED, MARY, and WRIGHT, LULA E.   The Beginnings of the Social Sciences. Scribner, New York, 1932.

> A description of kindergarten and first-grade curricula in the social sciences, organized around children's experiences. An exceedingly helpful reference.

RUGG, HAROLD, and SHUMAKER, ANN.   The Child-Centered School, Chapters VII–XII. World Book, Yonkers, N.Y., 1928.

> A discussion of subject-matter selection and an evaluation of the criticisms to which progressive schools are subjected. Interesting in connection with the question of integration.

ZYVE, CLAIRE, and MERRILL, MARIE.   "Analysis of Trends in an Informal Unit Teaching Program," *Teachers College Record* (January, 1934), Vol. XXXV, No. 4, pp. 293–309.

> This article is part of a report to be published by the New York State Department of Education, Albany. It presents evidence of integration as between lower and higher elementary grades and between subjects.

CHAPTER V

METHOD AND THE NEW CURRICULUM

In educational literature the word "method" has more than one meaning. Very often it is employed in the sense of a specific way to teach one of the school subjects. Sometimes "method" is used to denote a device, or series of devices, through which a school activity that is without intrinsic interest to the child may be forced upon him with the minimum effort on the teacher's part and the minimum resentment on the pupil's part. In its broadest sense method means the whole interaction between teacher and pupils in a learning situation. Accepted in this last sense, method must take account not only of the specific content or skill to be taught at the given moment, but also of all the habits, attitudes, and appreciations not directly related to the immediate lesson but affected for good or ill by the whole classroom setting. In this sense method is inseparable from subject matter, and method and subject matter are two complementary aspects of the new curriculum.

The educational reformers of the nineteenth century who were responsible for arousing interest in the study of method used the term in its several meanings at different points in their writings. Froebel thought of method in its widest implication as play, which he believed was the purest form of self-activity. Herbart, in his analysis of the "cycle of thought," broadly defined method as the process of leading the child, through a study of his physical environment and a study of the race, to a comprehension of the essence of the good life and the development of a good moral character. Pestalozzi, whose philosophical background was far less adequate than that of Froebel or Herbart, broadly defined his method as that of *Anschauung*, or education through the intelligent apprehension of the environment. Yet Froebel laid down definite rules of method in the narrower sense for the presentation of gifts, occupations, and mother plays in the kindergarten; and Herbart, in his careful analysis of the steps of a lesson, dealt with method in the restricted sense of technique. Pestalozzi described in detail the method, or technique, of object teaching. The followers of Froebel, and those who applied the methods of Herbart and Pestalozzi to public-school use, very often suggested games and other devices for inveigling children to participate in otherwise uninteresting gift sequences, history lessons, and investigation of objects. Such devices, of course, represent method in its most restricted sense.

Dr. John Dewey has defined method as "the continuous reconstruction of experience" by the learner through reflection and a progressive deepening of meanings, the whole process to be guided by the teacher, who represents adult society in its functions of nurture and selection. It is method in this broadest and most inclusive sense which is the main concern of this chapter, method in the sense in which it is virtually inseparable from subject matter, since both are simply means for releasing and encouraging the creative activity of the child. One cannot consider the whole interaction between adult and child in an educational situation without being forced to consider subject matter and method, "the what and the how," of education interchangeably.

To see method in the large does not rule out the need for good special methods of teaching the various traditional subjects; it merely places such methods in a subordinate position with respect to the whole aim and end of education. Problems of teaching reading, writing, number, — indeed, all the "school subjects," — are being carefully studied in laboratories and in the classrooms of progressive schools, with greatly increased efficiency of teaching as a result. There are, assuredly, good, better, and best ways of conducting arithmetic drill, of teaching spelling, of arranging first-grade reading material. The object of the progressive school is to use the best means of accomplishing minimum routine requirements, so that child energy and school time may be conserved and utilized to broaden and enrich the traditional school curriculum.

For "methods" in the sense of devices to keep children superficially interested in material which has no real appeal for them, or to maintain discipline in an overcrowded classroom, modern educational theory can find little place. When drills have to be kept going by tricks and games, our present conclusion is that drills are unsuitable in that time and place. Where order and attention have to be preserved by endlessly diverting the children through playful pastimes, there is something wrong with classroom organization. Whereas twenty years ago the good teacher was the one who had a thousand and one devices at her command, the teacher today who has to resort to such ruses frequently is suspected of being not quite so capable as the average. In the rare cases where devices are useful, because something difficult must be done to fulfill an arbitrary requirement or because the class is too large and heterogeneous to respond easily, they should be carefully chosen. A device is occasionally permissible if its interest can be subordinated to the requirements of the work to be accomplished. For instance, a relay race to speed up column addition is good if it helps the class to concentrate on number combinations. It is a poor device when the excitement of the game itself makes for careless work and the sacrifice of accuracy to speed. Properly speaking, the device occupies a very inconspicuous place in good teaching, appearing but rarely, and then as a subordinate part of technique.

The more radical changes in American school methods have resulted largely from the teachings of Dr. Dewey. There have been, however, some less far-reaching efforts to modify classroom procedure which have represented a move in the general direction of democratic organization and a different relationship between teacher and children. One of the earliest of these was the "socialized recitation," a product of the Herbartian influence. The socialized recitation was a plan by which more responsibility was placed upon the students of a class for the progress of the recitation lesson than they were obliged to assume under the old question-and-answer method. In the socialized recitation individual children are asked to volunteer reports, and sometimes the work of a small group is reported upon by a representing member. Occasionally the "socializing" of a recitation simply means allowing one of the children to take the place of the teacher in questioning the class. The socializing effect of this last procedure is not easy to see, for often the child "hearing" the lesson merely successfully apes the worst practices of particularly weak teachers. Sometimes, too, a bad situation is made worse by the teacher's failure to function in the group at all, allowing mistakes to creep in unchecked and, in general, failing to make sure that the group as a whole gains by the performance. The one unquestioned advantage of the socialized recitation is the fact that the teacher is encouraged to take her place as a member (albeit a leader) of a group, rather than as a mere hearer of lessons.

The method of object teaching influenced the lower school more strongly than the socialized recitation; but object teaching in America, as was mentioned before, was of the formal variety imported from England. As such, it was an adventure in method in the narrower sense of technique, although method in the broader sense also was involved because "object" teaching focused attention upon the child's self-active prehension of the world about him, in contrast with simple receptivity. Froebel's methods had little direct effect upon actual teaching in elementary schools. The influence of his educational theories upon the school, as appeared earlier, was exerted indirectly through the contacts between kindergarten and lower-grade teachers.

Before passing on to the "project method," or the interpretation for the classroom teacher of Dewey's philosophy of education, it may be well to mention certain administrative

devices which touch very closely upon the problem of method
in both its wider aspects and its narrower aspects. The platoon plan, the Winnetka plan, and the Dalton plan have
all three definitely affected the methods of teaching in our
public schools.

The platoon plan was urged by its advocates as a good
means of realizing Dr. Dewey's educational aims in dealing
with large numbers of children. In spite of this idealistic
purpose the plan has been severely criticized not only by
educators but also by organized labor as a mechanization of
classroom instruction and a reduction to a dangerous minimum of personal contacts between teachers and children.
Variations of the platoon plan are many, but its essential
principles are common to all varieties. Under the platoon
plan the school day is roughly divided into two sessions.
During one session half the school is busy in its home rooms,
learning the "tool subjects." The other half of the school is
passing from one special teacher to another for instruction
in history, literature, the fine arts, and other "special" subjects. During the second session the procedure is reversed:
the group which was engaged in home-room activities during
the morning passes from shop and laboratory to special classroom, to gym; and the special-subject group of the morning
returns to home rooms for drill in the three R's. By this
means every available bit of space in the school can be used
every minute of the day, and a home-room teacher can "take
care of" eighty or a hundred children instead of forty or
fifty. Teachers who have interests in special fields are released from the need of teaching all the subjects of the curriculum, and children are released from the tedium of one
teacher for six hours a day five days a week. In some schools
and systems the plan begins with the sixth grade; in certain
cities it begins with the first grade. The disadvantages of
such a highly mechanized way of dealing with hordes of
children are more apparent, of course, in the case of the
younger child then in that of the older. But the plan as
a whole can scarcely be advocated on the ground that it

approximates an ideal arrangement. It may provide better equipment and facilities, in some cases better teaching, but it cannot provide for the youngest children the amount of individual guidance and encouragement which little children need. Obviously, too, it makes for a cleavage between the three R's and the content subjects; between tools and their uses.

The Winnetka plan has been developed by Carleton Washburne in the schools of Winnetka, Illinois. It too divides the school day into two more or less discrete parts, giving half the time to drill subjects and half to content. In the drill subjects — reading, writing, number — individual children are allowed to progress at their own rate through a series of carefully planned practice drills. These are in constant process of refinement and improvement, and the Winnetka materials have been a great boon to teachers throughout the country. Content subjects, however, are taught to groups in the Winnetka plan, because in literature and the social studies the give and take of group discussion is believed to be indispensable. Like the platoon plan, the Winnetka plan makes for a cleavage between drill and content subjects, although it has the great advantage of saving the capable child's time by letting him go at his own rate in learning to read and write and use number, at the same time saving the slow child from pressure and a sense of failure.

The Dalton plan is a device for purely individual instruction, which has had more effect upon the course of events in upper elementary and high-school teaching than upon the primary school. In only a few instances has a real Dalton plan been attempted in dealing with the youngest children, and in the Dalton School of New York City no effort is made to teach children through a system of individual contracts until the fifth grade. The essential feature of the Dalton plan is that each child contracts to complete a certain number of carefully assigned lessons in a given time. He is supplied with "guide sheets," which give him every possible aid to study, and his teachers, of course, are always available for consultation. Like the Winnetka plan, the Dalton plan has the advantage of providing for a wide range of individual differences in ability. It is challenged by many on the ground that educational activity should go on in a group situation, and not in isolation : working mostly by himself, the child does not get the experience in group living and collective planning which seems essential for effective membership in a democratic society.

The platoon, the Winnetka, and the Dalton plans all represent administrative devices which are intended to promote efficient methods of teaching. Their adoption does not necessarily imply a radical reconstruction of one's educational philosophy.

The complete reorganization of school procedure, classroom method, and curriculum content which the educational aims set forth by Dr. Dewey demand was first carefully described by Dr. Kilpatrick in his monograph on the "Project Method." From this point of view the unit of all education is the purposeful act, carried on in a social situation under adequate guidance. Dr. Kilpatrick has shown in his book *Foundations of Method* the close affinity between the principles of the project method and the general trend of "stimulus-response" psychology. When a child purposes to act, all his pertinent inner resources are marshaled and alert to carry out his purpose. To act upon his purposes is pleasing to him ; to carry them through to a successful conclusion brings him concrete satisfaction. The processes through which the child passes in carrying his act to conclusion are these : first, the original purposing ; second, careful planning ; third, the carrying out of his plan ; lastly, the judgment of the results, which judgment often leads to a modification of original plans, a different form of execution, and a final result more satisfying to the child than the original effort.

Evidently a procedure like this, with all activity starting in the purposes of the children, demands a fundamental change in the attitude of the teacher. She becomes, in the first place, a student of child purposes, and then a guide in the planning, executing, and judging of these purposes. Classroom organization is necessarily flexible, for children must have a high degree of individual freedom within the social group to carry out their plans. Discipline is achieved through the happy concentration of children upon their own pursuits rather than through arbitrary requirement.

Evidently, too, the content of the curriculum must change when the child's own purpose becomes the unit of the teaching process. Children's interests cannot be expected to follow exactly along the line of the old curriculum requirements. With regard to content, Dr. Kilpatrick distinguishes four types of projects: the construction project, in the course of which the child makes something which he desires to have, either to help him in his dramatic play, or to give to someone, or to place in a school exhibit; the drill project, in which the child purposes to reach a certain degree of skill in some performance, for instance, to write as well as the third-grade standard performance given on a writing scale, or to complete a practice test in arithmetic in a given time; the problem project, in which the child purposes to find the solution of some problem which really interests him, either one which has arisen in connection with his work at school or one which has occurred to him in the course of his experience outside school; the appreciation project, in which the children and the teacher together purpose to enjoy some delightful experience, such as studying a picture or listening to a radio concert. These varied activities have in common their origin in the purpose or intention of the child or the group and the fact that activity on the child's part as well as on that of the teacher is taken as essential.

As the project method was introduced into the lower schools, the "construction" project became very popular. Young children delight in making things and doing things; they enjoy most a concrete, tangible result of their labors. The evaluation of construction projects was seen to be attended by great satisfaction; the standards of success were altogether concrete. If the child had made a stool, could he sit on it? If he modeled a dish out of clay, would it hold anything? If he cut and sewed a garment, did it fit? Could it be put on the person or the doll for which it was intended? Did it look like the sort of garment he intended it to be?

The suitability of these construction projects for the young child, and the fact that most "project" work was carried out in the lower grades, led to the mistaken assumption on the part of many that construction work was essential to the project method. Those who had not grasped the underlying theory, who failed to see project teaching in its true relation to "the continuous reconstruction of experience" and the laws of learning, jumped to the conclusion that the essentials of the project method were more moving about and more confusion in the classroom, regardless of how this activity was directed. A little more paste and a little less order, a little more activity and less achievement in the traditional subjects, unfortunately became associated with project teaching in the public mind. Such an interpretation is altogether foreign to the real theory of the project method. The essence of the project is child purposing: a child may purpose to read a book, or enjoy a story, or solve an abstract problem as naturally at certain stages of his development as the young child purposes to weave a hammock for her doll. Projects are not real projects at all, and most assuredly are not educative, unless they do involve serious planning, careful execution, and intelligent evaluation of the work accomplished.

The difficulties and dangers inherent in the project method were not overlooked by the people who first advocated its introduction into the schools. One of the most fundamental of these difficulties lay in the problem of selection. Children have many purposes, a large proportion of them very flitting. Who is to decide which of these many purposes shall be cultivated in the classroom, and by what standards should the selection be made? From the very beginning Dr. Kilpatrick and others interested in project teaching suggested certain ways in which teachers could make such decisions. Valuable projects should enlist the child's whole effort; they should enrich his store of meanings and increase his control over himself and his surroundings. The value of projects could also be partly determined by whether or not they generally led on into other valuable undertakings: if certain projects seemed to lead the child to repeat the same thing over and over again, or to turn to something trivial the minute a piece of work was finished, they could not be called valuable. The difficulty with these criteria lies in the fact that their application demands a great deal more of intelligence and foresight in the teacher than does the mere conscientious following of a definite course of study prepared in advance. "We desire to have a child wish what he does; we do not necessarily care to have him do as he wishes," Dr. Kilpatrick has explained. But project work has often been misunderstood to mean just exactly letting children do what they wish.

From the point of view of good curriculum making, the project method requires a great deal of thought in order to assure for the child a rounded school experience in any given year and also throughout his school career. There must be a development in the completeness and value of children's projects from month to month and from year to year. There must not be undue repetition in later grades of projects carried through in the earlier years. A great deal of consultation between teachers and supervisors and subject-matter experts is essential in order to plan for a well-balanced progress throughout the year, with enough continuity to ensure sound scholarship.

Teaching by projects requires a better training for classroom teachers than was needed under the old regime. Much more accurate general information and, above all, the ability to use sources wisely and expeditiously are required for project teaching in even the lowest grades. A lively, intelligent group of seven-year-olds, encouraged to express and develop their own interests, may well be a challenge to a college-trained adult. For the well-trained teacher the delightful thing about the project method is just this demand upon her scholarship and abilities as a leader; for the poorly trained the project method becomes an exhausting task if not an utterly impossible one. Some of the difficulties which have been encountered with project work have been due to the poor general background of individual teachers, and the failure on the part of administrators to realize that cultural background is essential for success in this work.

The method of purposeful activity can be carried out with success only by teachers who have a good working knowledge of child psychology and the psychology of learning. The ability to understand children as people, and the discernment to appreciate how much drill is needed before certain information is fixed and certain skills acquired, are essential for success. For at each point in the development of the purposeful act the teacher should function as a skillful adult guide. Among many purposes, she helps the child decide upon the most fruitful. From a "trial and error" system of planning she helps him progress toward intelligent forethought. When the child sees the need for a technique in executing his plan, the teacher is there to help him get it; when he does not see the need, she should point it out. In the judging of results it is the teacher's part to hold each child up to his own best standards and to see that his own best standards become progressively better. Although in all this she ideally functions as a guide rather than a taskmaster, she is none the less active and alert. Procedure of this sort requires real insight into the thoughts and feelings of children and real skill in giving formal training as it is required.

During the last few years there have been many criticisms of the project method and the philosophy of education which lies behind it. Some of these criticisms have been entirely just; for, as already implied in this chapter, much trivial, poorly organized classroom work was excused on the ground that the "project method" was being pursued. Moreover, in certain progressive schools where the purposeful act was taken as the unit of classroom procedure throughout the kindergarten and the elementary grades, poor scholarship was the result : there were great gaps in the children's preparation when they came to undertake the work of the secondary school. Six or seven years ago Dr. Harold Rugg, who is a most sincere and thorough student of curriculum theory and educational practice, remarked that one of the most serious criticisms of the so-called "progressive school" is lack of scholarship. However, Dr. Rugg and other openminded students of the matter agreed that this poor scholarship was not inherent in the method of purposeful activity, but traceable rather to a failure of teachers and administrators to appreciate the great demands which such a method places upon everyone concerned : school heads, classroom teachers, and pupils. The dangers to scholarship, and the difficulties of wisely guiding pupil purposing, had been overlooked, in spite of the warnings of Dr. Kilpatrick and other leaders of the movement.

Since about 1928 there has been a consistent effort to introduce the method of child activity into the public schools of the land, but to introduce it slowly and carefully, without jeopardizing good academic work. Partly because of the mistakes and misunderstandings which had grown up around the terms "project" and "project method," a new terminology has been used in connection with these more recent attempts, with the result that "activity curriculum," "unit of work," "centers of interest," and "child experiences" are now more frequent expressions. Progressive public-school men in many states are working toward the introduction of an activity curriculum which will gradually replace the old cut-and-dried courses of study.

The activity curriculum proceeds on the assumption that among the normal interests and play purposes of children there are many which have possibilities for real social and educational usefulness. These interests and play purposes may be, as it were, imported into the classroom and utilized by the teacher in constructive ways without sacrificing the formal training in skills which many people consider essential. Units of work may be planned which are altogether in line with the normal child's interests and which are also valuable from the standpoint of formal education; and, within certain wide limits, these units of work may be planned in advance. For example, experienced teachers know that little children are interested in playing, and incidentally learning about, family life and home activities, and that somewhat older children are interested in the community life about them. Many of the problems which society faces in providing food, clothing, and shelter may profitably be studied by boys and girls without departing in any large measure from the sort of thing they would like to do if left to themselves. The activity curriculum also implies that play is the most effective method of learning, and that play may be introduced into the classroom and directed toward desirable ends, the teacher deciding beforehand what general direction it is to follow. A unit of work around family life has excellent play possibilities for the younger child; a unit of work around air transportation can enlist the enthusiastic interest and play energies of the older child.

In the selection of units of work for the activity curriculum the minimum formal requirements for the different grades are kept in mind: reading, writing, number, and the social studies in the form appropriate to the grade in question are related to the unit of work as a center, or core. Sometimes practically all the work of a grade is fused in the unit; that is, each school subject is taught only as it affects the unit. For instance, if the second grade is studying Indian life, the reading and written English are carried on in the course of becoming acquainted with Indian legends; the oral-English teaching comes in connection with discussions or dramatization of Indian life; the arithmetic is taught as it is needed in the making of costumes, the arrangement of stage settings, the planning of a wigwam, and so on. As isolated subjects school activities thus lose their identity.

One of the immediate results of introducing even a conservative interpretation of the activity curriculum into the schools of the nation is just this breaking down of subject-matter barriers. From the first grade straight through to the senior year in college this is the tendency of contemporary educational experiment. As the child progresses through his school years this tendency toward fusion creates certain problems for him and for his teachers which do not concern us so much in our dealings with the younger child. This is assuredly a wholesome and interesting tendency, entirely in line with what we know of the way the human mind develops, and surely sound in early education. However, just as planning, executing, and judging projects require delicate guidance of the child by the teacher, so the whole attempt at correlation, or fusion, requires careful checking upon attainments in the specific skills. It may well be that the activity curriculum unavoidably sacrifices certain conventional standards of attainment in the skills, and that the sacrifices made are justified. The intelligent teacher should know the extent of the sacrifice, and the intelligent supervisor or administrator must decide whether in any particular class or individual case it is wise to make it.

Any sort of radical change in the curriculum should be accompanied by community education as to what is going forward. Parents, and even children, are sometimes very conservative; they assume certain things about school standards: that a first-grade child learns to read, that the third-grade child has made strides in writing and spelling and knows his multiplication tables. If the school does not achieve these results, the school's clients are entitled to an explanation, even though not to an apology.

The freer activity of the new schools makes it necessary to revise some of our popular notions about order and discipline in a classroom. Where there is play activity, there must be more noise than where children are all working "out of books." A very important part of the teacher's method lies in preserving an atmosphere of interested, active work and avoiding a general sense of confusion. Noise must not become so great that children's nerves are exhausted by the end of the day, but, on the other hand, an amount of noise which grates upon a teacher may not be at all confusing to the child. Teachers who work with projects and participate in an activity curriculum should give careful thought to the problem of classroom management. So far as possible children should aid in the making and enforcement of rules, but the teacher is finally responsible for the general atmosphere of the room.

A well-planned activity curriculum gives a variety of opportunities for individual children to contribute to the work of the group according to their special needs and abilities. Individualization of method is just as necessary here as in more formal school procedures; for many children it is easier to be passively receptive toward adult commands and suggestions than to take responsibility for independent choice and active participation in a group. Such children need special guidance in finding out what they have to contribute to group undertakings, and special encouragement to give it. Ideally, the education of the child for participation in group projects begins in the preschool period, but for children who have not had preschool training the adjustment must be made in the early grades.

The reader will see from this discussion that the project method and the activity curriculum are identical in their fundamental principles. Both call for purposeful activity on the part of children and for guidance on the part of teachers. Passivity and domination have no place in either. But it so happens that in some situations the project method was first attempted in a somewhat extreme form, with teachers afraid to plan their curriculum in advance and with bewildered children swinging from one project to the next without at all understanding where they were going, or why. On the other hand, the activity curriculum is associated with a much more conservative attempt to introduce child purposes into school procedure; in many of the present efforts the activities are frankly selected in advance by the teacher or a committee of teachers. In the days when we talked more about projects many people thought that projects should be selected in advance and suggested to the children by the teacher, just as many people today want very carefully adult-regulated activities. There are conservatives and radicals — if one likes those expressions — among leaders in the activity movement at present, just as there were in the first years of enthusiasm about projects.

A very complete account of the activity movement is given in the *Yearbook of the National Society for the Scientific Study of Education* for 1930. The identity of activity curricula with project curricula will be plain to anyone who studies these very thorough professional discussions. The yearbook also includes reflections upon the subject of the activity curriculum from leading educators who represent many different points of view, from conservative to radical. Margaret Pollitzer, head of the Walden School of New York City, for instance, thinks that the activity curriculum is too formal a conception for the Walden School. With justice she states that it could easily become just as dry, just as teacher-imposed as any course of study. This is certainly true if the cautious group who are afraid of any spontaneity get their way and swing the course of the movement.

In the last three years there have been many bitter criticisms of so-called "progressive education" on the ground that it stands for the selfish individualism to which we now trace so many of our social ills. Dr. Kandel has been especially caustic in his denunciations. Those who are deeply interested in American education are ready to give such an indictment full and careful consideration. But to this more serious criticism, as to the less serious remarks about poor scholarship as a result of project teaching, the answer is that where selfishness results the fault lies not in the underlying theory of the purposeful act as the unit of all true education. Rather does it lie in the inadequacy of teachers for the difficult leadership this method requires, or in a misinterpretation of the theory; for it must be borne in mind that Dewey and Kilpatrick have from the first insisted that purposing, to be fruitful, must go on *in and as a part of a social environment*, with all that human association implies in the way of co-operation and constant give and take.

The new curriculum, then, whether its units be called "projects" or "activities," calls for changes in both content and method, the "what" and the "how" of education. Its essentials might be summed up in the following manner: The content of the curriculum should be based so far as possible upon the normal interests of children. This content should be rich and varied; and gradually the social sciences, the skills of reading and writing and number, should enter in as they are needed to enrich the child's experience. There should be opportunity for as much initiative on the part of individuals as is consistent with the best good of the group. The results of the curriculum should appear in the form of better self-control on the part of individuals, a greater degree of intelligent co-operation in the group, a satisfactory amount of useful information gained, and an increase in command over socially useful skills.

In order that the aims of the new curriculum may be fully realized, certain changes in school housing, equipment, and schedules are highly desirable. These factors will be discussed in later chapters. But the essential points in the new procedure are comparatively independent of particular school surroundings. Rather are they contingent upon the intelligence, training, and social attitude of the teacher herself.

BIBLIOGRAPHY

BONSER, FREDERICK GORDON. The Elementary School Curriculum. Macmillan, New York, 1921.

> A discussion of the industrial arts in the elementary-school curriculum; the most complete published treatment of the subject.

COLLINGS, ELLSWORTH. Project Teaching in Elementary Schools. Chapter VI, "Teaching through Guidance." Century, New York, 1928.

> Presents very clearly the psychological processes involved in teaching and learning according to the newer methods.

DEWEY, JOHN. Interest and Effort in Education. Houghton Mifflin, Boston, 1913.

> One of Dr. Dewey's most important monographs for the library of the lower-school teacher.

DEWEY, JOHN. The Child and the Curriculum. University of Chicago Press, 1916.

> A clear presentation of Dr. Dewey's curriculum theory.

FOREST, ILSE. "The Activity Curriculum," *Educational Outlook* (January, 1933), Vol. VII, No. 2, pp. 86–94.

HISSONG, CLYDE. The Activity Movement. *Educational Psychology Monographs No. 30.* Warwick and York, Baltimore, 1932.

> A historical account of the movement and a discussion of its present values.

JOHNSON, ELEANOR (Compiler). "The New School: Its Philosophy, Teaching Technique, and Curriculum," *Childhood Education* (January, 1933), Vol. IX.

KILPATRICK, WILLIAM H. Foundations of Method. Macmillan, New York, 1925.

> A discussion, in dialogue form, of Dr. Kilpatrick's theory of method.

LANE, ROBERT HILL. A Teachers' Guide to the Activity Program. Macmillan, New York, 1932.

> A very helpful book. Chapter I ("The Background"), Chapter II ("First Steps"), Chapter V ("The Teacher at Work in the New School"), Chapter VI ("The Teacher Checks Herself"), of general value. Consult Chapter V also for time schedule.

MEAD, CYRUS D., and ORTH, FRED. The Transitional Public School, Macmillan, New York, 1934.

> Part I, theory and philosophy underlying the "activity" school versus the more conventional "subject-matter" school.

MELVIN, A. GORDON. The Technique of Progressive Teaching, Part I, "Basic Theories of Teaching," Part II, "Fundamentals of Technique." John Day Company, New York, 1932.

> Gives a good general discussion of method and the new curriculum.

MERIAM, JUNIUS. Child Life and the Curriculum. World Book, Yonkers, N. Y., 1920.

> Of historical interest as an early estimation of the project method. The school described is the laboratory school of the University of Missouri.

National Society for the Scientific Study of Education. Thirty-third Yearbook, Part II; Parts I–IV, "The Activity Movement." Public School Publishing Company, Bloomington, Illinois, 1934.

> A complete presentation of the theory and practice of such work. An invaluable reference for all those interested in activity work.

PORTER, MARTHA PECK. The Teacher in the New School. World Book, Yonkers, N.Y., 1931.

> A very interesting description of activity work in a third grade. A helpful reference from the point of view of teaching method, especially Chapters II, III, IV.

RUGG, HAROLD, and SHUMAKER, ANN. The Child-Centered School. Chapters I–V. World Book, Yonkers, N.Y., 1928.

> A general discussion of the new school's philosophy and its emergence in teaching method.

CHAPTER VI

PLANNING THE UNITS OF WORK

The activities of the new curriculum, planned and carried out by teachers and children with certain definite ends of accomplishment in view, are frequently called units of work. The Lincoln School of Teachers College, Columbia University, has published several units in very complete descriptive form, all the work described having been carried out under the unusually fine conditions provided by the Lincoln School itself. The Teachers College Bureau of Publications has put out a series of eighty-odd units, less elaborately described, and prepared by teachers in public and private schools throughout the country. The editors of the latter series have encouraged teachers everywhere to contribute, merely stipulating that the work submitted must always represent what has been achieved in a classroom situation. With such varied authorship, it is not surprising that the Teachers College units represent a wide range of educational theories and great variation of emphasis. Some are definitely teacher-planned activities, differing from the old-fashioned lesson plan only in name and rhetorical form; others are accurately descriptive of child activities, and are accordingly spontaneous and delightful.

Units of work, or, as they are sometimes called, centers of interest, as a method of planning the activities of the school year, do not necessarily imply a philosophy of education which gives the interests of children an important place in the construction of curricula and the determination of method. Neither is there much agreement as to the way in which the units may themselves best be written up for the guidance of teachers and the records of supervisors.

Experienced teachers whose work with children is really creative find it difficult to describe their activities in writing. No matter how beautifully the project or the unit is written up, something of the spontaneity which accompanied what was said and done by teacher and children is lost in the process of description. Yet descriptions of the newer type of work are very badly needed for the benefit of younger teachers and teachers in training, as well as for the purpose of clarifying the ideas of those who are engaged in constant experimentation. The modern lower-school curriculum needs protection from two opposing dangers: on the one hand, lack of coherence and definite objectives due to too little formal planning; on the other hand, a reversion to the old dry-as-dust course of study in modern dress through a formal, stereotyped description of units or through the arbitrary assignment, by supervisory officers, of activities to be carried on in each grade. Either extreme may be fatal for real progress.

A first step in the planning of activities, and one which offends neither by being arbitrary nor by a tendency to vagueness, is the setting up of standards in the light of which units may be judged. Such standards have been admirably worked out in several of the newer books on lower-school teaching. They may be briefly summarized here.

A unit of work should be intrinsically interesting to boys and girls of the age and school grade for which it is intended.

The subject selected should give the children the opportunity and incentive to acquire socially desirable habits, attitudes, and information.

The subject should be well chosen with respect to the particular environment of the children who are to participate in it. For instance, a center of interest such as "Studying the Boats in the Harbor" may be well suited to an intelligent five-year-old group living on the seashore, who are naturally familiar with and interested in boats. It would be too difficult a unit for a similar group of children in a

Midwestern town who perhaps had never seen a boat and to whom the whole business of navigation would be vague and unreal. The children in a city like New Haven, Connecticut, could learn much about boats through observation and first-hand experience. Such first-hand experience is very important for lower-school pupils, who easily form inaccurate and bizarre conceptions as a result of verbal description. Of course pictures and other illustrative material can be made very helpful, but even these do not compare with actual, immediate experience.

When the successful carrying out of a unit depends upon having the children get information through reading, the reading matter should be easily obtainable and well suited to the children's reading capacity.

A further standard which seems applicable is that a unit of work in first and second grades may well be directed in such a way that the children shall get practice in the basic skills of oral expression, reading, and number. This standard is actually a special case of one already mentioned, that a good unit promotes the acquisition of socially desirable habits, attitudes, and information. The restatement seems in place because many people seem to overlook the fact that reading and number are activities which are intrinsically interesting to children. To these people there appears to be an opposition between teaching the skills and carrying on interesting units of work. Such an opposition is apparent only. As a final criterion, a good unit of work should lead on to other interesting activities.

The standards so far mentioned are general and apply to centers of interest in any grade. When one turns to the consideration of how to plan a specific unit, it becomes really difficult to be definite without becoming dogmatic. In the opinion of the present writer, teachers — especially the less experienced teachers— need to plan units rather definitely in advance, picturing imaginatively the course they will take but remaining flexible about this course until they are actually working it out with the children. It is for this reason that the suggestions for planning a unit which appear below are offered for the reader's consideration.

The form for the writing up of a center of interest or unit of work should be so framed that the result is clear and satisfying to the teacher carrying on the work, as well as meaningful to the reader who has not seen the activity in progress. Information as to the age, general intelligence, and social background of the children participating is especially needed in the latter case. The purpose of the activity and the time spent in carrying it out should be stated; the teacher's activities, the children's activities, the materials and equipment used should appear also. The information gained by the children should be clearly and honestly stated. Suitable bibliographies for both teacher and children are an extremely valuable part of the record.

High-sounding objectives or outcomes should be avoided, or at least stated with care. We hope that children will develop "a spirit of co-operation" as a result of their group activities; we should like them to gain "worthy leisure-time interests"; but at the same time we know that only a tiny bit of progress in the general direction of these ideals is made by any one good teaching unit. Too much time and effort spent in formulating these fine, remote objectives, a too flowery description of outcomes in terms of character changes, tend to blind teachers to the plain, immediate ends which can be hoped for as the result of a few weeks' good teaching. In stating outcomes, especially, it is better to confine oneself to objective evidence rather than pious hopes. For instance, "Mary had no idea of 'taking turns' when the work began; at the end of this unit she was showing better co-operation by waiting for the hammer until another child had finished with it," states a fact; "Mary is much better adjusted socially" conveys a slight possibility.

The units which follow are offered in illustration of what is being done in good schools where teachers are conscientiously planning their work even while they give full play to the initiative and originality of their pupils. No one unit, as described, is considered a perfect model by its author. They are illustrations only; representing careful, honest teaching, carried on with an open mind.

THE ROGER SHERMAN KINDERGARTEN, NEW HAVEN, CONNECTICUT

Activities described by Miss Anna McManus

The Roger Sherman School is a demonstration school conducted by the New Haven State Normal School. For space the kindergarten is limited to one fair-sized, pleasant room, with two dressing rooms and a lavatory across the hall. The equipment is modern, but because of the limited space all the large apparatus has to be placed in the school yard.

The children come from comfortable homes, in some cases from wealthy homes. Their parents are lawyers, physicians, merchants, and college professors. Most of the mothers have active interests outside their own homes, some of them doing professional work and others being engaged in business. The majority of the homes are American, but there are a few children from French, English, German, and Italian homes. About half the families live in apartments; the others in private houses; many of them have summer homes in the mountains or at the seashore. The school has a co-operative Parent-Teacher Association. There are frequent conferences between parents and teachers, and the homes are visited at least once during the school year.

Problem cases are tested by the school psychologist, and each child is given the Pintner-Cunningham Test before entering the first grade.

There are two kindergarten sessions, forty children being enrolled in the morning group and forty in the afternoon. There are two teachers, each acting in the capacity of director for one session.

The following center of interest was developed during the opening days of school with the younger group of children, who are between four and five years old.

An Excursion through the School Building

The objectives which the teacher had in mind were these: to help the children develop a happy spirit in their new environment by getting them well acquainted with the school building; to have the children meet the principal, the school nurse, the librarian, the custodian, and some of the other teachers, so that these strange grown-ups would come to be recognized as friends of the children.

As her part in the activity the teacher planned little excursions through the building: to the principal's office, the nurse's room, the power plant, the library, the assembly room, and some of the other classrooms. In the course of their activities the children eagerly visited these places, asking questions and gaining useful information. They learned that the principal gives help to teachers and children, the nurse comes to keep children well, the librarian helps to choose interesting books, the custodian keeps the building clean. They began to develop the idea that the school building belongs to the children, who must help to take care of it.

They were encouraged to use their own library corner and had some first experiences in taking material out and putting it away after they had finished playing.

During four weeks later in the year the following center of interest was developed with the same group.

Learning about the Home and Family

Children of this age love to play house. The teacher planned to encourage their play with a view to realizing certain definite objectives. These were the following: to have the children learn how to take care of a playhouse; to wash, rinse, and hang up dolls' clothes; to wash and dry dishes; to use broom, mop, and dustpan correctly.

Accordingly, in the course of her own activities the teacher provided material for building a playhouse, and saw to it that dolls, dolls' clothes, dolls' dishes, and small-sized house-

The Playhouse, Four-Year-Old Group

keeping and cleaning utensils were available. She showed the children how to use the utensils, how to wash clothes, and, in a few cases, how to iron. She made occasional suggestions to make the play more interesting.

The children first built a playhouse with the teacher's help. Then they played house. In the course of their play they swept and dusted and tidied up, they washed and dried clothes and dishes, they set the table, they decorated the house. A few children, under supervision, used a small electric iron. As a special activity they made applesauce and cooked some cereal.

The outcomes of the activity were the building of a satisfactory playhouse, the acquisition of some skill in keeping their playhouse clean and in order, and the acquisition of skill in keeping dolls' clothes clean. This last outcome might be questioned by the skeptical, and many would doubt the wisdom of letting children iron. Of course the ironing was done under close supervision, but it is an interesting fact that it is no longer necessary for the teacher to take the

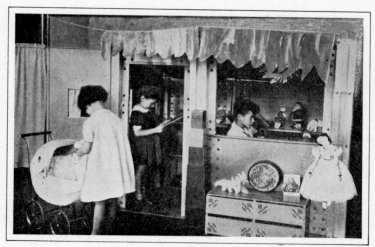

J. C. Neff

The Store, Five-Year-Old Group

dolls' clothes home for laundering. The children do it all. It is certain that they played together more and more happily as the days went on, and equally certain that they enjoyed their doll play very much.

The materials provided were two large cartons, some strips of wood, saw, nails, hammers, materials for curtains, and the equipment for playing house mentioned above. The two large cartons were taken apart and nailed to a light wooden frame made by the children under the teacher's guidance. A picture of the house appears on page 106.

The bibliographies used in connection with this unit follow :

Children's Bibliography

BESKOW, ELSE. The Tale of the Wee Little Woman. Harper.
FANGEL, MAUD T., and HIGGINS, ALICE. Picture Book of Babies (pictures by Maud T. Fangel, verses by Alice Higgins). Whitman.
FYLEMAN, ROSE. The Katy Kruse Dolly Book. Doubleday.
HADER, BERTA, and HADER, ELMER. Picture Book of Mother Goose. Coward-McCann.

Teacher's Bibliography

BAILEY, CAROLYN S. For the Children's Hour. Milton Bradley.

BIANCO, MARGERY. The Little Wooden Doll. Macmillan.

BRYANT, SARA CONE. Stories to Tell the Littlest Ones. Houghton Mifflin.

COLEMAN, SATIS, and THORN, ALICE. Singing Time. John Day.

Committee of A.C.E. Told Under the Blue Umbrella. Macmillan.

Committee of A.C.E. Told Under the Green Umbrella. Macmillan.

DALGLIESH, ALICE. The Choosing Book. Macmillan.

LINDSAY, MAUDE. Mother Stories. Milton Bradley.

McCONATHY, OSBOURNE, and others. The Music Hour in the Kindergarten and First Grade. Silver Burdett.

MAHONEY, WHITNEY. Realms of Gold. Dutton.

MILNE, A. A. When We Were Very Young. Dutton.

MITCHELL, LUCY S. Here and Now Story Book. Dutton.

ROSSETTI, CHRISTINA. Sing Song. Macmillan.

The children in the senior kindergarten of the Roger Sherman School are from five years old to five and eight months. They carried on a series of activities centering around the boats in the harbor, this interest being paramount for about eight weeks.

The objectives of this unit of work were to increase the children's interest in boats, and to add to their pleasure in taking boat trips by helping them to understand more about boats, their varieties, and their uses. The teacher provided pictures and books, also arranging to have on hand blocks, boards, wooden boxes, and other material for construction. Collecting steamship catalogues and pamphlets and selecting victrola records should also be included in this description of her activities.

The children told of their experiences on boats; they shared their pictures of boats and their storybooks. They expressed their ideas about boats, and recorded their own adventures with crayon and paintbrush; they listened to stories about boats, and learned boat songs. They made up some original poems and stories about boats. They built a vessel of large floor blocks, in which much interesting dramatic play was carried on. Then somebody complained that *all* the floor blocks had been used for the boat. "We could

J. C. Neff

The Boat

make a boat with boxes," suggested one of the boys. The next day boxes and crates began to arrive. After experimenting with boxes it was decided that a stronger cabin could be made with blocks, but that the boxes could be used for furnishing the cabin and for deck chairs. Boards were needed for the stern, bow, and gangplank. One of the fathers presented some wide boards which proved to be just what was needed. Two kegs painted red, white, and blue were used for smokestacks; paper circles were cut out and pasted on to represent portholes. The gangplank could be raised and lowered, and this led to much interesting dramatic play. A ticket office was made from two crates, and then the children became busily engaged in making tickets, pocketbooks, and sailor hats.

These children had previously carried on a series of activities relating to the home and family. As the boat interest progressed, the family planned to take a trip on the boat. The baby was dressed, the valise packed, and then, off to the ticket office! The sailors greeted the family and helped them on the boat. A sailor shouted "Pull in the gangplank!" The whistle blew, and they were on their way to New York.

There were many interesting discussions about different kinds of boats. The children learned that the canoe is sharp at both ends and tips very easily, and that it is propelled by paddles. They learned that the rowboat is a stronger and safer boat than the canoe; that the sail for the sailboat is usually made of canvas; that a barge is a small seagoing vessel, propelled by steam; and that an ocean liner is a large steam vessel.

They had a great deal of practice in the art of expression, and enjoyed their boat play a very great deal.

A picture of the boat appears on page 109. For the boat unit the following bibliographies were used:

Children's Bibliography

Anonymous. Big Book of Engines. Blackie, London.
CHATTERTON, E. K. Sailing Ships. Lippincott.
GABRIEL, SAMUEL. Over Land and Sea.
GRIMMAGE, PETER. A Picture Book of Ships. Macmillan.

Music

COLEMAN, SATIS, and THORN, ALICE. Singing Time. John Day.
GIDDINGS, T. P., and others. Music Education Series: Songs of Childhood. Ginn.
McCONATHY, OSBOURNE, and others. The Music Hour in the Kindergarten and First Grade. Silver Burdett.

Teacher's Bibliography

BRIDGES, THOMAS CHARLES. Young Folk's Book of the Sea. Little Brown.
CARTWRIGHT, CHARLES E. Boys' Book of Ships. Dutton.
COLEMAN, SATIS, and THORN, ALICE. Singing Time. John Day.
CURTIS, NELL C. Boats: Adventures in Boat-Making. Rand McNally.
GIDDINGS, T. P., and others. Music Education Series: Juvenile Music. Ginn.
HADER, BERTA, and HADER, ELMER. Picture Book of Travel. Macmillan.
HUBBARD, A. L., and BABBITT, A. The Golden Flute. John Day.
Manual of Physical Education, I–II. State Board of Education, Hartford, Conn.

MITCHELL, LUCY SPRAGUE. Here and Now Story Book. Dutton.
SMITH, CICELY FOX. Books of Famous Ships. Houghton.
Social Science Readers: Boats. Scribner.
WRIGHT, LULA E. The Magic Boat. Ginn.

LEARNING ABOUT THE CLOCK SHOP

Described by Miss Evelyn Schnitman and Miss Cecile Tansey

The children of Hamilton kindergarten come from foreign homes. The majority of the parents were born in Italy, and they adhere closely to their native customs and ways of living. The neighborhood is surrounded by factories, where many of the children's fathers make their living.

Often the children begin school with the handicap of not being able to understand English. One hundred and twenty children are registered in the kindergarten, sixty in the morning and sixty in the afternoon. There are three teachers.

A striking feature in the neighborhood is the clock factory. The children were taken on an excursion about the factory, and they decided to build a clock shop in the kindergarten. Materials for building the shop were supplied by various stores round about — orange crates, pasteboard boxes, etc.

When the building was finished, permission was obtained to visit the clock factory again and to see the clocks on display. In their turn the children invited the officials of the New Haven Clock Company to come to the kindergarten and see their clock shop. These gentlemen responded very cordially, and the children were greatly pleased with their guests. A very fine attitude toward the kindergarten was shown by the New Haven Clock Shop personnel.

The objectives of this unit were to help the children to gain interesting information about their own neighborhood, and especially about the New Haven Clock Shop, which is one of its most important features; to have them get some conception of the time and labor which go into the making of a good clock; to give them the opportunity to learn about different kinds of clocks; to help them to appreciate the use of the clock and to begin to tell time.

The children helped the teachers to plan the excursion to the clock shop. They learned something about how to conduct an excursion: how people should behave when taking a trip together. They built a clock shop and made clocks to sell in it. They dramatized buying and selling clocks, going to the factory to work, coming home. They entertained the personnel of the clock factory.

They gained much interesting information: It takes time to make a clock. Clockmaking is one way that fathers earn money. People in the clock factory are interested in the neighborhood children and like to show them their clocks. A clock has numbers, which make it possible to tell time; it has two hands, and a pendulum which swings constantly.

The teachers provided the following materials: wood of various lengths, cardboard boxes, pasteboard, and other material for construction, and isinglass for clockfaces.

The oral expression in connection with this unit was especially interesting in view of the children's foreign home background. These are some of their "stories."

We painted the clock shop red.
We mixed it up with brown.
The paintbrush went up and down.
And now it is all painted.

By four of the children

We went to get the boxes in the store.
Then we met Caroline's father.
He put the boxes in the truck.
The truck went brrp — brrp — brrp.

By three of the children

We took the saw and sawed the boxes.
We took the nails and hammered the boxes.
The saw went zipsaw, zipsaw.
The hammer went bang, bang, bang!

By the group

We went to get the boxes.
We met Caroline's father.
Caroline's father brought some boxes to school for everyone.
We built the clock shop.

By three of the children

We sawed the boxes with the saw.
We hammered the nails with the hammer.
We cut the windows with the scissors,
And pasted them on with paste.

By four of the children

The following bibliography was used:

BAILEY, CAROLYN S. Read Aloud Stories. Milton Bradley.
BAILEY, CAROLYN S., and LEWIS, CLARA M. For the Children's Hour. Milton Bradley.
CROWNINSHIELD, E. Mother Goose Songs for Little Ones. Milton Bradley.
CROWNINSHIELD, E. Songs and Rhymes for Little Ones. Milton Bradley.
GIDDINGS, T. P., and others. Music Education Series: Songs of Childhood. Ginn.
SHAW. Songs to Sing. Simcoe.

A FIRST-GRADE STUDY OF AIRPLANES

Described by Miss Helen Armstrong

The Haverford Friends School is situated on the old Haverford meeting grounds. There is much open space, with green grass and trees, and plenty of place to dig, plant, and tend gardens in the spring. The old wagon sheds are now a sunny outdoor play space equipped with junglegym, seesaws, swings, monkey ropes, ladder bars, and boxes and boards.

Having the privilege of using the Haverford College campus, the children have close contact with growing things, woods, pond, and familiar birds.

The first-grade room is large and sunny, with small tables and chairs; it is provided with a quiet library corner, in which books to meet the different interests of the children may be found. There is opportunity to work with clay or crayons, and a large easel, paints, and brushes are provided, also toys for dramatic play, trains, boats, planes, cars, etc. Opening out of the larger room is a workroom equipped with a workbench, tools, and different sizes and lengths of wood.

There were twenty-seven children in the group studying airplanes, many of whom had had previous school experience in nursery school and kindergarten. When they entered the first grade their chronological ages ranged from five years nine months to six years seven months. The mental-age range was from six years to eight years six months. The children come from homes where their physical and social development is given much consideration. Their leisure time is supervised, healthful eating and sleeping habits are established, they live a well-regulated life. Many have had experience in traveling; a few had been abroad, some to California. Almost every child in this group had had first-hand contact with farm life.

The school day begins at nine and ends at twelve thirty. There is a midmorning lunch, and a recess period with outdoor play whenever the weather permits. The program is a flexible one, providing for long uninterrupted periods during which the children may investigate, experiment, and create.

Three days each week the mornings are interrupted by the French teacher; once a week there is a long rhythm and singing period. Some of the time is used for games and story dances, often initiated by individual children. The work of this period is frequently a carry-over of a group interest.

Once a week there is a period for religious education, which is, as far as possible, a discussion of the daily school life together.

The unit was motivated by the group. The teachers had planned a unit on trains as a continuation of the transportation unit; we had worked on boats early in the year.

A child received a letter which her mother had sent her by air mail. The letter, brought to school, was the main topic of conversation that morning. Another child had an uncle who owned a plane; this increased interest and curiosity. During the week one boy brought in a magazine containing an article on airplanes; another offered a newspaper clipping of an airplane. The height of interest was reached when a girl brought a toy airplane and hangar and announced that she had actually made a visit to the airport. The unit was finally launched when one of the boys turned up with his large monoplane, declaring he would make a hangar for it.

Plenty of source books were available in the school library, and current magazines contained much material. To add to the interest, there was advertising in the sky, and the President had traveled in a plane. The child whose uncle owned a plane brought information from him received at the Camden Airport.

We could very easily visit an airport.

Most of the children had had some airplane experience: one had visited an airport, the mother of another had traveled by airplane, the lucky niece had been up in her uncle's plane. The teacher and the children decided to consider what they most wanted to find out about airplanes, and these questions were gradually made:

1. What makes airplanes fly?
2. How did people find out about airplanes?
3. How high can airplanes fly?
4. What does the inside of an airplane look like?
5. Of what are airplane wings made?
6. How does an airplane land?
7. Who first thought of airplanes?
8. What are the kinds of airplanes?
9. Why do airplanes have propellers?
10. Why don't gliders have propellers?
11. How do people learn to fly airplanes?
12. What makes an airplane go up?
13. How do airplane pilots see at night?
14. Can an airplane fly as fast at night as in day?
15. Are there any speed laws for airplanes?
16. Do airplanes carry anything besides people and mail?

The Activity Program

The group wrote for and obtained permission to visit the Camden Airport. They saw all they had hoped to see, — landing, take-off, a mail plane coming in and its mail taken off and put on. They saw an airplane that had been in a wreck. Best of all, they climbed into a plane. They watched planes being inspected and repaired before taking off for Florida and the West.

*All these experiences were recorded in a story written by the group about the excursion.

The children learned the names of the parts of a plane: wings, wingstrut, propeller, fin (or rudder), fuselage, landing gear, etc. They saw and acquired some knowledge of an airport's size, location, landing field, beacon, floodlight; they saw aviators, workers about the hangars, pilots, mechanics, and many more interesting people and things new to some of them.

As one result of the excursion, airplanes were made upon all sides. One boy tried to copy the plane which had taken off for Florida. Others made monoplanes, biplanes, trimotors; one made an amphibian, and one a glider. The group worked on a large plane constructed out of orange crates and beaverboard. This plane was large enough for a child to sit in.

Two other boys built a hangar to house the large monoplane and all the toy ones.

Airplanes were modeled from clay. Many airplanes were drawn. The children illustrated the story of their trip to the airport. They played take-off, landing, using the parachute, mechanics, and pilot. The airplane they made was by turns a pleasure plane and a mail plane, and once it was wrecked.

The unit presented excellent opportunities for the teaching of language. There were interesting and animated discussions of personal and group experiences. Accounts of trips to appear in the class book were dictated to the teacher by the group. Original verses were written, of which the following are examples:

> Come up in my airplane with me,
> We'll fly so high
> We'll touch the sky.
> We'll kiss the baby stars
> And ask the moon how to come back.
>
> *From Wharton*

I had a little toy dog,
His name was Johnny.
I put him in an airplane
To fly so far away.

From Betsy

My bear had an airplane.
He flew it every day.
He went to the Southland
To buy honey and to play.
He looked just like a bird
Flying up so high —
He raced the bees and all the things in the sky.

From Rachel

There was much reading for pleasure and information after the visit to the airport. Poems and stories from books, bulletin notices of news, weather reports, stories about airplanes, were found by the children and eagerly read to the group.

Number functioned in a lively fashion. Materials for plane construction had to be carefully measured. Everybody tried to read the numbers on all planes seen. Some idea of direction was developed: planes flying east, west, north, and south were observed. At the airport the children learned that every plane going up is equipped with a wireless set and that the pilot is informed of weather conditions every few minutes. They heard that under some weather conditions it is unsafe for planes to fly; that planes may fly around clouds; that an airplane must take off against the wind and turn with the wind after it has climbed to a certain height.

As a climax of the unit, the class arranged an exhibit of their modeling, drawing, and construction work. They sang their airplane song at the school assembly. One child suggested that an airplane movie be made, but this came too late to be attempted.

The airplane unit was a center of interest for about ten weeks.

Besides the definite information about airplanes gained through the visit to the airport and through reading, pictures, and class discussion, the teacher of this group thought that the children gained perceptibly in their ability to initiate and carry out projects independently. She also believed that the children saw the unit as a whole, not as a series of disjointed individual experiences and projects.

Children's Bibliography

An Airplane Picture Book. Made by another first grade.
BAILY. Aviation Book. Saalfield.
DIETZ. Good Times on the Farm. Newson.
DOBIAS. Picture Book of Flying. Macmillan.
HARDY. Best Stories. Wheeler.
HEIDERSTADT. Jimmy Flies. Stokes.
HOGAN. The Little Toy Airplane. McRae Smith.
JONES. An Alphabet of Aviation. McRae Smith.
LINDBERGH. We. Putnam.
MOUNTSEIR. Singing Youth. Harper.
National Geographic Magazine, May, 1933. National Geographic Society.
New Winston Book II. Winston.
PERSING. "A Trip to an Airport," *Normal Instructor*, April, 1929.
READ. The Airplane Ride. Scribner.
STONE. Webster Reading Book II. Webster.

Teacher's Bibliography

BUSWELL. Happy Days. Wheeler.
COMPTON. Compton's Pictured Encyclopaedia. E. S. Compton.
Country Gentleman, April, 1933. Curtis.
Hearst's Magazine, August, 1930. International Magazine Co., Inc.
HORN and McBROOM. Learn to Study Readers, Book III. Ginn.
ROMER. Sky Travel. Rand McNally.
TIPPETT. I Go A-Traveling. Harper.

The variety of setting, of topic, of procedure, and of description represented by the foregoing units will be apparent to every reader. And it is left to the reader to consider their relative value and significance for the children in each case described.

BIBLIOGRAPHY

BAXTER, T., and YOUNG, B. M. Ships and Navigation. Teachers College, Columbia University, New York, 1933.

> A unit of work for somewhat older children which may be stimulating and suggestive to lower-school teachers.

CAREY, ALICE E., HANNA, PAUL R., and MERIAM, JUNIUS L. Catalogue: units of work, activities, projects, etc. to 1932. Lincoln School Research Studies, Bureau of Publications, Teachers College, Columbia University, New York, 1932.

> An indispensable reference complete in every respect as a catalogue of the activity movement up to 1932.

CLOUSER, LUCY W., and MILLIKAN, CHLOE E. Kindergarten-Primary Activities Based on Community Life. Macmillan, New York, 1929.

> Good standards for selection of units and objectives in the first two chapters. Activities for kindergarten and first, second, and third grades well described.

CLOUSER, L. W., ROBINSON, W. S., and NEELY, D. L. Education Experiences through Activity Units. Lyons and Carnahan, Chicago, 1932.

> A record of primary-class activities. A good general discussion in Part I. Interesting units for the second and third grades.

EAKRIGHT, J. B., and YOUNG, B. M. Adventuring with Toys. Teachers College, Columbia University, New York, 1933.

HUGHES, AVAH W. Carrying the Mail: A Second Grade's Experiences. Lincoln School Curriculum Studies, Teachers College, Columbia University, New York, 1933.

Lincoln School Staff. Curriculum Making in an Elementary School. Ginn, Boston, 1927.

> Consult Chapter III for standards of selection in choosing activities.

McCALL, WILLIAM A. (Ed.). Teachers' Lesson Unit Series, Nos. 1–60. Columbia University, New York, 1932.

> A series of pamphlets describing units of work actually carried out in classrooms in various types of schools and different sections of the country. Teacher's Bibliography and Children's Bibliography accompany each. Nos. 6, 9, 13, 15, 17, 20, 29, 33, 36, 37, 40, 44, 47, 50, 53, 56, 57, 59, 60, are accounts of kindergarten-primary activities.

MEAD, CYRUS D., and ORTH, FRED. The Transitional Public School, pp. 165–181. Macmillan, New York, 1934.

> A description of activities.

National College of Education. Curriculum Records of an Elementary School, by members of the staff of the National College of Education, Evanston, Illinois, 1932.

> Consult for records of units of work.

PRATT, CAROLINE (Ed.). Experimental Practice in the City and Country School. Dutton, New York, 1924.

> A record of the seven-year-old group's activities.

PRATT, CAROLINE, and STANTON, JESSIE. Before Books. Adelphi, New York, 1926.

> A description of the work with children of four and five at the City and Country School.

STEVENS, MARION P. The Activities Curriculum in the Primary Grades. Heath, Boston, 1931.

> This book applies especially to the age group from five to nine, but would be most helpful also to teachers of children older and younger. An indispensable reference for lower-school teachers.

STOTT, LEILA. Eight Year Old Merchants. Experimental practice in the City and Country School Series, edited by Caroline Pratt. Greenberg, New York, 1928.

> A record of the eight-year-old group's activities in connection with the school store.

University of Chicago, Chicago, Illinois. "Selected References in Education, 1933." *Supplementary Educational Monographs No. 41*, January, 1934.

WRIGHT, LULA E. A First Grade at Work: A Non-Reading Curriculum, Lincoln School Curriculum Studies, Teachers College, Columbia University, New York, 1932.

> Content based on day-by-day description of group activities.

WYLER, ROSE. "Studying Rocks in the First Grade," *Science Education* (April, 1933), Vol. XVII, pp. 106–111.

> Describes the method by which the unit entitled "The Earth is Made of Rock" was developed in the first grade at Glens Falls, New York.

CHAPTER VII

PLANNING THE DAY IN THE LOWER SCHOOL

The changing curriculum is reflected in the newer ways of planning the younger child's school day. For the first-grade child the hours are shorter than they were a hundred years ago. In 1823 and 1827 he was expected to stay in school three hundred and seventy-five minutes, or six hours and a quarter a day; in 1926 the average length of his day was only two hundred and sixty-nine minutes, or about four and one-half hours. But while this lessened time is significant, it is nothing like so radical a change as that which appears in the way the modern school's day is divided.

Before beginning a discussion of the newer schedules and timetables, it is well to recognize the vast difference in both theory and practice as between the laboratory schools, the progressive public schools, and those schools both private and public where, because of existing conditions, it is necessary to schedule the day in a more or less arbitrary fashion. Regardless of these differences, the daily timetable in any school or class should reflect what the teachers and the school authorities really think about the comparative value of the different classroom activities for children of different ages, as well as their convictions about the length of time it takes to realize these values in the given school situation.

One of the conspicuous qualities of the newer time schedules is the effort of their makers to avoid breaking up the continuity of children's effort and activity. Once it was thought that a number of isolated periods, providing for frequent changes of work punctuated by "relief exercises," represented the best way of planning work in the lower grades. Now our thought is that reading periods which end with

"Put away your readers: take out your geographies," when
an arbitrary twenty-five minutes have passed, are hardly
conducive to good study habits; nor do we think it sensible to interject physical-training stunts to relieve strain.
Our present attempts are directed toward preventing strain
rather than relieving it. Therefore in many modern schools
we find periods of fifty minutes or more set aside, during
which the children may work freely on individual projects,
either closely related to the units of work being carried out
by the group or purely independent undertakings. Children
can work without fatigue for an appreciable length of time
upon work which really interests them and which they may
carry through in a variety of ways instead of only through
books. Drill periods, such as those required for learning
number combinations or word recognition, should of course
be very brief, but the tendency in the more modern schools
is to lessen the occurrence of such periods by postponing
formal work in number and writing until the child's skill in
reading is fairly well developed.

The average number of minutes devoted to reading in
our public schools is about eighty a day, or one fourth to
one third of the time spent in school. In one New England
city reported through a recent survey, a hundred and twenty
minutes a day are devoted to first-grade reading. At the
other extreme is the organization of such a class as the first
grade reported in Lula Wright's book *A First Grade at
Work: A Non-Reading Curriculum*. Working in the Lincoln
School of Teachers College, New York City, this group of
children devoted all their school day to the social studies,
the beginnings of the fine and industrial arts, rhythms,
music, stories, and various other fascinating activities.

The time schedule for Miss Wright's group appears in the
appendix to this chapter. Large blocks of time unassigned
to anything except group and individual project work make
for great flexibility; in fact, the only rigidity about it occurs
in connection with the definite arrangements which have to
be made for the use of the gymnasium and for the time of

special teachers. A situation such as that in the Lincoln School is of interest to the average primary-school teacher only because it shows the modern tendency toward freedom, flexibility, and the postponement of formal work in the three R's. It is significant; but other considerations besides laboratory-school practice are necessary in planning the day's schedule in the average situation. The needs and abilities of growing children must, of course, be given greatest weight. Physical and mental well-being should never be sacrificed to proficiency in the skills; but the well-developed six-year-old attacks a reasonable amount of work in reading gleefully, and can bear up under an appreciable degree of formal teaching. What the majority of public-school systems have found good — the average practice today — should surely be carefully studied. The relative difficulty of the different school subjects at different stages may not be ignored, and local conditions — the physical, intellectual, and social status of the children, the opinions of their parents, the resources of the school community — are also pertinent.

C. H. Mann has published a very interesting study of the time allotments in public elementary schools. His survey, entitled "How Schools Use their Time," includes the prevalent timetables in a number of communities with populations under 2500, as well as those in use in cities with a population of over 100,000. This study, the data for which were collected in 1926, shows that in the small communities first-grade children spent 52.0 per cent of their time in studying the three R's; in the larger communities 55.9 per cent of first-grade time was used for reading, writing, and arithmetic. The "special" subjects, including music and art, were pursued for 45.4 per cent of the time in the first grades of the smaller communities and for 39.5 per cent of the time in the city first grades. So-called "content subjects," or the social studies, occupied the remainder of the time in all the schools. Another interesting point brought out in Mann's tables is that by far the largest proportion of the time devoted to the three R's was used for reading.

In the kindergartens studied by Mann only about one fifth of the time was listed as "unassigned." This shows the tendency for formal time schedules in public-school kindergartens. As the comparative time allotments for the various school subjects in the kindergarten and Grades One, Two, and Three will perhaps be of interest to some readers of this book, three of Mann's most significant tables are reprinted by permission at the close of this chapter.

The actual organization of the school day, the way in which the individual teacher divides the time which she spends with her group, is quite as interesting and significant as actual quantitative time allotment. A description of typical days in the nursery school and in the five-year-old and the seven-year-old groups may be stimulating to thought on this subject.

The planning of a nursery-school day gives a good example of a situation arranged entirely with the growing child's needs in view. The child from two years to four years or thereabouts is enrolled in a nursery school, if he is enrolled, for certain main purposes: to give him a chance to go through the ordinary activities of a healthy toddler's day in the society of other children, and under trained supervision; to provide a suitable play environment planned for persons of his age; to reduce to the least possible the frets and jars and emotional upsets which come in the course of adjusting him to a home situation which is planned for adults and older children quite as much as for him; to give him a chance to gain increasing control of himself in a physical and social environment which is simple enough for him to enjoy and understand. Of curriculum pressure there is none; the nursery school is simply a place where the nursery baby carries on his legitimate, although entirely extracurricular, business under the best possible conditions.

As the baby's chief concern at the nursery age is to carry on successfully and happily those routines which help him to build a strong and healthy body, one third to one half of the nursery-school day (at a quite conservative estimate) is taken up with eating, sleeping, dressing and undressing, and bathroom activities; with taking cod-liver oil and orange juice; with sunning himself and generally vegetating. Some nursery-school timetables cover the two-year-old to four-year-old's whole day; others are arranged for two or three hours. The eight-hour and ten-hour schools are generally conducted in day nurseries; the so-called "all-day" nursery schools in the child-welfare research laboratories and private schools have sessions of six or seven hours.

A representative time schedule for an all-day school is the following:

8.45–9.30	The children arrive, are inspected by the doctor or the nurse, and then go to play, outdoors or indoors, according to the weather.
9.30–10	Wraps are removed, the children helping themselves as much as possible. They go to the bathroom, attending to the toilet and washing their hands.
10–10.30	Midmorning lunch — a very simple affair in the all-day school, followed by a brief rest on mats.
10.30–11.15	Play, outdoors or in.
11.15–11.30	Brief directed activity — music, or stories, or game, for those children who enjoy it.
11.30–12	The children wash for lunch and take a brief rest on their cots. Often they remove their shoes and put on bedroom slippers, so that they may get ready for their afternoon rest with the least possible confusion.
12–12.45	Luncheon. The children sit at tables with the nursery-school teachers. Usually they are served by an adult, sometimes carrying their empty plates back to the pantry. The children are encouraged to eat in businesslike fashion, without too much dallying. Pleasant conversation is encouraged. No one is expected to remain at the table after he has finished. He goes to the bathroom and then undresses and settles down for the long afternoon nap. Sometimes a slow child is given a few extra minutes to finish the main part of his dinner.

1–2.30 or 3 Most of the children sleep. Those who wake in an
hour may look at picture books or play quietly.

3 A glass of milk, and quiet play until called for to go home.

Evidently there is little about this time schedule which
differs from that of a well-ordered home nursery, except that
it is a schedule followed by a group of children rather than
by one child, and the group situation helps to make the
routine run smoothly.

The two-hour to three-hour nursery-school timetable does
not include the most important events of the day — the noon
meal and the afternoon nap. It is simply a well-planned
play morning, broken by a midmorning lunch, served with
some ceremony, and a rest of about twenty minutes on mats
or cots. The first three quarters of an hour is spent in health
inspection, indoor or outdoor play, and removing wraps; the
next three quarters of an hour goes for lunch, bathroom
routine, and rest; the remainder of the morning for play,
with a brief organized period for music, nature study, games,
or stories before going home.

Programs for the four-year-old and five-year-old preschool
groups — the age roughly corresponding to the kindergarten
age — vary greatly in the flexibility of their procedure. In
laboratory schools like the City and Country School of New
York they differ very little from nursery-school schedules,
merely including a little more provision for organized work.
In many public schools (where they are generally known as
kindergartens) these groups are as rigidly controlled as the
primary grades. In the study made by C. H. Mann, referred
to above, it appears that many public-school systems were
able to report the amount of time allotted in their kindergartens to reading, literature, phonics, arithmetic, in fact,
all the subjects reported upon by primary grades except
social science and supervised study. In the more progressive
public-school systems such detailed accounts of kindergarten
timetables are not provided for. In Seattle, Washington,
for instance, two hundred and fifty minutes a week of kindergarten time are given to free play, three hundred and

fifty to fine and industrial arts, and one hundred and fifty to reading and literature. Several different kindergarten or preschool programs appear at the end of this chapter; one of them is taken from the *Teachers' Guide to Child Development*, a bulletin put out by the California Curriculum Commission. Another of these timetables is taken from the account of work at the City and Country School, New York City, entitled *Before Books*. A third is the kindergarten schedule of a public school in New Haven, Connecticut.

The following schedule probably represents the usual practice in the more progressive public schools:

9–9.45   A self-chosen activity period, in which the child engages in his own work, frequently related to the unit of study then being carried on by the group.

9.45–10   A checking-up period in which the children and the teacher discuss the accomplishments of the work period. The room is tidied up, and a recess period is provided for.

10–10.40   A midmorning luncheon, carefully served, and a rest period.

10.45–11   Free play outdoors, or a vigorous game indoors if the weather is unsuitable for outdoor play.

11–11.20   Literature, or picture study, or nature study.

11.20–11.50 Music, including rhythm.

11.50–12   Dismissal.

In some kindergartens the day begins with a brief opening circle, in the belief that this helps to develop a good group spirit and also helps the children learn to get to school on time. The advantage of having the self-chosen activity period first is that it prevents waste of time on the part of children who come early and gives the child the right set for the morning by immediately enlisting his interest.

Presumably the five-year-old child goes from kindergarten to a hot luncheon and a suitable afternoon rest at home, followed by wholesome outdoor play. In a laboratory school he frequently has his hot luncheon and his afternoon rest at school, followed by outdoor play.

The entrance of the child into the first grade requires in most schools that a large percentage of his time be set aside for learning how to read. If, as is often the case, he must also have time for drill in writing and in number, then his school day must be quite formally and inflexibly planned. From 52 to 55.9 per cent of the school day in the public first grades of the country is devoted to the three R's; from 52.8 to 59 per cent of the school day is so used in the second grades.

When formal first-grade work is limited to reading, the schedule which appears in the *Teachers' Guide to Child Development*, blocking the day into large units of time, is practicable. Or a program something like the following one may be used.

9–9.30	Self-chosen activity period, to include special projects in industrial or fine arts or, in some cases, individual work in reading or number.
9.30–10	Class problems: discussion of work, hygiene, news items. Recess.
10–10.30	Midmorning lunch, rest.
10.30–11.20	Reading in at least two groups, the teacher dividing her time between them, the second group doing quiet seat work as she teaches the first, and vice versa.
11.20–11.40	Games, preferably outdoors.
11.40–12	Social studies, or elementary science, or nature study.
1.30–2.15	Fine arts, or literature, or dramatization.
2.15–2.40	Music: songs and rhythms.
2.40–2.50	Recess.
2.50–3.30	Reading, as in morning session.

The long afternoon period given to literature and the beginnings of the fine arts is planned to afford the child leisure for the enjoyment of these activities, and thus give him an incentive to do creative work.

The second grade's schedule differs little from the first, except that the opening period in the morning often includes time for individual study, and the leisurely afternoon periods might be curtailed to leave more time for drill. The amount of time devoted to reading drops when second-grade schedules are compared with those of first grades. In the forty cities having a population of over a hundred thousand, studied by Mann, 27.4 per cent of the time was used for reading in the second grades in comparison with 32.4 per cent in the first grades.

In public schools children six and seven years old usually go home for luncheon or eat at school a luncheon brought from home. Sometimes the school provides or sells hot soup or cocoa; often it assumes no responsibility except the most casual supervision of the young children who remain at school. An adequate afternoon rest is rare or unheard of. Yet in the laboratory schools and the progressive country day schools the hot noon meal is prepared and served at school, scientifically planned and carefully supervised; and in many schools of the latter types the younger children have an adequate rest on cots or in deck chairs after their luncheon.

From the standpoint of the welfare of the whole child there is little doubt as to which is the better plan. The usual public-school plan involves haste, strain, and tension; in many cases it makes for poor dietary habits too. It is a plan excusing itself on the old theory that the school is merely concerned with the child's intellectual growth or, perhaps, his intellectual and moral growth. And it is difficult for the home to supplement the school's work by providing the right noonday meal and an adequate rest during the hasty and unsatisfactory interlude of an hour to an hour and a half between morning and afternoon sessions, especially since part of the time must be consumed going to and from home and school. It is not necessarily true that all children thrive best on the country-day-school plan, but it is true that the child has as much right to consideration with respect to his physical requirements when he is six and seven as he has when he is two. If he seems better off at home in the afternoon, his day should surely be planned that way; if he must spend the afternoon at school, some arrangement should be made to give him adequate food and rest between sessions.

In summary, the principles of good daily planning are the following:

1. The intellectual, emotional, and physical aspects of the child's growth must be considered at all ages. While it is true that he requires a greater proportion of time for his physical routine at the nursery-school level than he does when he is seven, this does not imply that we can slight or ignore his physical requirements at the latter age. Outdoor play, experimentation with apparatus for the development of the larger muscles, adequate food, and sufficient rest are needed by the seven-year-old just as much as by his younger sister. All these things must be taken into account in planning the seven-year-old's day.

2. The developing intellectual life of the child must be fostered and encouraged by the provision of adequate time for individual study and creative work.

3. The learning of the fundamental skills must be provided for. Probably it is best to provide most generously for reading during the first school year. Current practice seems to indicate this.

4. Local conditions — social, economic, and climatic — must be taken into account in planning the child's day. Sometimes these local conditions have to be given deep consideration, especially during periods of stress and unemployment. Sometimes one needs to consider mostly the superficial questions relating to the sharing of a gymnasium with other grades, the sharing of lavatory facilities, the apportionment of the time of special teachers. But these conditions, whether permanent or temporary, deep-seated or superficial, must be regarded. To ignore local conditions and try to arrange a theoretically ideal time allotment in a most unideal situation is futile and stupid. Progress in education can never result from sporadic efforts to remedy the more unimportant aspects of the process. Time schedules must represent existing circumstances for teachers and children; they must be suitable for the curriculum as it is locally planned. They should always be a help to all concerned in making for pleasant, harmonious, and expeditious work. A school or class without any framework of time allotment would be chaos; one with a rigid timetable regulating every ten minutes is not conducive to good work and good thinking on the part of either teacher or children.

PROGRAM FOR THE KINDERGARTEN[1]

9–9.50   Self-chosen Activities. Woodwork, painting, modeling, sewing, care of pets and plants, block-building and construction or other work related to class activities.

9.50–10.05   Group Discussion. Examination and criticism of work and making further plans for work.

10.05–10.15   Recess.

10.15–10.45   Cleanliness Habits; Morning Lunch. Children serve themselves with orange juice; sit at tables in two groups, each with a teacher; conversation is carried on; habits of courtesy are observed.

10.45–11   Rest Period. Children lie down on mat on floor in relaxed position while music is played softly.

11–11.15   Literature, Science. Stories read by teacher; stories freely discussed by children; stories told by children; discussion of animals, plants, insects, brought in by children; etc. Songs chosen by children and teacher, rhythms, and imaginative, spontaneous expression of children's response to music.

11.15–11.25   Recess.

11.25–11.55   Music and Games.

11.55–12   Dismissal.

PROGRAM FOR THE B1 GRADE[2]

9–10   Industrial Period. Activities: woodwork, sewing, painting, clay modeling, nature-study excursions, care of pets and plants, and special-project activities. Conversation: criticism of work, plans for new work, and blackboard or chart reading as an outgrowth of discussion.

10–12   Literature Period. Divide as follows: period from 10.10 to 11, group reading from books and related handwork (directed or free); period from 11.10 to 12, writing, dramatization, reading games, and lunch.

1–2   Fine-Arts Period. Music and rhythms, art, individual reading, and dismissal.

[1] Teachers' Guide to Child Development, *United States Office of Education Bulletin No. 26*, p. 182, Department of the Interior, 1930.
[2] Ibid. p. 181.

A Laboratory-School Program for Four-Year-Olds[1]

9–10   Play indoors.
10–11   Play outdoors.
Midmorning lunch.
After lunch, reading of stories or sense-training games.
Play for thirty or forty minutes.
Mondays, Wednesdays, and Fridays, 15–minute music lesson.

Kindergarten Time Schedule[2]

Morning Session (Older Group)

8.45–9.40   Self-chosen activities, conferences, putting materials away. Excursions.
9.40–10.10   Personal hygiene, preparation for lunch, lunch.
10.10–10.25   Rest.
10.25–11.05   Music: singing, music appreciation, music interpretation, rhythms, games.
11.05–11.25   Group period: stories, poems, pictures, conversation.
11.25–11.30   Putting on wraps, and dismissal.

Afternoon Session (Younger Group)

12.45–1.40   Self-chosen activities, conferences, putting materials away (excursions).
1.40–2.10   Personal hygiene, preparation for rest, rest. (A lunch period is not included in the afternoon session.)
2.10–2.40   Music: singing, music appreciation, music interpretation, rhythms, games.
2.40–3   Group period: stories, poems, pictures, conversation.
3   Dismissal. (A longer period is allotted in cold weather so that the children may put on their own wraps.)
The activity period is conducted outdoors from April to June. Games and apparatus work are carried on outdoors when weather permits.

[1] Caroline Pratt and Jessie Stanton, *Before Books*, p. 137.
[2] Roger Sherman School, New Haven, Connecticut.

A Laboratory-School Program for Seven-Year-Olds[1]

A. The Week's Program

TIME	MONDAY	TUESDAY	WEDNESDAY	THURSDAY	FRIDAY
9	Discussion	Discussion	Discussion	Discussion	Discussion
9.20	Rhythms	(9.30) Writing	Music	Rhythms	(9.30) Number
10	Shop or free period	Shop or science laboratory	Shop or free period	Reading	Shop or free period
11	Reading. Shop open also	Reading. Shop open also	Reading. Shop open also	Free period	Reading. Shop open also
11.30	Number	Number	Writing	(11.45) Play in yard	(11.30) Writing
12	Play in yard	Play in yard	Play in yard	(12.15) Stories	(12) Play in yard
12.35	Lunch and rest period	Lunch and rest period	Lunch and rest period	Lunch and rest period	Lunch and rest period
2	Drawing	Stories	Stories	Drawing or clay	Play in yard
2.40	Stories	(2.15) Cooking	(2.20) Free period	Play in yard	(2.30) Science
3	Play in yard				Music
3.30	Home	Home	Home	Home	Home

[1] Caroline Pratt, *Experimental Practice in the City and Country School*, p. 237.

GRADE I. A NON-READING CURRICULUM[1]

Working Program, Grade I

TIME	MONDAY	TUESDAY	WEDNESDAY	THURSDAY	FRIDAY
9	(9–9.30) Rhythms				Science in connection with unit
10	9.30–10	9.30–10.00	(9.30–10.30) Household arts		Games and work with apparatus in gymnasium
10	(10–10.30) Play on roof			Play on roof	Painting, drawing, or clay work
11	10.30–11.30	Midmorning lunch. Discussion			
11	(11–11.30) Music	Painting, drawing, or clay work	Music	(11–12) Industrial arts	(11–11.30) Music
12	11.30–12.30	(11.30–12.15) Industrial arts	(11.30–12) Play on roof		11.30–12.30
12	(12.30–12.50) Business (class); appointing committees	(12.15–12.50) Nature study	(12–12.50) Painting, drawing, or clay		
1	Dismissal				

[1] Lula Wright, *A First Grade at Work*, p. 25. Lincoln School, New York.

FIFTY-ONE COMMUNITIES HAVING A POPULATION LESS THAN 2500[1]

[Percentage of time in each grade allotted to elementary subjects.]

	GRADE 1	GRADE 2	GRADE 3
Three R's	*Per Cent*	*Per Cent*	*Per Cent*
Reading	21.6	18.4	14.0
Phonics	6.0	4.0	1.7
Literature	1.6	1.3	0.8
Arithmetic	8.5	11.0	12.2
Language and grammar	5.7	7.1	9.1
Penmanship	5.7	5.1	5.4
Spelling	2.9	5.9	6.3
Total three R's	52.0	52.8	49.5
Content subjects			
Geography	0.3	0.5	4.3
History	0.8	0.9	1.9
Social science			
Citizenship and civics	0.5	0.5	0.6
Nature study and elementary science .	1.1	1.3	1.1
Total content	2.7	3.2	7.9
Special subjects			
Art and drawing	3.6	3.3	3.4
Music	3.5	3.6	3.0
Household and manual arts	0.2	0.1	0.1
Handwork	3.3	2.1	0.8
Projects and activities	0.7	0.7	0.6
Health education	1.8	1.9	2.6
Physical training	4.4	4.5	4.1
Recess	9.5	9.1	7.9
Opening exercises	5.4	5.2	4.7
Supervised study	3.9	4.7	5.0
Unassigned and free time	4.3	4.3	5.7
Miscellaneous	4.8	4.5	4.5
Total special	45.4	44.0	42.4
Total all subjects	100.1	100.0	99.8

[1] C. H. Mann, *How Schools Use Their Time*, Table 47, p. 170.

FORTY CITIES HAVING A POPULATION OF 100,000 OR OVER[1]

[Percentage of time in each grade allotted to the elementary subjects.]

	GRADE 1	GRADE 2	GRADE 3
Three R's	*Per Cent*	*Per Cent*	*Per Cent*
Reading	32.4	27.4	21.0
Phonics	1.8	1.4	0.7
Literature	2.0	1.7	1.6
Arithmetic	4.2	9.7	13.2
Language and grammar	8.5	8.3	9.4
Penmanship.	5.3	5.1	4.9
Spelling	1.7	5.4	5.8
Total three R's	55.9	59.0	56.6
Content subjects			
Geography	0.4	0.7	3.8
History.	1.2	1.1	2.3
Social science	0.1	0.2	0.3
Citizenship and civics	0.8	0.7	1.0
Nature study and elementary science	2.0	2.3	1.9
Total content	4.5	5.0	9.3
Special subjects			
Art and drawing.	6.3	5.9	5.6
Music	5.1	4.8	4.7
Household and manual arts	0.2	0.2	0.5
Handwork	1.2	1.0	0.8
Projects and activities	1.0	0.8	0.6
Health education	1.5	1.4	1.5
Physical training	7.5	7.1	6.7
Recess	7.5	7.3	6.8
Opening exercises	3.5	3.3	2.9
Supervised study	0.1	0.1	0.6
Unassigned and free time	3.7	3.0	2.5
Miscellaneous	1.9	1.3	0.9
Total special	39.5	36.2	34.1
Total all subjects	99.9	100.2	100.0

[1]C. H. Mann, *How Schools Use Their Time*, Table 42, p. 165.

Minutes per Week devoted to Elementary-School Subjects in Kindergartens in Cities of Larger and Smaller Populations[1]

	100,000 AND OVER	30,000 TO 100,000	10,000 TO 30,000	5000 TO 10,000	2500 TO 5000	UNDER 2500
Reading		40	110	80	230	
Phonics		30		25	73	
Literature	90	76	60	76	73	105
Arithmetic		25	48	30	70	70
Language and grammar	110	103	68	70	90	
Penmanship				25	105	
Spelling						
Geography				10		20
History			25	10		30
Social science						
Citizenship and civics	25	33	25	22	40	20
Nature study and elementary science .	38	55	50	50	52	20
Art and drawing . . .	105	73	95	65	90	55
Music	123	90	102	103	90	73
Household and manual arts	100					
Handwork	108	175	127	165	155	75
Projects and activities	205	175	130	130	152	145
Health education . .	53	25	31	53	45	35
Physical training . .	120	104	105	102	105	35
Recess	77	90	74	76	104	153
Opening exercises . .	56	72	75	71	58	50
Supervised study . .						
Unassigned and free time	73	117	147	77	130	70
Miscellaneous . . .	50	165	90	78	75	145

[1] C. H. Mann, *How Schools Use Their Time*, Tables 48–53.

BIBLIOGRAPHY

Armentrout, W. D. A Comparison of Time Allotments in Primary Grades, Colorado State Teachers College, *Bulletin 26, No. 4*, 1927.

Ayer, F. C. Time Allotment in the Elementary School Subjects, *City School Leaflet No. 19*, United States Bureau of Education, February, 1925.

California Curriculum Commission (R. M. Hockett, Ed.). Teachers' Guide to Child Development, pp. 345–383. California State Printing Office, Sacramento, 1933.

CASWELL, HOLLIS L. Program-Making in Small Elementary Schools, Public Division Surveys and Field Studies, George Peabody College for Teachers, Nashville, Tennessee, 1930.

HUGHES, AVAH W. Carrying the Mail: A Second Grade's Experiences. Bureau of Publications, Teachers College, Columbia University. For the Lincoln School of Teachers College, 1933.

A tentative daily program, Grade II, p. 12.

KEELOR, KATHARINE L., and SWEET, MAYME. Indian Life and the Dutch Colonial Settlement. Teachers College, Columbia University, New York. For the Lincoln School of Teachers College, 1931.

A daily program, p. 56.

LANE, ROBERT HILL. A Teachers' Guide to the Activity Program, Chapter V. Macmillan, New York, 1932.

Lincoln School Staff. Curriculum Making in an Elementary School, Chapter V, pp. 58–145. Ginn, Boston, 1927.

MEAD, CYRUS D., and ORTH, FRED. The Transitional Public School. Macmillan, New York, 1934.

Chapter V, "Programs and Schedules for Kindergarten and Grades I, II, and III." Including activities and "typical days."

National Society for the Scientific Study of Education, Twenty-eighth Yearbook (Public School Publishing Company, Bloomington, Illinois, 1929), "Preschool and Parental Education," pp. 253–256.

Activities of a typical day in a modern kindergarten.

PARKER, S. C., and TEMPLE, ALICE. Unified Kindergarten and First-Grade Teaching, pp. 110–126. Ginn, Boston, 1925.

PRATT, CAROLINE (Ed.). Experimental Practice in the City and Country School, with a Record of Group VII by Lula Wright, p. 287. Dutton, New York, 1924.

PRATT, CAROLINE, and STANTON, JESSIE. Before Books, p. 337. Adelphi, New York, 1926.

RUGG, HAROLD, and SHUMAKER, ANN. The Child-Centered School, Chapter VI. World Book, Yonkers, N.Y., 1928.

STEVENS, MARION. The Activities Curriculum in the Primary Grades. Heath, Boston, 1931.

Chapter VI, "The Program for an Activity Curriculum," gives a full and excellent discussion of this topic.

WRIGHT, LULA E. A First Grade at Work: A Non-Reading Curriculum, p. 24. Teachers College, Columbia University, New York, 1932.

CHAPTER VIII

THE HOUSING AND EQUIPMENT OF THE LOWER SCHOOL

Modern science constantly reminds us that growing children share with other organisms the need for certain indispensable conditions of growth: the need for sunlight, nourishment, shelter, and protection from blights. The housing and equipment of the lower school should be planned with these needs in mind.

Schoolrooms for little children should be spacious, sunny, adequately heated, well-ventilated, and pleasing to the eye. If fairly ideal conditions can be provided, it is well to have two rooms available for each group: a "quiet" room, where reading and other quiet occupations are carried on; and a "noisy" room, where hammers, saws, wagons, and other equipment which makes for noisy play may be used without disturbing those who desire quiet. Often it is possible to have two of the lower-school groups share a workroom, but in this case the groups should be nearly of an age. Nursery-school children cannot profitably share a workroom with primary children, for the older boys and girls make so much noise that the situation is overstimulating and exhausting to the three-year-old.

The minimum size for a public-school classroom which is intended to house a given number of children is regulated by law. Generally modern schools provide space much in excess of this minimum, for most school authorities have come to recognize the small child's need for unhampered play. However, there is a point at which size becomes a disadvantage. A room should not echo sounds, and it should not be so big that it seems cavernous and unfriendly to the small child. Especially for nursery-school groups it is desirable to have several small rooms available rather than one large room. It is good for little children to play by themselves or in small groups, away from the noise and confusion of a large classroom. A private house turned over wholly or in part to a nursery school is sometimes more desirable than the more spacious and pretentious quarters provided in elaborate school buildings.

For many reasons it is frequently planned to house the youngest children in the school on the ground floor. Such an arrangement is considered safest in case of fire or other emergency, and it obviates the need for passing through the crowded halls of a typical elementary-school building. On the first floor, too, the running about of the youngest children may be less disturbing to the routine of the school, and the time it takes for small children to get safely up and down stairs is saved by obviating the need for stair climbing. Actually, the climbing of stairs is excellent exercise for little children, but it is well to provide for it apart from the pushing and jostling that are likely to ensue when the youngest classes must use the same stairs as vigorous nine-year-olds and ten-year-olds.

In the best-equipped buildings schoolrooms for young children are provided with special window glass allowing violet rays free passage. The windows are so arranged that the maximum amount of sunlight may enter, and are provided with shades or curtains for the control of glare. The floor covering of the newest rooms is sanitary and relatively noiseless; battleship linoleum is a favorite material. Heating systems should be so arranged that an average temperature of 68 to 70 degrees may be maintained with proper ventilation provided for, and adequate moisture should be assured.

Plato, in his *Republic*, stressed the importance of beautiful surroundings for small children. Nearly every writer on the education of the young since the days when the *Republic* was written, has dwelt upon the significance and importance of the aesthetic element in early education. Our first fine modern classrooms were usually finished in neutral tints, relieved by soft gold or other pastel colors. Recently stronger colors have found their way into schoolroom decoration. Observers of young children have found how much the littlest ones enjoy bright color. In nurseries and kindergartens one now frequently finds tables and chairs painted in different harmonizing colors. Such a scheme is often very pleasing if the person planning it has a good color sense and if the bright colors need not remain too constant. For instance, Chinese-red chairs had better be shifted about and occasionally replaced with others of a soft green. Too much color can become irritating and wearying. The advantage of a good neutral color scheme is that it provides an excellent background for pictures and other decorative effects and that it is easily planned and maintained by the teacher of average artistic taste and ability. It is much easier to make mistakes in the use of more pronounced color schemes.

Movable furniture is gradually replacing screwed-down desks in most lower schools. Such furniture lends itself much better to a free sort of organization and to the carrying out of interesting class and individual projects. Chairs and tables should be of suitable size, and varying heights should be provided for. Children should be encouraged to select appropriate chairs and thus assist the development of good posture. This becomes more important in the grades than in kindergarten and nursery school, because in the grades the children sit still for longer periods of time.

An important characteristic of the good lower-school environment is an arrangement which makes children feel that the building is *their* school. In one nursery school visited by the writer this standard is so thoroughly worked out that adults are obliged to stoop in order to enter the door, which is built low for the sake of the children. Few adults stop to realize how overpowering to the child two or three years old is an environment built on a scale of size suitable for grown men and women. From the point of view of good teaching, it is, above all, necessary to arrange rooms so that small children may help themselves as much as possible. Lockers and hooks should be easily accessible to the child; lavatory fixtures should be in proper proportion. Where special fixtures are not available it is possible to do a great deal to make it easy for the child to help himself by a wise use of low benches and simply built removable platforms. Nursery schools provide an excellent example in this matter for kindergartens and primary schools to follow. The reason for this is that the provision of an environment in which the preschool child can help himself and feel truly at home is one of the important aims of nursery schools.

The equipment of the lower school should include a piano and a good victrola, easily accessible for use where one cannot be provided for each separate group.

So-called "permanent play materials" and equipment for the lower school may, for convenience, be discussed under the following heads: apparatus for vigorous play, wheel toys, construction materials, toys to aid dramatic play, materials for art and the industrial arts, musical toys, books. In the selection of equipment certain general standards must be kept in mind which are important in the choice of any of them. Appropriate equipment and play materials should stimulate desirable activity on the part of the children. They should be durable, hygienic, and reasonably safe and should be well selected from the point of view of economy. Anything approaching a complete list of equipment and play materials for the child from two to seven is far beyond the scope of this chapter, but the special bearing each of the standards suggested has upon the different varieties of materials is worthy of discussion.

In the selection of equipment for vigorous play, one thinks at the outset of the junglegym, the seesaw, the rope-and-board swing, the slide, and the merry-go-round. The junglegym provides plenty of opportunity for good climbing, for strengthening the muscles of the arms, and for developing good co-ordination in the use of arms and legs. It also provides practice in balancing and in accustoming the child to high places. From the point of view of reasonable safety it is excellent because of the many chances to hold on and ascend or descend very gradually. Of course the child should never be lifted to the top of the junglegym by any well-meaning adult: he should do his own climbing, so that he may understand that ascending and descending demand cautious, piecemeal effort. Otherwise, if he is a little child, he may attempt to step off the top, expecting to descend as easily as he rose. The junglegym is fairly durable if kept indoors; and, properly painted, it weathers reasonably well outdoors if it is not kept in too exposed a place. Economically it requires a rather large original outlay; but where funds are available, it is an excellent investment from the point of view of its play possibilities.

The seesaw, or teeter, is a piece of apparatus which may be bought at a comparatively small cost. It is greatly enjoyed by the children and affords much opportunity for co-operative play. In fact, it is impossible to play on a seesaw and *not* be co-operative! However, the seesaw requires rather more adult guidance than the junglegym. Little children need to be taught the seesaw's principles of operation rather definitely, especially if more than two children want to play on it. It provides less variety of muscle activity than the junglegym, although it gives splendid experience in maintaining balance. Plenty of good dramatic play originates with the seesaw. The seesaw is quite durable, and of course simple varieties of it may be easily home-made.

The rope-and-board swing is a perennial favorite. Economical and safe if properly adjusted to the children, it gives experience in hanging by the arms, in co-ordination and control, and in delightful rhythmic motion. It affords some opportunity for co-operative play; for turns must be taken and children may push each other.

Slides of various heights have of recent years become a familiar bit of lower-school equipment. They are always great favorites. Fairly durable and not overwhelmingly expensive, they are perhaps the best single gymnasium equipment for children from two to five years old. Slides provide for climbing and the excitement of coasting down again. A fairly large group may take turns in playing on the slide at any one time, and it is quite safe equipment if the most rudimentary rules of taking turns and not pushing are taught and insisted upon. Of course a slide should be of appropriate height for the children who are to use it. The very high slide is not suitable for the young child. When high slides are used, even with older children, the adult must be on the alert for possible difficulties on the top platform — for skirts and panties getting caught and impaling the child and for panic due to real or fancied danger. Though climbing the slide is excellent for giving confidence and a sense of poise and security on a height, one accident or near-accident on a dangerously high slide may shatter the security of an individual or group. Adventure at too high a cost is not desirable.

The merry-go-round is well liked by some teachers, but, on the whole, its popularity seems to be waning. The activity it provides is fun, but of a very limited sort. Because of the element of danger the merry-go-round has to be hedged about with restrictions, and the adult is obliged to give the enforcement of these restrictions a great deal of attention. The merry-go-round requires a fine, rowing motion, but other articles of equipment provide equally good exercise with greater safety and less adult interference. Somewhat older children, it is true, get good co-operative dramatic play from a merry-go-round. It is a rather expensive piece of apparatus but fairly durable if well taken care of.

With the exception of the homemade seesaw and the rope-and-board swing, the equipment so far mentioned requires a considerable outlay from the school funds. Such funds should be available within reasonable limits; the younger child needs his play apparatus quite as much as his high-school brother or sister needs expensive laboratories and libraries. But where funds are stringently limited it is pos-

Using the Library Furniture Made by the Class

sible for a teacher with imagination to use homemade equipment with great success. Well-painted packing boxes of varying sizes encourage climbing and provide "houses" and "caves" which start excellent dramatic play. A simple straight ladder supported on large packing cases provokes varieties of climbing; a plank raised on low supports provides a favorite walking board, enjoyed by children both older and younger. Especially in these days of economy the labor and ingenuity of the local carpenter should be enlisted whenever possible.

Wheel toys — kiddy-cars, scooters, wagons, and velocipedes — are very important additions to the play life of children. They are good for both indoor and outdoor use, but they must be kept in good condition from the point of view of both economy and safety. The writer thinks that even a very restricted number of toys of good quality, safe, and durable are to be preferred to a large number of cheap varieties. The express wagon seems the most valuable of all because of the variety of play which it suggests: hauling cargoes of different sorts, playing train or taxi, pulling the baby doll, moving the furniture, and so on. Even when adequate funds are available, it seems unwise to purchase so many toys that no sharing is required. On the other hand, one lone wagon or velocipede for a large group provokes many conflicts, too many for educational purposes unless they are very wisely handled.

Of the wheel toys listed kiddy-cars are an item suitable only for the nursery-school level. They should not be used too constantly by individual children; and when one or two children become too firmly attached to a kiddy-car or, for that matter, to any other bit of equipment, it is well to have such equipment whisked away to be "fixed," or otherwise eliminated for a time.

Materials for block-building may now be purchased in great variety. Adequate lists of what is available may be found in Garrison's book *Permanent Play Materials for Young Children* and other references. The following standards for selecting building materials for different age levels are here suggested: First, there should be considered what the children will gain just from the manipulation of the material, apart from any planned building. At the nursery-school level children enjoy pulling and hauling large blocks which are not too heavy. For this reason the hollow wooden blocks are very desirable. Nursery-school children also like to pile blocks one on top of the other for the pleasure of tumbling them over. For this activity floor blocks of sufficient size to be easily handled and easily retrieved are good. Then, little children like at times to handle little blocks, just because they are little. Blocks of the "gift" size are good for this purpose. As a second principle of selection one must consider the buildings children like to make at different age levels. The plans and interests of nursery-school children are very fleeting. The kinds of building which they enjoy are few. Simple floor blocks serve well for making the "railroad tracks," "sidewalks," and crude "houses" children two and three years old like to build. On the whole, very little children do not care for having their work preserved for any

A Safe Place for a Dollhouse

length of time, so that blocks with corner pieces or more elaborate devices for providing stability are not needed at this level. Little children's ideas are crude and simple; variety of shape is not called for in their building material.

Older preschool children and younger school children desire permanence for their buildings. They also want a fairly finished product: a house they can get into, a wagon that can be pulled, a boat that can be used for a period of time as the center of dramatic play. For such children the Hill Floor Blocks, with their sturdy corner pieces and supporting rods, are a delight. Still older children like more diversified building materials, with a yet greater feeling of permanency in the finished product. Stability Blocks and Bilder Boards and Lincoln Logs are therefore desirable for the child six or seven years old.

In the selection of blocks economy is an important factor, for some of the larger sets require a large expenditure. If a large outlay is to be made for the purchase of an expensive set, it is important to answer a number of practical questions before investing. Are these blocks really important for the child at this age? Are his ideas such that he can really use them as a play medium? Is the space in the room such that large building blocks can be used with profit without curtailing other desirable forms of play? If when the block building is completed it must be immediately torn down because the room must be cleared for another use, is it worth while to buy the blocks? If a "store" or "house" will take up so much of the room that no other valuable piece of work can go on while it remains, should the blocks required for such building be purchased, or should they perhaps be borrowed for very occasional use from another grade? Against the undoubted value of many elaborate block-building projects must be weighed the curtailment of other activities necessitated by such block-building.

A standard which applies to any equipment or material provided by the school, the application of which is particularly well illustrated in connection with blocks, is that good equipment should lead to a growth in planning and executing as it is used in the course of the year. Well-selected blocks stimulate progress in building; poorly selected blocks result in a dearth of ideas and in aimless manipulation amounting to fooling. When children are ready for the making of buildings with stability and permanence, it is wasting their time to let them play with floor blocks having no corner pieces and no other provision for the development of new ideas. When appropriate blocks cannot be provided because they are too expensive or there is no room for them, probably blocks should not be provided at all.

Dramatic play has been mentioned in several connections in this chapter. Such play is natural to children; and normal, active individuals will engage in it, no matter how poor their environment. Witness the elaborate dramatic play which our grandmothers recall, even though it was carried on in a day when children did not have many ready-made toys, but had to imagine or create their own. However, a wise selection of play materials greatly assists this very important means of growth and expression. All the equipment

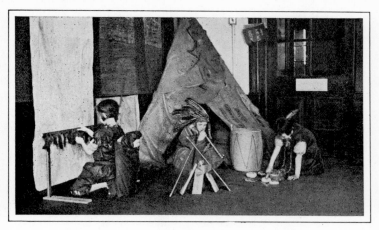

An Indian Scene

so far mentioned contributes to dramatic play of one sort or another. Apparatus for vigorous play, wheel toys, and blocks, as well as the other play materials yet to be discussed, are incentives to good dramatization if they are not so numerous and complete as to stultify the child's own active fancy.

In well-provided home nurseries the needs of children's dramatic play are met through a variety of toys. Dolls and doll furniture, railroad trains and toy villages, and all the other fascinating wares of the toy shops are bought by delighted relatives and given to delighted children at Christmas and birthday times and other occasions. These attractive toys have only gradually found their way into the school through the nursery school and the kindergarten. The principles of wise selection for school use are not very different from those which should guide intelligent grown people in buying toys to provide fun at home. For instance, a doll with simple, well-made clothing which the child can put on and take off and wash and iron is preferred to a doll whose very fancy frock is sewed on or, if removable, is so fragile that when removed it is in shreds. Also a doll with a limited wardrobe, which suggests making additional things for her, is more fun and has more educational possibilities than a doll with such a complete wardrobe that nothing else is needed. A fully furnished playhouse or dollhouse is not so good as one for which certain things need to be made.

A very complete mechanical toy, from a motor car that goes "by itself" to an elaborate electric railway, has no play possibilities for the younger child, once he has seen it work a few times, except the possibility of taking it apart to see how it is made. So a toy of this sort has only a limited use at home, and certainly no use at school — unless you can call amusing the adult who buys it a use.

In purchasing varieties of toys for the school environment, economy, durability, and play possibilities should be carefully considered. Furthermore, the environment should not be overcrowded with toys. Some nursery schools are almost oversupplied in this respect. Usually, too, it is well to have few toys in the beginning of the year and to increase the number and variety as group play develops. Given an adequate budget to begin with, the teacher should see that the playroom is adequately stocked and not "littered." The five-and-ten-cent stores provide an excellent source of supply for the accessories of play equipment. All sorts of housekeeping appliances — for the children to use themselves, and in Lilliputian size for use in doll play — may be purchased for nickels and dimes. Most of the toys are of good artistic standard.

The sand box is a very important item of equipment. Outdoors it provides for much good free play, with or without water; indoors its use is more restricted, but it is still a great deal of fun if properly supervised. Both outdoors and in, the sand should be kept clean and should be renewed from time to time. Indoors, sand should not be swept up from a playroom floor and returned to the tray. Outdoors, there should be an adequate cover to protect the sand pile when not in use. Playing in the sand in the late fall and early spring re-

The First Grade Furnishes a Living Room

quires supervision from the point of view of health. Even if the children are adequately clothed, the sand pile encourages too much quiet and sedentary play outdoors for chilly weather.

Both outdoors and in, the sand pile should be provided with toys to stimulate desirable play and crowd out throwing the sand about. Dishes and cooky tins, pails and shovels, are needed for good sand play. Throwing sand should never be permitted. A little water adds greatly to the joy of the play, but too much messing about with water is not wise in cold weather.

Materials for the fine and industrial arts form an important part of lower-school equipment. In addition to directed work with crayons, paint, and clay, even the more formal schools are beginning to appreciate the wisdom of exposing children to plastic materials and encouraging their spontaneous reactions. Sheets of drawing paper (of varying sizes, running to the large), crayons (with extra large ones for the younger children), easels, show-card colors, and boxes of water-color paints are commonly provided, and children are permitted to use them during free-play periods. Scissors, blunt for the two-year-olds and three-year-olds and pointed for the older child, are recognized as useful tools. Clay is furnished, and

Limited Space does not Prevent Varied Activity

children's spontaneous use of it is encouraged. Carpenter's tools, wood, and workbenches are the rule in progressive schools, although not so lavishly provided in the more conservative ones. Children are encouraged to work with these materials, in the belief that the work is valuable for their development and that their creations greatly enrich their play life.

There is much to be said on both sides concerning the use of sharp tools in the classroom. Such tools teach control and careful handling, thus giving the child an acquaintance with danger which may prevent his incurring accidental harm. But the risk of serious injury is likewise great; and for this reason sharp tools should not be used by the youngest children except under the direct supervision of an adult, and they should be removed at any time that the children ignore necessary restrictions. For this reason the value of carpenter's tools for nursery-school children, other than small hammers, with nails to be hammered into bars of soap, seems doubtful. It is a good principle to avoid activities and materials which require constant direction and supervision. On the other hand, in those progressive schools where children have *begun* the use of tools at two and three, they are capable of using them with a much greater degree of safety at four and five than children of the same age who are unused to handling such equipment. Two facts about young children in situations involving danger need to be considered in making plans for the use of tools. On the one hand, children trained from their earliest years to be self-reliant, to use judgment and skill, can be relied upon to a surprising extent to manage themselves and avoid personal injury. On the other hand, a very slight accident may under certain circumstances lead to serious or even fatal consequences. We desire children with characters which are cautious rather than timid; we hope that our children will be self-reliant and capable. Too great caution on our part defeats these worthy ends, but carelessness may lead to disaster. Between the two extremes lies reasonable procedure, but what such reasonable procedure is must be decided by each teacher in her own situation. The number of children in the group; their age, discipline, and previous experience; the degree of freedom to which they are accustomed at home; the teacher's own alertness, poise, and rapidity of movement, — all these must be taken into account in introducing tools into the equipment of the classroom.

Sewing and weaving materials have some place in the equipment of the lower school, from the five-year-old level on. But the kind of sewing encouraged should be that which is done with worsted or coarse thread and large needles, and weaving should be carried out with roving or with rags. The old fine sewing and weaving materials are out of place in the modern school. On the whole, even more modern sewing and weaving materials do not seem very useful for the child under six years old unless there is a dearth of other possibilities.

The presence of musical toys in the school environment is a source of joy to certain children; and if these toys are in good condition and well selected, they may be of educational value in the more formal sense of the word "education." Bells, a xylophone, a drum, cymbals, as well as improvised

Getting Ready for an Indian Play in Grade II

musical toys, such as glasses of water containing various amounts of liquid, give the opportunity for play with sound. If such equipment is at hand, it should be in tune or in such condition that a true and pleasing tone may be called forth; otherwise it is the reverse of valuable from the musical standpoint. Generally, too, it should be used under supervision; for noisy misuse of such toys results very easily, if for no other reason than that children do not possess the knack of handling them so that a pleasing tone may result.

It is customary in many kindergartens and nursery schools to allow children to touch the piano at certain times during the morning if they do so gently and create real tone rather than mere noise. Such a privilege seems preferable to the provision of a toy piano, which is never in tune, and lends itself mostly to banging noises.

Picture books and storybooks belong in every nursery and classroom. They should be of good aesthetic standard, and children should be taught the right method of handling them. For this reason, even in the nursery school there should be plenty of regular picture books made of paper as well as those of linen. Only by using perishable books does the nursery baby learn how to treat books with care. Illustrations should be colorful, simple, and clear. Distorted interpretations and adult sophistications generally have no place in the books for little children. Bright colors are probably enjoyed more than pastel tints or black and white. There is one school of art teachers which warns us that too many picture books in the environment have a hampering effect upon the pictures the child is able to create himself. Concerning this theory more will be said in a later chapter. The point here is that the well-equipped nursery or lower-school classroom provides, and should provide, a good selection of picture books and storybooks. These delight the children and also develop that readiness for reading so dear to the heart of the average parent and primary-school teacher.

Good, well-illustrated books may be obtained at relatively small cost or at a considerable outlay. Many good ones may be procured at the five-and-ten-cent stores. Not only are these books interesting to children, but many of them are also of good artistic standard.

There is another group of playthings which the resourceful teacher provides, and that is the miscellaneous material to be used in baby scientific demonstrations. Soap-bubbles are a never-failing source of delight; there should be occasional opportunities to "sail" boats, if only in a basin; magnetic toys are of interest to children five and six years old, — to mention only a few possibilities.

Games and picture puzzles also have their place, although for the nursery child the place is a small one. For children two and three years old the simple puzzle of a few pieces, with the matrix of the form to be made enclosed on a board, is the only suitable one. Some children at four and five years like more complicated puzzles, and these perhaps serve the purpose of a quiet occupation to relieve strain on a rainy day indoors; but more complicated puzzles easily create nervousness, and require a fine muscular co-ordination which should rarely be encouraged in preschool children. Children five, six, or seven years old are interested in number games and matching games — games which may provide both fun and practice in accurate perception. The attention of the five-year-old to such activities is flitting, but older children in the first and second grades may concentrate upon them very well.

Bead-stringing and peg-tiles as materials for very little children should perhaps be mentioned. Bead-stringing is a soothing occupation for the four-year-old; but the finished string affords little satisfaction, for if it is made with the wooden beads, which alone are appropriate from the hygienic standpoint, it must be immediately unstrung and the beads returned to the school box. Yet in groups of four-year-olds wooden beads have their uses, because they provide an activity in which nervous and shy children find satisfaction. Peg-tiles are on a very low level, for their educational possibilities in the way of variation and invention are almost nil. Like beads, they provide occupation, only on a more infantile level, for the insecure and unhappy baby in his process of adjustment to the group.

No discussion of play equipment is complete without some mention of the toys children bring from home. The old-fashioned kindergartner rejoiced when children began to bring things from home, because this showed that they were making a connection between home and school. This was quite true, although perhaps in a different sense from what was originally intended. To bring toys from home gives the child a sense of security — makes him feel at home in the school. Sometimes, too, it gives him the respectful notice of other children, and occasionally the satisfaction of sharing what is his with someone else.

In some nursery schools and primary classes teachers discourage the bringing of things from home, even insisting at times upon putting away the child's personal possessions in a safe place until he goes home. The difficulties in allowing personal possessions to be used by the group are many. Breakage causes distress to the child and, if the toy is an expensive one, to the parent. It is also difficult to manage the group situation, especially in the case of the youngest children. If this is John's wagon, why, if he wishes, shouldn't he play with it all day without letting anyone else have it? If he wants to keep it for himself, and the teacher, by suggestion or other pressure, prevails upon him to share it, there is an element of artificiality in the situation which is quite undesirable. If other children take it away by force, the adult feels called upon to interfere.

In a few cases parents who understand the school's difficulties, and are willing to stand the odds in the way of damage or loss, encourage children who have plenty of toys at home to bring them to school and share them with children who have not so many. Unless such sharing gives the child who possesses the toy too much prestige, the benefit to the group of having more to play with may compensate for the difficulty of managing personal possessions. But on the whole (except as a temporary measure, to give a shy child new security or to give an underprivileged group an advantage) it is better to have children use school equipment in school and learn the principles of sharing and fair play through an impartial use of the school equipment.

The planning of housing and equipment for the modern lower school, then, includes the provision of many facilities which the older school would have considered outside its province. A wide variety of child interests must be encouraged and stimulated, and the hygienic conditions planned with the child's all-round good in mind. In days of economy the tendency of the unenlightened is to think that some of the equipment which has been discussed — let us say slides, and varieties of blocks, and toys — are extravagances. This is true only if such equipment is not purchased with due regard to the child's need and to the durability of the equipment in relation to its cost. Toys are as necessary for the young child as books; outdoor-play apparatus is as necessary as spinach and orange juice. In some form these facilities should be provided, even if for economical reasons they must be makeshift and homemade.

The modern school must provide a normal environment for growing children; it should supplement the home, without attempting to duplicate the home's facilities. The ideal school environment provides a variety of incentive and opportunity for work and play; it avoids waste, the confusion of overabundance, and the danger of overstimulation.

There is here appended a list of kindergarten equipment prepared by Miss Anne McManus, who has contributed also three of the units of work described in Chapter VI. This list seems to represent an excellent selection for a school with a generous although not unlimited budget.

EQUIPMENT IN OUR ROOM

Twenty movable tables (oak-stained and varnished; several heights)

Forty-five chairs (rubber-capped and varnished)

Low cupboards (for the children's materials)

High cupboards (for supplies, books, materials)

Piano

Victrola

Gong (for signals)

Sand table (equipped with cover and rubber casters)

Workbench: vise, brace and bit, three hammers, three saws, drills, sandpaper, large-headed nails, glue, dustpan, brush, large box for wood

Blocks: Patty Hill Blocks, Hennessey Blocks, enlarged gifts, smooth boards

Two easels for painting: uniform jars for alabastine, long-handled brushes

Two jars for clay. The jars are kept on a stand provided with rubber casters

Blackboard

Bulletin boards

Pictures (framed, mounted)

Play corner: table, chairs, dish cabinet, dishes, stove (electric), chest for clothes, bed, carriage, three dolls, washtub and board, clothesline, pins, basket, ironing board, iron, broom, dustpan, duster

Library corner: table, eight chairs, book rack, books, bulletin

Nature materials: plants, aquarium for fish and turtles, cage for pets

Toys: wooden trains, wooden animals, furniture (small), balls, hoops, jump ropes, puzzles, dominoes, tenpins, galvanized tub for boats and celluloid animals

Milk stand (equipped with rubber casters)

Boxes: wooden, cardboard; lumber and wheels for construction work

Apparatus: two rope swings, slide, junglegym, packing boxes, balancing board, seesaw, barrel, and ladder. (This apparatus is outdoors)

BIBLIOGRAPHY

California Curriculum Commission. Teachers' Guide to Child Development. California State Printing Office, Sacramento, 1930.

> Consult Chapter III. Descriptions of developmental activities in kindergarten-primary groups.

DAVIS, MARY DABNEY. Housing and Equipping the Washington Child-Welfare Research Station. *United States Office of Education Bulletin No. 13*, 1930.

GARRISON, CHARLOTTE G. Permanent Play Materials for Young Children. Scribner, New York, 1926.

KNOX, ROSE. School Activities and Equipment, Part II, "General School Equipment and Practical Problems." Houghton Mifflin, Boston, 1927.

> Discussions of equipment needed in connection with various activities appear throughout the book.

MEAD, CYRUS, and ORTH, FRED. The Traditional Public School, Chapter XII, pp. 286–339, "The Utilization of Discarded Material in Elementary Handwork." Macmillan, New York, 1934.

National College of Education, Curriculum Records of the Children's School, by members of the staff. Bureau of Publications, National College of Education, Evanston, Illinois, 1932.

> Consult descriptions of units of work.

National Society for the Scientific Study of Education, Twenty-eighth Yearbook (Public School Publishing Company, Bloomington, Illinois, 1929): "Preschool and Parental Education," "Nursery School Equipment," pp. 235–238.

STEVENS, MARION P. The Activities Curriculum in the Primary Grades, "Equipment," pp. 403–437. Heath, Boston, 1931.

CHAPTER IX

THE FINE ARTS IN THE LOWER SCHOOL

I want to know a butcher paints,
A baker rhymes for his pursuit,
Candlestick-maker much acquaints
His soul with song, or, haply mute,
Blows out his brains upon the flute!

ROBERT BROWNING

Modern education is completely in accord with the poet's dream of a world in which "a butcher paints, a baker rhymes for his pursuit." Many of us who are today grown up, perhaps middle-aged and a trifle drab, would be happier, more delightful people if the creative spark within us, no matter how slight, had been fanned to a flame instead of extinguished by ridicule. One does not need to be a great artist to enjoy painting pictures, or a finished musician to sing or play with enjoyment to oneself and with no real violence to the sensibilities of others. The creative spirit, so we have come to understand, is not purely the endowment of a selected few but is present to some degree in each individual. Some small thing that is true, some bit of expression that has the spark of originality, can be contributed by everyone who approaches normal mentality. But the result of school education in bygone generations was that the small contributions the average child was capable of making were discouraged by holding up arbitrary standards of achievement, by teaching difficult techniques which most children could not grasp, or by coldly ignoring his efforts.

In progressive educational theory the fine arts are assigned, as their prime function, the release of creative energy and the awakening of appreciations in all children, not merely in the gifted few. Therefore an atmosphere of freedom should distinguish all good art teaching. Technique should be taught when the child needs it to express that which he knows and feels, but it should not be intruded into his spontaneous work at the risk of extinguishing the original flare which is peculiarly his own. Sympathetic recognition of true expression, no matter how crude or limited that expression may be, should meet the child's efforts.

Thomas Munro, in the symposium *Art and Education,* says:

The chief aim of education should be the development of the individual's own aesthetic powers, with emphasis on clear, spontaneous feeling and ability to organize experience creatively, rather than on the memorizing of facts about art or the acquiring of technical skill along stereotyped lines. Pupils should be encouraged to look at nature and their own affairs with a fresh, untrammeled vision, and to devise by experiment the means most appropriate to express this vision. . . .

For exceptional students, and to a large extent for all students, little positive instruction in art is desirable. The basis of the procedure should be to surround the child with stimuli to artistic experiment, including tools, materials, and a few simple and varied examples of the use of these materials according to the chief artistic traditions. Thus provided, he should be left to play with these articles when and as he wishes.

In the lower schools of today there is a wide divergence in both theory and practice. Differences in method go all the way from the completely untrammeled freedom which is characteristic of some experimental schools to the definite training given four-year-olds and five-year-olds in some city school systems. A review of these different methods would be fascinating to attempt but quite beyond the scope of this book. The reader is urged to consult the volume *Creative Expression: The Development of Children in Art, Literature, Music, and Dramatics.* This reference includes all the material published in the *Progressive Education Magazine* and is extremely interesting and valuable. For our purposes here it will be best to discuss the small child's creative work and some of the more practical questions of method.

A child's drawing develops through a series of stages analogous to those through which his language passes. First he scribbles, just as a tiny baby plays with sound. Then "he draws that which he feels," which stage is equivalent to egocentric speech, when the child is merely talking and doesn't care at all whether you listen to him, agree, or disagree. Finally the child draws what he knows; he makes an effort to make himself intelligible through plastic material as through speech. Certain psychologists have made studies to determine the degree to which the child's drawing may be an indication of his mental development. Dr. Florence Goodenough has shown that the number of precise details which children include in their drawings of the human figure is an indication of mental maturity. If asked to draw a man, the very immature child merely produces a scribble; the somewhat more mature may produce a vague elliptical or rectangular outline, with a suggestion of a head appended. Older children include the extremities, the features, and various articles of clothing. Those details which a child has recently discovered and in which he is most interested are drawn very large, quite out of proportion to the other elements in his picture. When he is interested in buttons, tremendous buttons appear in his drawing of a man; or, later in his development, he hits upon a scheme of indicating eyebrows, and greatly enlarges this detail. Goodenough and others think that the kindergarten child's strange drawings are in the first place a mode of expressing ideas, and only secondarily an effort to make something beautiful.

Probably the first really good artistic effects the child achieves with his plastic materials are accidental. Through a sense of pleasure in having produced something which he himself appreciates, the child is encouraged to experiment further. Adult praise and the approval of companions add to his pleasure, and still more pleasing effects are created. While, as has been said, there is much diversity of opinion as to the place of any downright teaching in art, all modern authorities in this field differ from older authorities in appreciating and encouraging these experimental efforts. In order to give the child plenty of opportunity to manipulate, a variety of plastic materials is provided. For painting in nursery school and kindergarten, there are provided paints in jars and large brushes, to be experimented with on big sheets of paper tacked to floor or blackboard or easel. In addition, many nursery schools and some primary grades are using a fascinating new medium, the "Shaw Finger Paints." Devised by Miss Shaw at the Dalton School, New York City, these paints admit of direct use with the fingers and palms of the hands, without the intermediary work of a brush. Putting the child in such close touch with his actual medium encourages much joyful manipulation and experimentation; using the paint with fingers, palms of hands, and even elbows creates big effects which are quite lovely, and which also provide for the play of large muscles rather than the fine co-ordinations required in using even a large brush.

Paint boxes, with their possibilities of mixing colors, are a joy to older children. Tempera and oil paints — difficult to manipulate and expensive — are included in the environment in some upper primary grades. For drawing, large crayons and charcoal are replacing the old small crayons, and the child is encouraged to experiment with these as he does with paint.

The teaching technique which is most effective in encouraging young children's art work is so much a matter of opinion at the present time that one hesitates to be dogmatic. The following suggestions, however, are universal enough in their application to be offered here: First, the teacher of young children must know how to appreciate art, in order to recognize what is fine and spontaneous in the child's first crude attempts. Secondly, she must understand child psychology and the special psychology of children's drawings enough to sympathize with the stages through which the child passes — from mere manipulation to expression of feeling, to definite expression of thought, to a recognition of the aesthetic. Finally, she should be intelligent and ingenious in providing the best media at each stage in the development of an individual or a group. Indications that children need such a medium as the Shaw Finger Paints, or that they need more play with large paintbrushes, should be heeded and acted upon in the planning of the environment. Again, the moment for helping the child is a matter for study. When does he need a technique in order to say what he wants to say, to achieve the effect in color or arrangement which he patently desires? When does he need to be diverted to an entirely different sort of medium, such as clay? When would it be well to encourage rhythmic dancing and listening to music rather than work with any plastic materials? Intelligence and fine discrimination of values are needed for good art teaching with the youngest children; in the lower school a large measure of technical skill is probably far less necessary. The too intrusive teacher and the one who adopts an attitude of complete *laissez faire* are, in the writer's opinion, alike unsuccessful. Again quoting Mr. Munro's article: "Reliance upon freedom and 'self-expression' may . . . be carried to excess. To leave children entirely unguided and uninspired is an extreme of anarchy that defeats itself," just as "the standards and laws of good art now generally taught in public schools . . . are false and obstructive to originality."

Schools of art teaching are not in agreement as to the place of classical pictures and models in schoolroom surroundings. An extreme point of view adopted by some is that no models should be shown, no masterpieces of art should be placed in the environment, lest the child's originality be hampered by the thought of others and lest he be discouraged by a model of perfect technique. One enthusiast discourages children from looking at picture books too much. Others adopt a more reasonable middle ground, giving the child the opportunity to see and enjoy great and lovely things, but never discouraging him by overt comparisons between the perfect piece of work and his own crude efforts. Although one sincerely desires to create a neutral atmosphere, giving the child no models, the aim is impossible of achievement. Consciously or unconsciously he will be influenced by other children, failing more inspiring suggestions. The fact that the pictures by Franz Cizek's pupils are distinguished by so much similarity, in spite of the fact that the children were discouraged from going to art museums or studying models in school, illustrates this point rather vividly.

Most of the observations which have been made on drawing and painting so far apply equally through the nursery and the primary school. It should be added that the younger the child, the more conclusive are the arguments for complete freedom unless materials are abused. In the upper primary grades the adult may well help in enhancing appreciations by commenting appreciatively on the strong points in an individual child's work or bringing out the fine points of beauty in some picture universally recognized as good. With the youngest children, only the simplest comments, such as "That is a fine, clear color," or, "I like that dark stem; it makes the flower stand out," are appropriate; and even these easily become artificial. Appreciations develop gradually; there is little to be done in the lower school beyond providing fertile soil for them. Like the seeds which cease to grow when the child digs them up out of his garden, appreciations go stale when they are pried up forcibly and discussed. A small child should be allowed to look at a flower without having some great, awkward adult say, "How pretty the flower is!" or watch the glittering goldfish flashing through the globe without being reminded, "See the pretty goldfish!"

Are there specific results, the reader might well ask, to be expected in the lower school from art teaching of the almost passive sort we have been discussing? There should be definite results unless the teaching has failed of its mark. The child should have a more critical sense of color, form, and arrangement from year to year. This should show itself in his own work and in his comments upon the work of others. On the whole, the variety of feelings and ideas which he seeks to express should grow richer and more varied with the years of play with plastic materials. Sincerity and clarity should distinguish his work at each age level, and when for some reason these qualities are absent he should himself become increasingly sensitive to the lack. That these results, together with a gradual increase in technical skill, do come about in some schools where a high degree of freedom is permitted and the teacher is virtually passive so far as criticism goes, is the writer's conviction. But an intelligent planning of the environment and a certain amount of discerning suggestion seem to be indispensable.

Plastic material is used in the schools from two nearly related and yet distant points of view: the point of view of the creative artist and the more utilitarian outlook of people interested in the products of industrial art. Both seek to achieve as a result a pleasing object, but in industrial-art work it is essential that the child obtain some insight into the processes by which articles of food, clothing, and shelter, tools, utensils, and decorative objects are produced for the world's use. In fine art the aim is more directly upon expression and original creation; in industrial art, upon the production of things both beautiful and useful for the needs of life. To quote once more Mr. Munro's article:

No sharp distinction should be made at first between the fine and useful arts, the emphasis being rather on disclosing the principles of design common to both. In useful art the student should be shown how an artist takes a practical need, a utilitarian object, as an occasion for realizing at the same time a beautiful form: how the dictates of utility may function as themes and inspirations, rather than as limits, in the creation of beauty.

The aims of both fine and industrial art appear with great clarity in the use made of clay and plasticene. Such a medium is particularly suited to manipulation and experiment by the younger children, which result either in purely imaginative productions or in crude pieces of pottery.

The child's play with it follows much the same stages of development as his use of paint and crayons. At first, and for a long while, the pure joy of manipulation absorbs his whole attention. He pounds the material, pats it, pokes holes in it, and rolls it about with great vigor. The first meaningful form which emerges as a result of pommeling the stuff is probably produced accidentally, unless some adult or some other child has given him a suggestion or unless he has watched someone else produce a definite form.

Real clay is a satisfactory material at the five-year-old and six-year-old levels. For twos, threes, and fours some sort of plasticene, which retains its plasticity indefinitely, is probably better. Simple clay dries out very quickly and is difficult to keep in perfect condition. It should therefore be used when the child is ready to make permanent things — things which can be allowed to dry and perhaps be painted, shellacked, and taken home. Unfortunately clay work as a product to take home is peculiarly unsatisfactory; it breaks "if you look at it" and, when it breaks, creates a great deal of mess, bringing down the wrath of tidy parents or nurses. When children can be persuaded to donate their creations to a permanent class or school exhibit, this is probably the best disposition of them.

Industrial-art teachers have often criticized primary class-room teachers for permitting children to think that a clay dish or other object, dried and shellacked, is truly finished. Such a process is altogether different from the real way dishes are made, such critics say. There is some force in the criticism, at least for six-year-olds and seven-year-olds, if not for younger children. But a homemade kiln is always difficult to achieve, and in many situations absolutely impossible. One sometimes wonders if what children gain from having their productions fired by an improvised kiln is always worth the time and energy expended by both teacher and child.

There comes a time in the average child's experiment with clay when intelligent guidance is needed to assure continued growth. This is perhaps especially true in the case of the child whose interest is in making dishes, bowls, and other commonplace objects. The possibilities of crude experimental manipulation are usually exhausted by the child of six if he has had plenty of experience at the four-year-old and five-year-old levels. Some concentration on technique becomes necessary in order to reach the child's own best standards. When the firing process is a possibility, he can get plenty of practice in smoothing and refining his work to the point where there are no cracks. If there are cracks and holes his product will not withstand the heat. He may perhaps also be taught to build up his pottery by a coil method, thus acquiring better technique and a more satisfactory product.

Like experimentation with plastic materials, music has an important place among the lower school's activities. The progress in America toward making fine music available for all has been enormous in the last decade. Through the efforts of devoted leaders like Dr. Walter Damrosch, music has been finding its way more and more into the hearts and homes of the American people. Recently more and more adequate radio programs have aided the work of musical education for the public. Within the schools great changes have been made, with the result that music is taught much more for the joy and emotional release it offers than to achieve the technical ends which were once thought so important. Rote singing is the accepted musical activity for the kindergarten and first grade. Music reading is gradually introduced in the second grade, with a continuance of rote singing in order to make the music period more varied and attractive.

Even the first generation of American kindergarten teachers used a great deal of music of a sort. Many of the songs and rhythms were totally unsuited to the children. Although progressive kindergarten teachers have learned from musicians and from teachers of music much about the proper selection and use of musical material for young children, the credit for the improvement in the kind of music offered is due to a general raising of the standards and ideals of music teaching in the schools, and this has been fostered by the Music Educators' National Conference. The same thing is true for primary-school teachers, although these can more frequently call upon specialists for constant guidance and suggestion.

Musical activities in the lower school are of the following varieties: rote singing; tone matching; rhythmic dancing or "rhythms"; the band; play with musical toys and instruments; making instruments; quiet listening to music performed by others to furnish a basis for genuine music appreciation. Good discussions of these activities may be found in the special references listed at the end of the chapter; a brief mention of the values of each of them will therefore suffice here.

In selecting songs for rote singing the purpose is to have children sing sweetly and truly songs which they thoroughly enjoy. If they are to sing well and enjoy what they sing, the songs must be very short, must be within a very limited range of the scale, must have simple words about familiar topics, and must be melodious and rhythmic. It goes without saying that they should always be good music. Many excellent collections of simple folk tunes and classical melodies have been made; it remains for the taste and the discretion of the individual teacher to select for her group songs which are suitable and pleasing.

In the old days the teacher of young children acted on the assumption that a large number of her pupils were monotones; therefore, it was thought, nothing could be done about them. Sometimes these children joined the singing and spoiled it; at other times they just sat; at still other times they presented a problem in discipline. Investigations have shown that there is probably no such individual as a complete monotone among average groups of children, or, if such a creature does exist, he is very rare. This discovery has been interesting and helpful, because teachers now feel they must do something about the child who cannot sing. Accordingly, it is customary to divide children into groups:

those who sing well, those who sing a little, and those who are near-monotones. Each group, through games and other playful devices, gets some experience in the matching of tones. No one is left out of the music activities.

There are, however, a few points about this undoubted reform which call for comment. Though monotones are rare, if not nonexistent, children who are very nearly lacking in tone discrimination are fairly numerous. How much time and energy, on the part of both teacher and child, should go into helping this group sing a very little is at times a question. Probably it should be answered in terms of the child's interest in learning. It is not very sensible to nag him into an activity the main purpose of which is enjoyment, although we do not wish to abandon lightly the task of teaching him something which might eventually be a great joy to him. Most five-year-olds and six-year-olds want to keep on trying, but it takes a tactful and interesting teacher to carry them through to anything like a pleasurable result if they are seriously deficient in tone recognition.

"Rhythms" in the kindergarten of yesterday were — and perhaps in some kindergartens and primary classes are today — far from really musical experiences. The tunes were ugly and commonplace; the responses the children were taught to make were stereotyped. There has been a gradual progress in the direction of using good music. Owing to the influence of the several schools of rhythmic dancing, "rhythms" in the lower school approximate real musical expression more nearly than once they did, and in many progressive schools they provide a true outlet for the creative impulse under the guidance of trained teachers. As a means of dramatization, rhythms add variety and refinement to the child's spontaneous dramatic play.

The rhythm band is dear to the heart of many lower-school teachers, and without doubt it has brought joy to numberless children. Various percussion instruments, either legitimate or homemade, are given the youngsters, and they are permitted to accompany the music played by the teacher on a piano. A child is chosen as conductor and is asked to lead the band. The unquestioned values of this activity lie in the pleasure it gives the children and in the excellent experience of group co-operation which it affords. Musically the rhythm band is open to some question, especially when crude, makeshift instruments, emitting horrible sounds, are included in the program. On the other hand, where only a few children accompany the piano, and where these children are provided with good cymbals, a drum or tom-tom, and well-tuned bells, the effect can be quite pleasing, and the values probably outweigh the disadvantages.

Children love to play with sound. In infancy they play with their own vocal apparatus; when they are a little older they enjoy rattles and like to pound on resounding surfaces. Musical toys are a source of pleasure. The horns, mouth organs, and other wind instruments our parents and grandparents enjoyed are taboo in the modern nursery because they are unsanitary, since they are always passed from one to another. But toy pianos, drums, cymbals, bells, and xylophones provide similar delights. Their actual educational value to the child is small, and if they are out of tune, as they usually are, it is simply nonexistent. Drums, cymbals, and bells may be used occasionally in the nursery and the kindergarten; the wooden xylophone has value, and some children like to experiment with it. However, if one must economize on the equipment of the lower school, it would probably do small harm to cut down on musical toys.

The making of instruments may be a valuable experience in the child's musical education. Well-made instruments, constructed by children under the direction of a teacher, help the child to appreciate something of what goes into the development of a modern band or orchestra, and they give him a simple means of musical expression which he entirely understands and can fully control. Mrs. Satis Coleman has made a real contribution in this field. She and a few other gifted teachers are able to direct an activity of this sort with great profit to their pupils. Other teachers less musically gifted, and less capable with their hands, do not have such marked success. Sometimes, it is true, an average teacher accomplishes something in the making of instruments with the children; but all too often the music period, or most of it, is used up in this manual activity and in fooling with strange sounds. When this is the result, the effort enlisted seems misplaced. Music periods are assigned in the lower school for the teaching of music, not for manual dexterity.

Of the newer methods of teaching music in the lower school several are exceedingly interesting, and most of them may be found described in the bibliography of this chapter. Teachers of music, like specialists in the plastic arts, differ a great deal among themselves as to the place of technique in the child's musical education. At one extreme are a few who would encourage creative expression, unhampered by formal training; at the other are those who would give children the advantage of careful training from nursery-school days. To many of us a degree of freedom which seems altogether desirable in the plastic arts is difficult to accept when suggested for music. But although instrumental music seems to demand at least a minimum of technical instruction from the beginning, complete freedom of expression may be provided through rhythmic work. Such work directly encourages the child to respond with his whole body to music, expressing the *feeling* which this music awakens *in him*.

In the nursery school the beginnings of the fine arts are very, very small. Teaching is entirely indirect, through the provision of an environment aesthetically pleasing and through such simple means as sympathetically (but without sentimentality!) sharing the child's joy in bright sunshine, in vivid color, in the song of the robin and the softness of the rabbit's fur. The four-year-old and the five-year-old gradually begin to investigate the possibilities of plastic materials, to listen with pleasure to instrumental music and to songs, to respond rhythmically to music upon suggestion, to sing the simplest of melodies. Children six and seven years old are ready to learn some simple techniques and to respond to training which by degrees helps them to achieve some of the formal standards which they have learned to appreciate. The crux of the teaching problem is to meet the child's growing needs and demands for formal training without spoiling the freshness of his product. It takes faith and patience to stand back and forbear from the suggestion, or the tiny stroke of a brush, which may transform a child's crude but honest expression into a finished but artificial adult product; but such faith and forbearance are essentials for good teaching in the fine arts. What matters first, last, and all the time, is that the product shall be sincere and true and shall represent the child's own best standard and be satisfying to his creative impulse.

The development of appreciations is the ultimate aim of all artistic training; the creative impulse itself is but a striving toward that end — toward clearer vision, deeper feeling. What we hope as the result of our training is that the child may sense the harmonies of nature in a noisy, radio-infested world; that he may see, in spite of all the electric arc-lamps and the headlights of automobiles, "the light that never was, on sea or land." What we wish to avoid is the fate of the "Financier" in Humbert Wolfe's little poem, who, wandering through a garden in the spring-time, completely unaware of its loveliness,

> . . . looked importantly about him,
> While all the spring went on without him.

BIBLIOGRAPHY

ACKLEY, EDITH FLACK. Marionettes. Stokes, New York, 1929.

  The simplest reference on marionettes.

BROWN, CORINNE. Creative Drama in the Lower School. Appleton, New York, 1929.

  Covers the field of dramatics for the younger children, including play presentation, dances, puppets, and pageantry.

DEWEY, JOHN, et al. Art and Education. Barnes Foundation Press, Merion, Pennsylvania, 1929.

DIXON, MADELEINE. Children Are Like That. John Day, New York, 1930.

> A good book for parents and teachers, with excellent advice concerning the guidance of creative expression.

GOODENOUGH, FLORENCE. Measurement of Children's Intelligence through Drawing. World Book, Yonkers, N.Y., 1926.

HARTMAN, GERTRUDE, and SHUMAKER, ANN (Ed.). Creative Expression: The Development of Children in Art, Music, Literature, and Dramatics. John Day, New York, 1932.

> A compendium of the material published in the *Progressive Education Magazine*. Describes work with students of all ages — nursery school through college. References to the lower school are scattered throughout, but the reader who wishes really to appreciate the material should browse without regard to age levels. Pages 1–68, Art: drawing, painting, plastic art; pages 69–142, Music; pages 143–258, Literature; pages 258–344, Dramatics.

Lincoln School Staff. Curriculum Making in an Elementary School, pp. 74–130. Ginn, Boston, 1927.

> Discussions of dramatic play.

MATHIAS, MARGARET E. The Teaching of Art. Scribner, New York, 1932.

NAUMBERG, MARGARET. The Child and the World. Harcourt Brace, New York, 1928.

> The fourteenth dialogue tells of play making in the Walden School.

RUGG, HAROLD, and SHUMAKER, ANN. The Child-Centered School. World Book, Yonkers, N.Y., 1928.

> Chapters XIII–XIX concern the fine arts and are especially helpful in their treatment of rhythm.

SCHWIN, HELEN L. "Music in the Nursery School," *Music Supervisors Journal* (March, 1934), pp. 36–38. National Music Educators' Conference.

THORN, ALICE. Music for Young Children. Scribner, New York, 1929.

CHAPTER X

LITERATURE AND THE ART OF EXPRESSION

Elementary schools the world over devote a large proportion of their time to the language arts: literature, oral and written expression, and the technique of reading. Not only are language activities of immediate significance to the child in and of themselves, but the command of language also is fundamental to the progress of his general education.

The influence of literature upon character and personality in the early years of life has been appreciated from the beginning of conscious education. The stories and poems which the child learns to know and love in his nursery and early school days play the same part in his life that adult literature plays in the lives of men and women. Literature, for both child and adult, provides relaxation and aesthetic pleasure. A delightful tale takes us out of ourselves and gives re-creation in the fullest sense of the word. The sound of well-chosen words, the rhythm of prose and verse, the happy metaphor, give sheer pleasure. Through the vicarious experiences with which good reading provides us we enter into the lives of others, gaining some insight into the motives of great men, the springs of tragedy, the conflicting purposes which make for human weal and human woe. To the very young child his own self, his wants and purposes, are the only vivid realities. Gradually, as time goes on, the "not-self" takes more definite form, and he is able to feel some objective interest in the world of other people and of things. But almost until the close of the period which we are here discussing, the lower-school years, children live in a very narrow world. Their concepts of human nature and human life are constructed wholly from their experiences in their own immediate surroundings. Through stories and anecdotes of other people, other surroundings, other times, this childish horizon is gradually broadened and expanded.

According to the best current opinion, stories for the very little child should deal almost entirely with the here and now. For the nursery baby, anecdotes about his own experiences are suitable, and they are very much enjoyed. As he grows older, stories less intimately related to his own life and dealing more widely with the interesting elements in his environment are appreciated. Modern theory holds that both the content and the form of the story for the little child should be determined through a study of child life itself. This study seems to show that the vivid sensory and motor experiences of his everyday life are the high points in the child's appreciation. Anecdotes which relate and expand such experiences, which give the chance to re-enact their thrilling moments, are surely suitable in content. The form which such stories take in the best modern collections is the form the child himself gives them : a simple, clear-cut form of episodes loosely and naïvely connected and rhythmically told. Wealth of detail, expansion and elaboration, all the things which an adult mind yearns to do to a simple story, are beside the point and tend to spoil it for the child, who is easily confused by many words.

It is the contention of Lucy Sprague Mitchell and other experts in the field of children's literature that the purpose of the story is to help the child get clearer ideas about his environment, to help him interpret his world. Therefore he should not be confused by fanciful tales nor encouraged to read the bizarre and highly imaginative fairy story until, through many "here and now" stories, his feet are firmly upon the ground of the world in which he lives.

This point of view represents a reaction from certain grievous mistakes which adults heretofore have made in their selection of stories for children. For instance, in the past, instead of studying the child himself in his own surroundings and taking from this the content of his literature, unthinking people have diluted great stories to what they considered a suitable consistency for the infant mind. There was a prejudice too against negative stories; and so good, sturdy folk tales were mutilated by some juvenile authors to produce happy endings. The canons of simplicity and cheerfulness were responsible for much that was insipid, inartistic, and sentimental in the children's books of yesterday. At one stage in the development of children's literature, almost anything couched in short words that was simple, saccharine, and highly moral in its tone was supposed to be ideal literary material for the young.

Even if one is not disposed to hold entirely with the theory that the here and now is the only appropriate setting for little children's stories, it must be admitted that the value of the fanciful story has been greatly overrated. In fact, in many cases the fanciful has been overdone, to the psychological detriment of individual children. In childhood the imagination is very vivid and riotously active. Fantastic images are unchecked by experience with the workaday world, and fairy tales seem quite normal and possible because the child has no knowledge of real life adequate to check their vagaries and impossibilities. It is a psychological fact that the early stage of confusion between the fairy world of fancy and the matter-of-fact surroundings to which the child must adjust in everyday life is outgrown very slowly. An exclusive diet of imaginative literature only prolongs this stage of confusion and puts off the day when a prosy reality is frankly faced. Highly imaginative material, if included at all in children's literature, should be wisely chosen and sparingly used.

Alice Dalgliesh, in her book *First Experiences with Literature*, writes:

Folk tales, such as "The Three Bears" and "The Three Pigs," very simple, fanciful stories, fairy pictures, and poems, these are all the fanciful material that a child under six needs. They constitute a delightful introduction to the world of fancy. Later, the fairy tale proper, with its kings, queens, witches, dragons, and delightful "shivers," takes its rightful place in the child's experience, but at all ages a wholesome balance should be kept between fact and fancy.

Stories about animals have a great appeal for children older and younger. True anecdotes and fanciful tales, grotesque fables and humanitarian appeals, all have their fascination. The work of Ernest Thompson Seton, the tales of Uncle Remus, *Angus and the Ducks*, and *A Dog of Flanders*, each at one time or another has its great appeal. The overwhelming success of Beatrix Potter's stories, the achievement by "Dr. Doolittle" of a place among the immortals, the charming picture books, such as *Millions of Cats*, bear witness to the enduring popularity of the animal tale. Partly by reason of this interest in animal stories, the fable maintains its popularity in the modern nursery. However, there are some stories about animals which impress the intelligent critic as being distinctly meretricious. It is not easy to set up satisfying standards, but it may be helpful to suggest the following pertinent questions: Is the story a true anecdote and an accurate description of the qualities and behavior of the animals it describes? If not true in fact, is the story true to the general qualities of kittens, Scotties, and rabbits as we know them? Do the animals in the story speak and think as we speak and think, as the child thinks, or as we imagine kittens and Scotties would think, if they could?

Are the illustrations in the story artistic, realistic, humorous, or simply silly? Are the animals dressed in conventional human clothes? In general, is the effect of the pictures that of sympathetic interpretation, wholesome fun, accuracy, or burlesque? When stories about animals verge on the funny-paper type of buffoonery, when they are misleading and attribute to their four-footed characters traits which are altogether *out* of character, they are inartistic and trashy; when they are true to nature, or imaginatively sympathetic, or subtly humorous, they are a valuable addition to children's libraries.

The charm of Mother Goose and the fascination of the several excellent illustrated editions now on the market are admitted by the modern critic of children's literature. Mother Goose rhymes are a sort of standard reference for the home nursery and the modern nursery school. However, Lucy Sprague Mitchell has pointed out with considerable justice that the fascination of Mother Goose lies as much in the form as in the content; in fact, in many Mother Goose favorites probably the form alone is really enjoyed by the child.

In her very helpful book *First Experiences with Literature*, Alice Dalgliesh classifies juvenile stories as "Real and Almost Real," "Fairy Tales," and "Tales of Laughter." The older collections of children's stories used the captions "Mother Goose," "Fable," "Folk Tale," "Legend," "Fairy Tale," and "Myth." The distinction between the folk tale and the fairy tale lies in the fact that fairy tales are more fantastic. They are also more sophisticated than folk tales, with a magic or fairy element introduced to explain marvelous happenings. For example, in folk tales like "The Three Little Pigs," "The Three Bears," and "Billy Goats Gruff," no attempt is made to explain why animals talk and how trolls can live under bridges. The fairy godmother, however, with her magic wand, whisks Cinderella to the ball; and the witch builds the house of bread and cake and sugar in "Hänsel and Gretel." It is because of its highly fantastic element and its sophistications that the fairy tale seems to the modern critic unsuitable for the young child.

Myths, both classical (Greek and Roman) and Norse, have little place in the lower school. Rather do they belong to the literary experience of the third and fourth grades, many of them to that of the fifth and sixth. Instead of using these stories at intervals and out of context, with one or two exceptions they are best read or told in connection with a study of the lives of the people who conceived them. So told, the child is able to appreciate their meaning and beauty. Legends — the fanciful tales with a religious element, which lie, as it were, on the fringe of true mythical and religious literature — have an occasional place among the stories told to children. When they are tinged with the ghostly and the horrible, they are definitely unsuitable. They should always be selected with care and with tactful consideration of children's religious training. The legend of St. Christopher and some of the legends of St. Francis are among those sometimes much appreciated and enjoyed by children of the first and second grades.

For "nature stories" about the "waking up of the seeds," "how the caterpillar became a beautiful butterfly," and analogous themes there is, in the opinion of modern critics, little use. The world about him provides the child with one vast nature story, for the appreciation of which he needs guided observation rather than fictitious anecdotes. Until he is mature enough to appreciate the great nature myths, his own observations and his own naïve reactions are the best guides.

Realistic stories may include some accurate descriptions of events in nature. Such stories lend themselves to original composition by teachers who have a gift in this direction. Especially in dealing with nursery-school children, spontaneous accounts of the events in a child's day, or the interesting behavior of the family cat, or the birds building a safe nest way up in the tree, are very successful. Such stories should contain a great deal of repetition, and are especially enjoyed if they include some rhythmic refrain. In Miss Dalgliesh's helpful book there are some very good suggestions about making up one's own stories.

Telling stories to younger children is on the whole more effective than reading them. The rapport between the storyteller and her audience is more readily established if no printed page intervenes, and it is interesting to the children to watch the facial expression and gesture of the storyteller, to which they respond sympathetically. It is a much more direct way of imparting a tale and a much more natural one. The storyteller should be unaffected and not overdramatic in her manner, fulfilling the rôle of the simple raconteur rather than the professional entertainer. A story must be thoroughly mastered before it can be told effectively. It need not be memorized entirely, but it is well to learn by rote a good opening, an effective close, and a few good guiding sentences throughout. However, in using a story the charm of which lies in its language, the whole tale should be memorized or else it should be read from a book. No liberties, for instance, may be taken with such material as Kipling's *Just So Stories*.

The reading of stories has the undoubted advantage of securing complete adherence to the author's literary form. For this reason, reading to older children is a very important part of teaching literature. The same general comments about simplicity of manner hold good here as in the matter of telling stories; and with younger children a special effort must be made to keep up a good rapport between reader and audience in spite of the intervention of a book. When illustrations are to be shown, the group should be so arranged that it is possible to see the pictures without confusion and crowding.

In summary, it may be stated that the best modern opinion holds that the "here and now" story, grounded in the world of reality, is the most suitable for the young child. The content for this story is found in the child's own vivid experiences; the form follows the pattern in which these experiences occur. Of traditional children's literature, Mother Goose has unquestioned value for its masterly form, if not always for its content. The fable has occasional uses; the folk tale is conceded to be the best form of imaginative literature for the younger child. Fairy tales belong to the older child, whose hold on the world of actual things is already firmly established, rather than to his younger brother and sister, to whom the world of fancy is more vivid than the world of fact. Myths and legends, expressing, as they do, the innermost dreams and profoundest struggles of the human mind, are on the whole unsuitable for children and, with perhaps one or two exceptions, are altogether out of place in the lower school.

According to Lucy Sprague Mitchell the most important aim in telling stories to children is to get the children to make up stories of their own. Creation and expression are at once the goal and the method of progressive language teaching. Well-chosen literature is a most valuable stimulus.

One of the most delightful discussions of the young child's language development is found in Harriet Johnson's book *Children in the Nursery School.* Miss Johnson believes that the love of playing with sound, the sheer pleasure of exercising the vocal apparatus, is an important factor in the nursery-school child's language. The desire to communicate is not, by any means, the only motive for vocalization, nor is it at the early stage of a child's language development the most important. During the nursery-school years, Miss Johnson thinks, it is very unwise to stimulate and encourage precocious ability in communication. Such precocity, the records of her nursery school seem to show, means that "a stage in growth, the locomotor stage, and constructive abilities likewise, suffer in consequence." When children are absorbed in some postural activity, language responses are few; but once the technique has been mastered, and the activity has become automatic, like sliding down the slide, there is a great deal of vocal activity. The observation of nursery-school workers generally bears out the latter of Miss Johnson's conclusions.

The little child's love of play with sound often prompts him to repeat over and over again some "big" word the mere sound of which has attracted his fancy. One gifted four-year-old, the child of parents who were engaged in scientific research, would skip along the street to nursery school chanting, "I will de-sensitize it, I will de-sensitize it." A meddlesome neighbor asked the school psychologist if the little girl were mentally deficient!

As was intimated above, the small child's desire to use speech as a means of communication is very limited during the early preschool period. The egocentricity of his speech, that is, his tendency to talk for his own benefit without regard for anyone else, has been remarked upon by numerous investigators, of whom Jean Piaget has made the most distinctive contribution to our understanding of the functions of speech in early childhood.

The use of speech as a means of communication, and the ability to make his wishes and reasons intelligible to others, little developed in the two-year-old, develops rapidly during the ensuing eighteen months in the case of the intelligent child. This is especially true of nursery-school children. Miss Johnson's belief that this social function of language should not be overstressed by nursery-school workers followed upon her theory that socialization is not the most important aim during these nursery years. Other nursery-school workers take a different point of view and make a decided effort to help the child make himself intelligible to others.

Numerous interesting studies have been made of the language development of young children. Among them Dorothea McCarthy's study, *The Language Development of the Preschool Child*, is significant and especially interesting from the point of view of the investigator's technique. All the data for this study were gathered by Dr. McCarthy herself in conversation with young children, and the groups used in the research were very carefully selected and defined.

The general conclusions of research workers concerning the language development of young children should be known by teachers. A very brief summary is offered here. (1) The child's vocabulary at the age of one year consists of but one or two words. During the next few years it grows rapidly until at four and a half or five years the average child has a vocabulary comparable in size to that of the average adult. (2) In general, as common observation will bear out, substantives are employed first; the use of verbs develops gradually, and so does the use of qualifying adjectives and adverbs. The correct use of prepositions and conjunctions indicates that thought and language have matured beyond the babyhood level. (3) There is a positive correlation between socioeconomic status and language development; that is, *on the whole*, children from cultivated homes outstrip the underprivileged groups in their language development. (4) Language does not function only as a means of communication: the fun of using the vocal apparatus, and the love of sound and rhythm, are often ends in themselves. (5) The questions of the child are frequently asked just for the sake of making a social contact with an adult, not because an answer is desired. Miss Johnson says that one can frequently satisfy a child's wish more completely by turning the question back to him than by answering it. (6) The child's language deals largely with his own activities and experiences. (7) Children tend to use words that recall sensory and motor experiences and to attend to and respond to such language.

These conclusions give the teacher valuable suggestions as to intelligent language teaching in the lower school. Progressive teachers utilize the natural tendencies of children in cultivating language expression. The more stereotyped aims of language teaching — increasing the child's actual vocabulary, teaching him to express his thoughts clearly and in good form, helping him to eliminate bad language habits — are secondary to the prime aims of encouraging him to use language creatively, to express his images vividly, to play with sound and indulge his love of rhythm. This does not mean that the more prosaic aims will be overlooked; merely that they will be subordinated. Baby talk must still be actively discouraged, ungrammatical expressions eliminated, and the less gifted child supplied with incentive to carry out the ordinary usages of language acceptably. The gifted, creative child himself needs some routine training in reporting an event accurately and discussing commonplace matters clearly and capably.

The discouragement of baby talk must often be carried out in the face of secret opposition at home. Parents and affectionate relatives like to listen to baby talk; it is *so* cute! The nursery-school worker enjoys "cuteness" too, but she knows that it is not her business to enjoy it at the child's expense. Baby talk is undesirable from two points of view: it is an infantile habit, and should be discarded along with other baby ways as the child grows older. Moreover, baby talk, when it persists, can develop into a real speech defect. At best, it is a source of embarrassment to the child himself when he reaches the mature age of five and six and still lisps like a baby. Therefore the adult trained in child psychology recognizes the encouragement of baby talk for what it is — a piece of grown-up selfishness, indulged in because it amuses. Without being pedantic, the professional nursery-school worker tries to teach correct enunciation and pronunciation from the very start, uses simple and correct language in conversing with the child, and helps him gradually to increase his vocabulary by the addition of useful words. Besides, the trained worker restricts the amount of talking she herself does, or tries to restrict it. She does not shower the child with profuse words of praise, nor make an issue in many words of his mistakes and misdeeds.

Many children five and six years old have formed some bad habits of speech other than baby talk. Errors in pronunciation, ungrammatical forms, slang, and occasional profanity give the average lower-school teacher plenty of incentive for corrective work. But such corrective work should be begun only when the need for it has been observed and recognized. In schools where children come from cultivated homes such work is quite unnecessary; in other localities it is very much needed. Typical errors, too, vary in their appearance and frequency in different parts of the country.

It is a customary procedure with classes five and six years old to encourage the child to express his thoughts and opinions clearly to the group. He is invited to tell his experiences over the week-end, to describe what he intends to accomplish during a given work period, to explain why he thinks a class meeting needs to be called. These opportunities are very valuable and should be used freely, especially among children who do not get much training in language at home. The aim of this work is to help the child to express with increasing effectiveness what he is thinking and to assist him to keep longer and longer trains of thought in mind. It should not, however, be carried on to the exclusion or detriment of really creative work, nor should it be permitted to hamper the child in making up original stories and poems. He should never be discouraged from using new expressions simply because he cannot spell the words.

Children who have a stimulating home background, with a life interesting and vivid enough to provide them with material for expression, naturally progress more rapidly in their oral and written language than children of more meager background. For the children of limited opportunity the school must make special effort to provide experiences which the home is unable to give. An interesting physical environment, walks and more ambitious excursions, discussions of classroom happenings, and even rather formal picture study should be called upon to give the child something to express. No one, child or adult, whose surroundings are circumscribed can be an interesting conversationalist. When direct experiences, like excursions, are precluded, vicarious experience must be generously supplied through books and pictures. One must always remember that the first essential for expression is that the child have something to express. Also, children and adults both require an interested and sympathetic audience to do themselves justice. Such an audience the school group provides.

Dramatics in the lower school should grow out of the simple dramatic games of the children, such as playing house, playing school, playing train. Encouraged by progressive teaching in music and rhythm and art, growing by degrees more complex and varied as the children's possession of ideas increases, these games are the natural beginnings of drama. Stories and poems provide new imaginative themes, and the social studies gradually acquaint the young dramatists with more of life's activities, giving them the impetus to portray a wider range of experiences.

The direction of dramatic work should be carried out with the least possible adult interference. Every effort should be made to keep the spontaneity and lack of self-consciousness which are at once the essence and the charm of children's play. With gifted groups the teacher need do little beyond recognizing the interest of some dramatic game and taking the part of a sympathetic audience. The suggestion that someone else be invited to see the "play" often comes from the children themselves; if it does not, the teacher may suggest that another group — the kindergarten, if the play arises in the first grade — might like to see it too. Where people who really understand children are in charge of a school's policy, little children are never invited or encouraged to put on a show. They are simply given plenty of opportunity for dramatization which is interesting to themselves. When at the age of five or six they begin to feel themselves part of a school and *want* to do something for the rest of the school, small and sympathetic audiences may be invited. These should come not to see a performance, but to find out what the five-year-olds or six-year-olds are doing in their grade.

In less gifted groups, where intelligence and spontaneity are lacking, or when language difficulties cause constraint, the adult may be permitted to encourage dramatization by suggesting that the children dramatize a poem or a simple story. The steps in this dramatization include, first, telling the story; then helping the children to memorize the important points; then letting them tell the story; finally, telling the story in action. There is some difference of opinion as to how much teaching may be permitted; many people who have worked in progressive schools would wish to exclude, at least for the five-year-olds, any teacher-motivated dramatizations, except perhaps Mother Goose rhymes.

Shy and constrained children may sometimes be encouraged by acting in pantomime rather than in dramatization with a verbal accompaniment. Shadow pictures, produced by pantomime behind a sheet, with the light from the window behind the actors, are effective and serve a useful purpose in freeing the timid from self-consciousness. Actually, dramatics should be regarded as a division of the fine arts: they should be associated with music and dancing — not, as is so often the case, with lifeless teaching of oral English. Dramatics should call forth the child's creative ability, his power to express his feeling. They should not be debased to a method of memorizing commonplace stories.

Little children are content with very few properties; their active, untrammeled imaginations easily see the teacher's desk as a cave or a house, and a chair as a galloping steed. Children six and seven years old often respond well to a property box containing pieces of fabric, perhaps a gilt-paper crown, a wreath, and some other baubles. These fascinating accessories stimulate their imaginations and lead to more varied and elaborate dramatization. At all times care should be taken not to overstimulate, and at no time should an adult audience be invited to come and applaud. When parents and other adults visit well-managed lower schools, they should be warned beforehand to treat the children and their work with respect, never thoughtlessly applauding or laughing or remarking about "cuteness." In even the simplest dramatics adults must be on guard against exploiting children whose appearance or histrionic ability tends to push them into the limelight. All the children, not just the "cute" ones, must have the opportunity to express what is within them through the medium of gesture and language; so far as it can possibly be avoided, no child should be permitted to show off.

The program of the modern school postpones the teaching of writing until the end of the first-grade year, in many instances until the second and third grades. Writing is not a suitable activity for kindergarten and young first-grade children, because it requires a fine co-ordination which is difficult for the child and which fatigues him. So oral expression takes undisputed precedence over written in the primary years. Sometimes the first grade composes a group letter of invitation or thanks, or a request to the principal for permission to go on a trip, or what not. Occasionally a group composes an experience story. These are the first steps toward written expression, for the children get the experience of selecting what they shall say and putting it into proper form for the teacher to write. In some schools, too, during free periods, a lower-school teacher lets the children dictate stories and takes them down in shorthand or rapid writing. But no real, appreciable practice in written expression can be provided until the upper primary years. Then there ensues great difference of opinion between teachers who believe in teaching accurate spelling and proper form and those who believe in sacrificing these goods to free, spontaneous composition. Into that controversy it is not necessary to enter here; it is pertinent merely to insist that the essential factors in written expression, as in oral, are interesting things to express, an interested audience, and a growing command of the mother tongue. As the aims of language teaching in the lower school, clarity, fluency, and originality seem more essential than mechanical drills in correct use of language.

BIBLIOGRAPHY

ADAMS, EDITH E. A Guide to Children's Literature in the Early Elementary Grades, revised edition. George Wahr, Ann Arbor, Michigan, 1933.

Discusses types of suitable literature for young children, with selected references to each.

Association for Childhood Education, Literature Committee. Told under the Blue Umbrella. Macmillan, New York, 1933.

"The Experience Story," by Eloise Ramsay, pp. 155–159.

BILDERSEE, DOROTHY. Teaching the Primary Grades. Appleton, New York, 1932.

Psychological principles and methods of experimental schools at kindergarten-primary level.

DALGLEISH, ALICE. First Experiences with Literature. Scribner, New York, 1932.

> Literature and methods in nursery and lower school. Indispensable as a reference.

DEVEREAUX, SISTER MARY CECIL. "Children's Literature: Annotated Bibliography of Books and Periodical Articles about Children's Literature and Reading," *Children's Library Yearbook No. 4*, pp. 125–168. American Library Association, Chicago, 1932.

> Studies relations between language patterns of the preschool child and his age, sex, and intelligence. Also gives some interesting lights on his egocentricity. Interesting data.

HARTMANN, GERTRUDE, and SHUMAKER, ANN (Ed.). Creative Expression. John Day, New York, 1933.

JOHNSON, HARRIET. Children in the Nursery School, pp. 103–150, 253–281. John Day, New York, 1928.

MABIE, ETHEL. Language Development in Primary Grades through School Activities. Public School Publishing Company, Bloomington, Illinois, 1930.

> An attempt to have language growth the direct outcome of the child's interests.

McCARTHY, D. A. The Language Development of the Preschool Child. University of Minnesota Press, Minneapolis, Minnesota, 1930.

> One of the most interesting and convincing studies of preschool development.

McKEE, PAUL. Language in the Elementary School. Houghton Mifflin, Boston, 1934.

> An excellent text. Little discussion of lower-school problems — except in Chapter VII, "Oral Composition."

MITCHELL, LUCY SPRAGUE. The Here and Now Story Book. Introduction. Dutton, New York, 1921.

> For children from two to seven years old.

MOORE, ANNIE E. Literature Old and New for Children. Houghton Mifflin, Boston, 1934.

MOORE, ANNIE E., and BETZNER, JEAN. "Primary Language and Literature for Primary Children," in *The Classroom Teacher*, published by The Classroom Teacher, Inc., Chicago, 1927.

PIAGET, JEAN. Language and Thought of the Child. Harcourt Brace, New York, 1926.

> A most interesting discussion of the function of language.

TROXELL, ELEANORE. Language and Literature in the Kindergarten and Primary Grades. Scribner, New York, 1927.

> A conventional treatment, with little emphasis on creative work.

CHAPTER XI

THE TECHNIQUE OF READING

Many excellent books have been written on the subject of reading. The general character of reading methods has improved steadily in the last twenty-five years; in fact, the technique of teaching reading has been refined to a high degree of excellence. The experimental work of Judd, Buswell, Gray, and Gates, and the artistic classroom demonstrations of Miss Marjorie Hardy and other gifted teachers, have given a tremendous impetus to really fine work in beginning reading. There are several excellent manuals on the market for the guidance of teachers, and the primers and readers which these manuals accompany are artistic and attractive to children as well as carefully planned in the light of scientific studies of the reading process. Not only are the vocabularies of these books selected with a view to children's needs and the relative difficulty of the single words, not only are plans made for repetition to insure sufficient drill, but type, spacing, alignment, size of page, and quality of paper are determined by the best available information about the length of eye span, the character of eye movements, and the best methods of avoiding eyestrain. Furthermore, colorful pictures and a generally attractive format add to the value of the books as additions to a child's library.

Several methods of teaching reading have enjoyed popularity in American classrooms: the alphabet method, the phonetic method, the whole-story method, the opportunistic method, and the intrinsic method. The alphabet method is rarely used now except as a remedial measure with children who present special reading problems.

Against the alphabet method as it was used in our schools

generally thirty or forty years ago the several phonetic methods which were developed in the ensuing period of our educational history were a great advance. Phonetics was introduced as an important part of the teaching of reading in the belief that in phonic analysis the child could be given a key through which he might overcome his difficulties himself, thus achieving independence in reading. Children were carefully drilled in the proper sounding of vowels and consonants through a variety of games, and then were taught to combine the sounds to form familiar words. Words which did not lend themselves to phonic analysis were taught by a sight-recognition method, and intelligent, conscientious teachers began to show excellent results. Many children gained great assurance in reading in a comparatively short time, and the method became extremely popular.

Because of the success which attended the phonetic method, some school systems and many individual teachers became so enthusiastic that they carried the teaching of phonics to rather extreme lengths, so that phonics as a bit of gymnastic drill became in certain cases an end in itself rather than a means for the teaching of reading. Where this sort of teaching was overemphasized, subsequent study of the results showed that phonic analysis accentuated too much may well lead to slow and labored reading, and that it can exaggerate a natural tendency to move the lips while reading silently. For these reasons, and also because of the steadily increasing interest in the project method and progressive-school organization, the popularity of the phonetic method showed a marked decline in many places from about 1920 onward. Getting the children down to definite drill in phonics did not fit in with the programs of the laboratory and progressive schools. It was difficult to see how such drill could really be related to the child's spontaneous activities. Accordingly, the so-called whole-story method was for a short time much in vogue among the more progressive schools. This method stressed the enjoyment of reading and emphasized the need for interesting, continuous content.

The essentials of this method (it had many variations) were the accurate memorization of a whole story or poem, and its subsequent "reading" from an illustrated chart. Like the phonetic method, it gave the child a sense of mastery, for he found himself almost immediately able to "read" a whole story. Unfortunately the child's mastery, although less laboriously achieved, was far less real than that which he acquired through phonetic training. The procedure really did encourage rapid reading, it emphasized the joy of reading, and it minimized the habit of "word calling," which is disastrous to the acquisition of efficiency in reading. The gifted child, provided he were attentive and self-critical, learned rapidly; but the less gifted, the careless, and the inattentive developed some very shiftless habits.

The whole-story method, of course, did not stop short at whole stories. As common sense would demand, the child was drilled in the recognition of individual sentences, phrases, and finally words. A duplicate chart was made and cut into pieces for purposes of drill, and flash-card exercises were a part of the regular procedure. But rapid progress to a second and a third story, repeating certain of the phrases of the first, was usual where the whole-story method was in vogue, and many children were able to memorize the stories so thoroughly that they could effectively simulate reading when, in fact, they were only repeating parrot-fashion material which they had learned by rote. The advocates of the whole-story method, because of their interest in developing speed and the rapid reading of enjoyable material, encouraged silent reading, sometimes almost to the exclusion of oral reading. It seemed to many that the old-fashioned methods of oral reading — one child reading aloud, thirty-nine others "following," presumably — were deadening to interest, and that oral reading should be restricted to audience situations, when the reader himself had some reason for reading aloud and the group for listening. Where silent reading was overstressed, naturally enough all sorts of habits of mispronunciation developed. Most serious of all was the case of the bright but careless individual who deluded himself into thinking he could read — had, in fact, read a primer and a first reader — when he had simply memorized all the stories and could read just as well with the book turned upside down. His awakening was very painful, and the process of his re-education was laborious and difficult. It is as a result of misuses and mistakes in connection with the whole-story method that many progressive teachers have turned to phonics with renewed interest during the last few years.

The opportunistic method should not, in one sense, be discussed as though it were a co-ordinate of other definite methods of teaching reading. This method is rather an expression of the philosophy of certain progressive schools and teachers. These progressives felt — perhaps one should say *feel* — that reading should be taught only when the incentive to learn comes from the child's own interests. On the whole they regard the teaching of reading as an incidental matter, rather than a main purpose, with children six and seven years old. Accordingly, in schools where the opportunistic method was or is in vogue, the teacher merely plans a classroom environment supposedly rich in possibilities for interesting children in reading, and virtually leaves the decision as to when formal teaching shall begin to the children themselves. In such situations reading practice would be given only when the child himself felt the need for it and came to it of his own wish. Years of experience in the use of this method have convinced many thoughtful teachers that it does not provide enough drill in reading for the average child. Inasmuch as he does not get enough practice, the pupil does not get the success and satisfaction which he needs as encouragement to go on. He becomes disheartened, and easily gets a set against reading which develops into a real reading problem. As time goes on and the child reaches the age when his playmates who do not attend progressive schools are quite advanced in their ability to read, he develops a sense of inferiority. Furthermore, if he does not really get down to reading until he is seven or eight years old, the very easy material of a primer is most boring to him. Some exceedingly superior children who failed to learn to read in the first grade or two of a progressive school, simply because they liked the school's other activities better, are still seriously handicapped in speed and accuracy in the fifth and sixth grades. The one unquestioned advantage of the opportunistic method appears in the case of the superior child whose extraordinary intellectual aptitude enables him to read with very little drill, and whose literary interest is keen. Such a child is inclined to read too avidly, neglecting other valuable activities. A classroom which tempts him to neglect reading a bit and attend to other things is perhaps better for such a child. However, one can scarcely believe that a thoroughgoing opportunistic method will be necessary for these rare children when teachers become more skillful in providing varied classroom activities and are less tempted to exploit the very able pupil.

The so-called "intrinsic method," as developed by Dr. Arthur I. Gates and others, purports to give children careful and thorough training in reading, to avoid the dangers of slowing up speed by too much emphasis on phonic analysis, and to relate reading closely to the child's natural interests. In Gates's words:

The implication of this theory is that children are no longer to be required to study phonics, or study words, or study reading in the older sense of the term "study." They are, on the contrary, to be introduced to a related series of projects in which their inclination to engage in varied linguistic, dramatic, artistic, constructive, and exploratory activities are given play. In these natural and satisfying activities should be encountered situations so arranged that [quoting Dewey] "pupils will make the responses which cannot help having learning as their consequence." The development of all reading abilities, in other words, should be the "natural and necessary result" of doing the things which the series of situations calls for, instead of the outcome of forced and effortful teaching and study.

The essential points of an intrinsic method may be summed up as follows: (1) The method is based upon a thorough and extensive study of the interests of lower elementary-school children. (2) Reading material provided in primers and readers is selected in terms of these interests. (3) Practice material too is selected and arranged with a view to interest and is closely related to actual reading material. Drill material is planned to give direct practice in *thought getting*, and in actually reading from the printed page rather than from charts and flash cards. (4) Well-standardized tests are available for use in connection with the intrinsic method and are so planned as to be diagnostic of the individual child's strengths and weaknesses in reading. The tests show how the ability of a certain child to recognize words compares with that of other children of his age and grade, and give separate evidence as to how well he is progressing in the recognition of phrases and the mastery of content.

Protagonists of the intrinsic method are open-minded on the question of teaching phonics. Quoting Gates once more, from his book *Interest and Ability in Reading*:

> We need a method that will develop phonetic skills so that they work when and where needed, namely, in the actual process of reading for thought. . . . In a sound system, the "mechanical" and "thought-getting" training will not be separated, but combined."

This is an ideal which all forward-looking teachers and supervisors of reading would surely wish to achieve.

The development of methods of remedial teaching has progressed rapidly during the last few years. This is a highly specialized field, challenging the effort and attention of leading psychologists. Significant contributions have been made from various research centers. Remedial teaching under the direction of a clinical psychologist is a most interesting specialty for the lower-school teacher whose tastes run in this direction and who has done more study than the average in psychology, mental hygiene, and child guidance.

A detailed discussion of the teaching of reading and an evaluation of available teaching material are beyond the scope of this book. We are here concerned with the place of reading in the school curriculum for the child under eight in schools where, presumably, the aim is the normal development of children and their progressive adjustment to the demands of contemporary social life. From the point of view of normal child development, as we have stated in another connection, a mental age of approximately six years is required for successful progress in beginning reading. However, no intelligent student of child development would deny that not only the mental development of children but also their physical and emotional development must be taken into consideration when the lower-school curriculum is planned. Let us consider briefly some of the practical implications of these statements. If a mental age of six is required for learning to read, then a certain proportion of any unselected group of six-year-old children are not sufficiently mature to make it advisable to press them. The child who is even slightly retarded is apt to have difficulty and to experience a great deal of discouragement unless he is an unusually persevering child and has a sensible, sympathetic teacher. If things can be adjusted so that he does not begin reading until he is six months older, the chances of discouragement are much lessened, and the adjustment is well worth making. Studies of young school failures show very clearly that a large percentage of them are owing to initial difficulties in learning to read.

On the other hand, the average six-year-old who comes into the first grade is able and also eager to learn to read if he is approached through any of the several good methods now at our command. A little distaste at the start, or after the novelty has worn off, may well be overcome by kindly but consistent pressure to join in reading activities. Many of us who have been working with young children for a number of years can recall the day when our sympathies with the opportunistic method were very strong, and when we recoiled at the suggestion that pressure be used to induce children to read. Experience has shown most of us that in the majority of cases, at least, our misgivings about the disastrous effect of a little urging are unfounded, and that nothing is gained through letting the child avoid tackling reading if he is physically well developed, mentally competent, and emotionally reasonably well poised. There are exceptions, and a modern school is prepared for those exceptions, but the exceptions are few. By the time he is six, the normal child has a healthy desire to learn how to read. Many normal children balk a little at the requisite effort, but if they are sensibly handled they soon overcome this bit of indolence and find both pride and pleasure in their achievements.

Another point to be considered is the wisdom of encouraging the child who is mentally six, and chronologically five or a little less, to learn to read. This is indeed a debatable point, especially in view of the question already raised as to means of enriching the curriculum from year to year for the child who attends nursery school from the time he is two. One hesitates to be dogmatic, but the following suggestions appear of sufficiently general validity to be entitled to consideration. Five-year-old children who are mentally accelerated, physiologically mature, and exceedingly keen to learn to read might well be permitted to do so, provided other activities normal for five-year-olds and of educational value are not neglected. But the bright, well-developed five-year-old who wants to learn to read and who has difficulty in interesting himself in other activities should not be permitted to take up reading by way of escape. The teacher of bright five-year-olds who lacks the ingenuity to plan varied activities should, on her part, not be allowed to escape by teaching the children reading. There are many interesting possibilities for five-year-olds other than reading, *but these activities are a greater tax* on the teacher's resourcefulness than teaching beginning reading by a good, standard method. People who urge reading as an activity for gifted five-year-olds should keep this fact in mind, no matter how many valuable arguments they can produce to justify beginning reading at this age level. The point is not that we may not eventually approve the earlier introduction of reading into the school curriculum, but that at the moment we are forced to admit it is an innovation of doubtful value, although an easy way out for the teacher and lower-school administrator.

Another point to be considered is that reading activities should be introduced gradually, and not all at once when, so to speak, "the clock strikes six." Reading is one of the language arts, intrinsically related to the other language arts of oral expression, dramatization, and writing. Reading, moreover, involves the care and appreciation of books as a part of the environment and, as an introduction, some appreciation of what books can give us in the way of information and delightful entertainment. Progressive lower-school teachers are realizing this fact; and interesting activities, far removed from the formal teaching of reading and yet definitely conducive to the development of *reading readiness*, are being developed in many five-year-old groups.

Such an activity was a library project carried on in the Abraham Lincoln School, New Haven, Connecticut.

LIBRARY PROJECT

Setting

Our ·kindergarten group consisted mainly of children of American, German, and Irish extraction. The parents were very co-operative and interested in the educational advancement of their children.

At the beginning of the school year attractive Mother Goose pictures were displayed on our bulletin board. Many children were eager to tell the familiar rhymes that were illustrated in the pictures, and this led to interesting discussions about their Mother Goose books at home. Bobby suggested bringing his Mother Goose book to school. As a result, several books were brought in and shared with the group. The teacher then presented four or five picture books that had been carefully selected at the public library. The children, delighted with the books, decided to have a library of their own.

Their library was situated in a well-lighted corner of the kindergarten, away from all other activities. This gave a restful atmosphere needed to complete a library situation. A table and four chairs were painted light green, and colorful cretonne covered the backs of the chairs.

Books were lent by the teachers and children and were changed frequently as interest indicated the need.

The care and handling of the books were stressed, and the children took great pride in keeping the books neatly arranged on the table.

No reading was taught, but a valuable provision for reading readiness was gained through this unit of work.

Outline of Project

I. Objectives:
   1. To provide enjoyment for the children.
   2. To create an interest in books.
   3. To develop a repertoire of good stories.
   4. To teach the children how to care for books.
   5. To familiarize the children with many books.
II. Procedure:
   1. Simple Mother Goose rhymes were used almost solely at first.
   2. Mother Goose pictures, cut-outs, and songs stimulated an interest in the library.
   3. Several different Mother Goose books were placed in the library.
   4. Our library and conversation hours were closely correlated at this time.
   5. We next presented many interesting picture books to stimulate an interest.
   6. The old folk tales were then brought out.
      a. The Three Bears.
      b. The Three Little Pigs.
      c. The Gingerbread Boy.
      d. The Three Billy Goats.
      e. Little Black Sambo.
   7. Holidays were utilized. Books having pictures about the various holidays were supplied.
      a. Halloween.

    b. Thanksgiving.

    c. Christmas.

  8. Books were brought in by children.

    a. Two books about trains, probably stimulated by the trains which pass near by.

    b. Books of familiar stories.

  9. As the year progressed newer books were presented.

    a. The Angus Books.

    b. Millions of Cats.

    c. Johnny Penguin.

    d. Once There Was a Big Crocodile.

10. From time to time books that were especially enjoyed by the children were returned.

11. Books were changed frequently as interests indicated the need.

12. No more than six books were presented at any one time.

13. Certain rules were set up; both children and teachers checked on them; for example, four children in the library at one time.

NOTE. Pictures from the Zoological Garden in New York were introduced into the library from time to time. Two or three children had visited there during the year and enjoyed looking at pictures of the animals they had seen.

III. Teacher's activities:

  1. Supplying books for the library.

  2. Frequent change of books.

  3. Telling stories selected from books that had been placed in the library.

  4. Bringing in material from the public library.

  5. Familiarizing children with the care of books.

  6. Checking on the use of books.

  7. Enjoying books with children.

IV. Children's activities:

  1. Looking at books.

  2. Caring for books properly.

  3. Bringing books from home for other children to enjoy.

  4. Making scrapbooks to take home.

V. Outcomes:

The following information was gained by the children, and suitable attitudes and habits were initiated in connection with it:

  1. The library should not be crowded. Four children might use this library at once.

2. Readers must be quiet in a library.
3. Books must be taken care of. Backs should be held carefully, and pages turned without tearing them.
4. The library is a place for the enjoyment of books.
5. It is a pleasure to share books.
6. It is desirable to learn to read.
7. New words may be added to each child's vocabulary, and thus oral expression comes to be more rich and varied.
8. Books are the source of pleasure and information.

VI. Children's bibliography :

AMEND, OTTILIE. Jolly Jungle Jingles. Volland, Chicago, 1929.

BANNERMAN, HELEN. Little Black Sambo. Harter, 1931.

BESKOW, ELSA. Aunt Green, Aunt Brown, and Aunt Lavender. Harper, New York, 1930.

BRANN, ESTHER. Bobbie and Donnie were Twins. 1933.

BROOKE, A. LESLIE. Johnny Crow's Garden. Warne, New York, 1925.

BROOKE, A. LESLIE. Ring o'Roses. A nursery-rhyme picture book. Warne.

BRYAN, DOROTHY and MARGUERITE. Johnny Penguin. Doubleday, Doran, New York, 1931.

BRYAN, DOROTHY and MARGUERITE. Michael and Patsy on the Golf Links. Doubleday, Doran, 1933.

DALGLIESH, ALICE. The Little Wooden Farmer. Macmillan, New York, 1930.

DONALDSON, LOIS. In the Mouse's House. Laidlaw Brothers, New York, 1930.

DUPLAIX, GEORGES. Gaston and Josephine. Oxford University Press, 1933.

EVERS, HELEN and ALFRED. The Happy Hen. Farrar and Rinehart, New York, 1933.

EVERS, HELEN and ALFRED. This Little Pig. Farrar and Rinehart, 1932.

FLACK, MARJORIE. Angus and the Cat. Doubleday, Doran, 1931.

FLACK, MARJORIE. Angus and the Ducks. Doubleday, Doran, 1930.

FLACK, MARJORIE. Angus Lost. Doubleday, Doran, 1932.

GÁG, WANDA. Millions of Cats. Coward, McCann, New York, 1928.

GÁG, WANDA. Snippy and Snappy. Coward, McCann, New York, 1932.

Happy Hour Books : The Three Bears. The Three Little Pigs. The A B C Nonsense Book. Macmillan.

HIGGINS, VIOLET MOORE. The Gingerbread Man. Retold and illustrated by V. M. Higgins. Whitman.

LINDMAN, MAJ JAN. Snipp, Snapp, Snurr and the Magic Horse. Whitman, 1933.

LORD, ISABEL ELY. The Picture Book of Animals. Selected and translated by I. E. Lord. Macmillan, 1931.

"Margaret." Once There Was a Big Crocodile. Macmillan, 1931.

MARTIN, MARY STREICHEN. The First Picture Book. Harcourt, Brace, New York, 1930.

MOORE, CLEMENT C. "'Twas the Night before Christmas." Mother Goose Rhymes.

NICHOLS, RUTH ALEXANDER. Nancy. Macmillan, 1933.

NICHOLSON, WILLIAM. Clever Bill. Doubleday, Doran.

PETERSHAM, MAUD and MISKA. Auntie and Celia Jane and Miki. Doubleday, Doran, 1932.

PETERSHAM, MAUD and MISKA. The Christ Child, as Told by Matthew and Luke. Doubleday, Doran, 1931.

PIPER, WATTY. The Brimful Book. Platt and Munk.

PIPER, WATTY. Gateway to Storyland. Platt and Munk, New York.

POTTER, BEATRIX. The Tale of Peter Rabbit. Warne.

RICHARDSON, FREDERICK. Old, Old Tales Retold; eight best-beloved folk stories for children. Volland, 1923.

SARG, TONY. Tony Sarg's Book of Animals. Greenberg, New York.

SEWELL, HELEN. A Head for Happy. Macmillan, 1931.

TOWSLEY, LENA. Sally and Her Friends. Farrar and Rinehart, 1932.

Many paper-bound books with favorite stories and pictures were used early in the year. These we found to be uninteresting and unsatisfactory to the children as the library unit progressed.

VII. Teacher's bibliography:

Association for Childhood Education, Literature Committee. Told Under the Blue Umbrella. New stories for new children. Macmillan, 1933.

Association for Childhood Education, Literature Committee. Told Under the Green Umbrella. Old stories for new children. Macmillan, 1930.

BAILEY, CAROLYN S., and LEWIS, CLARA M. For the Children's Hour. Milton Bradley.

CURRY, C. M., and CLIPPINGER, E. E. Children's Literature. Rand McNally, New York, 1923.

This activity has been a great joy to the children. They browse in the library before and after school, and they take great pride in their collection of books. Yet the library corner does not detract from the interest in their other activities.

One group of children who participated in the library activity last year has been promoted to the first grade. They do not differ in any distinctive way from other groups who have gone to the first grade from the Abraham Lincoln kindergarten; in intelligence, home background, and physical development they are roughly comparable with the other first-grade entrants. But the first-grade teacher reports that they are more interested in reading, and that they are making better progress in learning to read than any of the other groups who have passed through her hands.

The children in the group just mentioned had not been in nursery school; they came directly from their homes to the kindergarten. One may, however, picture how, in a progressive lower school where the children were admitted to nursery school at two, the library project would have been preceded in earlier years by even simpler methods of introducing children to the delights of picture books and storybooks. At two, for instance, the children would have handled many linen books and a few paper-bound books; at three and four they would have handled more books, looking at them singly and in groups, by themselves, and over the teacher's shoulder; at five they would greatly enjoy a well-conducted library and would have many suggestions to offer for its organization and development.

The progressive lower school regards the teaching of the technique of reading as one of the school's most important activities. Proceeding on the assumption that normal young children love stories and pictures and soon learn to love books, the school provides abundant opportunity for handling books and enjoying them before formal teaching begins. Knowing that the possession of a fairly large vocabulary and the information which is gained through many interesting group activities are valuable assets in learning to read, the school encourages language expression and plans an environment rich in possibilities for doing interesting things. Knowing also that the acquisition of reading skill requires a certain degree of mental and physical development, the progressive lower school does not encourage children to read until they have achieved the development of the average six-year-old. And understanding that normal six-year-olds are both able and willing to learn to read, the progressive lower school attempts by a wise planning of the environment, by good teaching, and by the exercise of reasonable persuasion to give children a good start in reading when they are approximately at the six-year-old level.

As we have indicated, the special methods of teaching reading represented by good manuals and attractive children's readers are many. Among these, school systems and individual schools, administrators, supervisors, and teachers may jointly or severally choose. One basic set of readers, supplemented by several others to give variety and encourage rapid reading, is a general rule in progressive schools.

The well-informed modern school administrator does not judge a first-grade teacher wholly on the percentage of children who learn to read during their first school year. Nor does he expect every six-year-old, even every so-called "average" six-year-old, to learn to read during the first-grade year. He knows that there are exceptions to every rule of child development. However, he inclines to the opinion that most capable teachers will achieve a high degree of success in teaching their first-grade pupils to read, without sacrificing other valuable school activities, and that the overwhelming majority of normal six-year-olds will have no difficulties about learning to read.

Reading is not the be-all and the end-all of the primary grades. It is one activity among many; but it is a very important activity and to most children a highly entrancing one.

BIBLIOGRAPHY

BONAR, HUGH S. "Systematic versus Incidental Training in Reading," *Elementary English Review* (April, 1933), Vol. X, pp. 90–94, 112.

Summarizes the results of investigation.

BONEY, C. DEWITT. A Study of Library Reading in the Primary Grades, Teachers College Contributions to Education No. 578. Columbia University, New York, 1933.

Recommendations and conclusions, pp. 58–62.

CORDTS, ANNA, and MCBROWN, A. M.   "Phonics," *The Classroom Teacher*, Vol. II, pp. 389–419. The Classroom Teacher, Inc., Chicago, 1928.

A clear explanation of what the term "phonics" means, with some reasons for teaching phonics.

DEPUTY, ERBY CHESTER.   Predicting First Grade Reading Achievement, Teachers College Contributions to Education No. 426. Columbia University, New York, 1930.

DOLCH, E. W.   The Psychology and Teaching of Reading. Ginn, Boston, 1931.

A good general discussion. Chapter IV, on "Phonics," and Chapter V, on "Combining the Methods," interesting to the general reader who wants to know about phonics.

GATES, ARTHUR I.   The Improvement of Reading. Macmillan, New York, 1927.

GATES, ARTHUR I.   New Methods in Primary Reading. Teachers College, Columbia University, New York, 1928.

GATES, ARTHUR I., and BENNETT, CHESTER C.   Reversal Tendencies in Reading. 33 pages. Teachers College, Columbia University, New York, 1933.

A brief and readable discussion, stressing prevention and remedial work.

GIST, ARTHUR S.   The Teaching and Supervision of Reading. Scribner, New York, 1927.

GRAY, WILLIAM S.   Summary of Investigations Relating to Reading. University of Chicago Press, 1925.

GRAY, WILLIAM S.   "Summary of Reading Investigations" (July 1, 1931, to June 30, 1932), *Journal of Educational Research* (February, 1933), Vol. XXVI, pp. 401–424.

GRAY, WILLIAM S., assisted by WHIPPLE, GERTRUDE.   Improving Instruction in Reading: An Experimental Study, *Supplementary Education Monographs No. 40*, September, 1933. University of Chicago, 1933.

A study subsidized by the Commonwealth Fund. Chapter IV gives an interesting summary.

GRAY, WILLIAM S., and ZIRBES, LAURA.   "Primary Reading," *The Classroom Teacher*, Vol II, pp. 39–370. The Classroom Teacher, Inc., Chicago, 1928.

A very clear and helpful discussion of aims, activities, diagnosis, and testing.

HARDY, MARJORIE.   First Grade Manual for The Child's Own Way Series. Wheeler, Chicago, 1929.

An exceedingly helpful manual. See especially pages 44–56, "The Five Stages of Learning to Read."

HARDY, MARJORIE (Ed.).   Reading Emphasis in School Activities, *Bulletin of the Association for Childhood Education*, 1933.

A summary of the discussions at the Cleveland meeting of the association in 1931 and at the Washington meeting in 1932.

HUGHES, MARIE M. Teaching a Standard English Vocabulary with Initial Reading Instruction. Bronson Printing Co., Las Cruces, N. M., 1932.

A plan of procedure designed to meet the needs of non-English-speaking children. A very interesting and suggestive bulletin.

McKEE, PAUL. Reading and Literature in the Elementary School. Houghton Mifflin, Boston, 1934.

A complete and scholarly treatment of the subject, including summaries of important pieces of research. Chapters V, VI, VII, deal, respectively, with the kindergarten and the first and second grades.

SMITH, NILA B. "Successive Emphases in American Reading Instruction," *Teachers College Record* (December, 1932), Vol. XXXIV, pp. 188–203.

Traces the historical development, identifying important emphases.

STORM, GRACE E., and SMITH, NILA B. Reading Activities in the Primary Grades. Ginn, Boston, 1930.

A very helpful reference.

TEAGARDEN, LORENE. "Kindergarten and Reading Reversals," *Childhood Education* (November, 1932), Vol. IX, pp. 82–83.

Describes reversal tests for school entrants.

TERMAN, L. M., and LIMA, MARGARET. Children's Reading. Appleton, New York, 1926.

WHEAT, H. G. "Examination Analysis versus Phonic Analysis in Primary Reading," *Elementary School Journal* (December, 1928), Vol. XXIX, pp. 256–266.

ZIRBES, LAURA. Comparative Study of Current Practices in Reading, with Techniques for the Improvement of Teaching. Teachers College, Columbia University, New York, 1928.

A very important study by a recognized authority. Chapter II, "Reading Activity Recommendations," and Chapter III, "Purposes and Objectives in Progressive Reading Programs," are especially interesting for the general reader.

ZIRBES, LAURA. Practice Exercises and Checks on Silent Reading in the Primary Grades. Lincoln School of Teachers College, Columbia University, New York, 1925.

A record of experimentation in the second grade of the Lincoln School.

The reader who is interested in educational developments during the last half-century should consult this reference also:

Alphabet-Phonetic Method. McGuffey's Complete Set of Readers. First appeared between 1836 and 1844. Last two editions for public-school use appeared in 1896 and 1907. Henry Ford had a private edition printed in 1925.

Drill on naming and sounding letters and spelling words. Unit of approach: letters.

CHAPTER XII

NUMBER, SCIENCE, AND HEALTH EDUCATION IN THE LOWER SCHOOL

NUMBER

"Good old-fashioned arithmetic drill" was an important activity in the schools of yesterday, and it is still a popular activity in many primary grades. However, the psychology of arithmetic has been subjected to a very searching scrutiny in the last twenty years, with the result that methods of teaching number work, especially in the early grades, have undergone numerous changes. Good authorities differ in their opinions as to the exact age at which formal work in arithmetic should begin; but all are virtually in agreement that the most important part of number work for the young child is his introduction to number relations through concrete problems involving arithmetical concepts.

On the whole the kindergarten gives much more opportunity for learning the meaning of number relationships than does a formal first grade. In the old, conservative kindergarten program the Froebelian gifts gave the child innumerable experiences with number in all its relationships — serial, group, relational, and proportional. He had ample opportunity to count; ample practice in forming and counting groups of objects. He spent at least half his building time in drilling on halves, quarters, thirds, and so forth, and he had plenty of chances to see that a half-cube was half as big as a whole cube. In the modern kindergarten the child uses number in a variety of ways. He counts children, chairs, tables, crackers at lunch time. Through his industrial-art projects he learns to use a foot rule, gets some concept of the size of an inch in comparison with a foot, and learns to divide blocks, crayons, and many other things into equal parts. These are valuable experiences for him, being most helpful in giving him clear and useful concepts of number. The wise preschool teacher arranges matters so that every suitable opportunity to clear up the child's idea of number is utilized: she does not teach arithmetic lessons, but she is alive to the possibilities of all the kindergarten activities with regard to number teaching. The more varied the activities and the more alert the teacher, the more opportunity the children have to count and estimate and see distances, groups, and quantities in relation to each other.

The freely organized primary grade, like the kindergarten, is rich in opportunities for the development of number concepts through informal activities. Children of five and a half and six are more capable of forming abstract conceptions and are readier than younger ones to be interested in projects involving an appreciable amount of number activity. Number games, such as dominoes and lotto, are exceedingly popular. Beanbag games involving the keeping of scores and the marking of goals provide valuable practice, and in the course of constructive activities many good opportunities arise to practice reading numbers and learn the simplest number combinations. The general trend of opinion in the more progressive schools is strongly in favor of omitting any formal teaching of arithmetic until the second grade or even until the beginning of the child's third regular school year. In such schools, however, this postponement is compensated for by abundant number experiences of the informal sort we have mentioned. In progressive schools the teacher of younger children is not released from teaching arithmetic; in fact, she is urged to teach it more thoroughly than it was taught in conservative schools. But she is expected carefully and intelligently to develop number concepts through helping children to appreciate the meaning and value of number in concrete situations. Formal drill in number combinations is not to be introduced in advance of such thorough and careful preliminary work.

The teaching of number in an entirely informal way is altogether defensible from the point of view of present-day psychology; but it is essential that teacher and children realize that a number fact is not *mastered* simply because it has been encountered and perhaps at the moment fairly well understood. There is no royal road to the learning of mathematics, and no way of avoiding drill in the long run. Countless number facts have to be learned, actually memorized, before real facility is achieved. A second-grade teacher was demonstrating for a class of students who were studying methods of teaching arithmetic in the primary grades. She was intelligent, alert, and ingenious, and planned many situations in which the children encountered number facts and understood their significance, although as a group they were not especially gifted or extraordinarily well trained. A very nice project centered about the giving of a party to the grade mothers. With the teacher's help the group estimated the number of lemons and the amount of sugar needed to make lemonade, the amount of water to be added, the price of the fruit and sugar, the expense of providing wafers to eat with the lemonade. The children were very much interested and worked with fine co-operation on the plans for the party, the preparation, and the actual entertainment. The teacher wrote up the results for the class in "Methods of Teaching Arithmetic"; among them she listed the learning of how to read and write sums of United States money, the relation between pint and quart, the meaning and relation of ounce and pound. Now the children had certainly watched the teacher write on the board sums involving United States money. Their attention had been called to the dollar sign and the decimal point, but these experiences were repeated only once or twice and were a small part of an absorbing activity. The children had distinctly *not* learned to write United States money; they had not even learned to read it with any accuracy. They had not memorized the tables of dry and liquid measure; rather had they merely seen the significance and usefulness of such tables. For what it was, the whole project was very valuable, and it had served a purpose in helping the children to develop concepts of number, quantity, and relationship. But few if any *number facts* had been *fixed* by the group. Arithmetical facts and processes have to be learned through drill, and the difference between the new methods of teaching arithmetic and the old is not, as sometimes is supposed, that the new way eliminates drill whereas the old way stressed it, but rather that the new way employs scientifically planned drill and attempts to eliminate waste effort. One way of eliminating waste effort is to postpone practice exercises until the child has an adequate understanding of the meaning and uses of number in life situations. Then drill is an intelligent and purposeful activity, not mere drudgery.

In his *New Methods in Arithmetic* Dr. Thorndike takes the position that arithmetic strongly appeals to two fundamental human interests — interests which manifest themselves in children as well as in adults. These are mental activity for its own sake and the sense of achievement. As to mental activity, arithmetic affords the best intellectual stimulus of any subject in the elementary school. As to the sense of achievement, arithmetic also has special contributions to make. The child, for example, knows precisely where he stands. Almost every exercise affords him an opportunity for recording his success. He can work with full consciousness of the results he is getting.

The newer methods of teaching number are planned with a view to meeting and developing these interests. Many appropriate procedures are recommended. Good teachers will be alert to use childish interests in life both in school and out of school. They will seek "vital and engaging problems" as a way of introducing the child to new processes. They will be resourceful in devising and selecting problems and, indeed, whole units of instruction which relate to the present and probable future interests of the pupils. They will supplement drill with team play, individual games, recording devices, charts, seat work, and all the variety of intriguing procedures which modern pedagogy has developed not only in arithmetic but in other subjects as well. They will seek to invest the subject with human appeal — with sympathy, with satisfaction of curiosity, with the sense of wider horizons. They will not only seek to impart substantial strength to arithmetic but will even attempt to give it charm and humor. They will, at least in their own thinking and as far as possible in their presentation of the subject, realize its contribution to orderly thinking, to the unique human concepts of system and precision.

For little children in the preschool and early primary grades, number begins to find a place in games and in simple problems of buying and selling, as well as in measurement of size, distance, and quantity. Any number of "vital and engaging problems" may be drawn from these sources. Games are highly appropriate; humor and sociability should be the order of the day.

If the teacher of young children must do some formal teaching because of school or community demands, she may get the best of suggestions for interesting, intelligent, and economical drill procedures from reading Dr. Thorndike's *New Methods in Arithmetic*, even though the discussion there applies to children from the upper half of the second grade on. The underlying principles are the same for the littlest ones, but it is difficult or impossible to provide formal work for them which would entirely meet Dr. Thorndike's standards of interest and suitability.

SCIENCE

Science in the early school years has been rather generally taken to be synonymous with "nature study." For purposes of this discussion it will be more broadly defined to include physical science and health education as well as simple lessons in the biology of plants and animals.

The possibilities of the physical sciences for enriching the curriculum at the lower age levels have been but imperfectly

explored. For one thing, teachers of little children are themselves usually not especially strong in the field of the physical sciences. Yet the active, eager, inquiring child has many
questions the answers to which are to be found in this field
of knowledge. "Where does the water go when the kettle
boils dry?" "Can you make ice?" "Why will a cork float?"
and so forth, not to mention the endless questions about
cars and airplanes and what not. Dr. Gerald Craig has
developed a most interesting series of lessons in science for
use in the early grades. Within the series he has included
several items which are important in connection with safety
education, such, for example, as the effect upon a flame of
being smothered or exposed to a draft; the effect of water
upon burning oil, and the contrasting effect of sand. In
laboratory schools young children are encouraged to set up
simple bells and light effects in the shop, and the science
teachers stand ready to help them in exploring the possibilities of the physical environment.

The test of value in such work with children is whether
they gain from it clear, useful, or interesting ideas; whether
it is of practical value to them or perhaps stimulates them
to undertake other interesting experiments. Demonstrations and experiments have to be very simple to register
clear impressions with young children. It is possible to
spend a great deal of time in rather aimless fooling if these
standards are not kept before the teacher. Some children
will watch a grown person manipulate apparatus, and will
fiddle with wires and batteries and magnets themselves for
astonishing lengths of time if they are permitted to do so.
For the unusual child such watching and aimless trying out
may be valuable, but for many it amounts simply to waste
of time.

The teaching of nature study has undergone great changes
in the last generation. At one time it consisted of sentimental, semiaccurate accounts of plant and animal life, with a
strong religious-moral flavor, supplemented by rather aimless observations of trees, birds, and flowers. The possi-

bilities of a rich, varied nature-study program are just beginning to be realized, and from the nursery school on through the grades very interesting projects have been carried out. Especial emphasis has been placed of late upon the possibility of teaching children the facts of mating, procreation, gestation, and birth through the observation of animal life. Many preschool groups are encouraged to care for and observe families of guinea pigs, rabbits, or white mice, in the belief that protracted observation satisfies the child's natural curiosity in the best possible way without arousing the morbid interest which sometimes surrounds the phenomena of life. The care of plants and the making of school gardens have long been favorite activities for children, and sometimes particular groups and their teachers develop particular hobbies, such as collecting turtles or goldfish or other interesting or exotic specimens of life.

The aims of work in nature study in the modern lower school might be stated as follows: (1) Nature study should result in deeper appreciation upon the part of children of the beauty and interest of natural phenomena. This appreciation should be cultivated and encouraged by the teacher, but sentimentality should be avoided. (2) Nature study should serve as a means of satisfying the child's curiosity about the processes of life. (3) Through the care of plants and animals the child's impulses to nurture and care for helpless living things should be stimulated. (4) In the course of nature-study observations certain children should become interested in the making of collections or develop other desirable hobbies.

Nature-study activities should include the observation, care, and nurture of plants and animals, the spontaneous drawing or painting of pictures, the spontaneous production of poems and stories, observation by the children with intelligent guidance by the teacher, and interesting excursions.

Excursions have long been an important school activity. Their value as educational procedure, however, depends upon how well they are selected, planned for, and carried out. Teachers of little children often exhaust themselves over excursions, with little gain to their young charges. Two kindergarten teachers cannot conduct forty-five or fifty five-year-olds through the city streets or on trips requiring the use of trains or trolleys, with anything like safety. Avoidance of accident is a matter of good fortune or perhaps the result of almost superhuman exertion on the part of the adults. Tempers grow short in the process; energy which should be used for instructive explanations is used up in counting heads. Moreover, little children get too tired on long walks or train trips to gain much from them.

Excursions for the lower school should be short and easy to carry out, involving the minimum of physical strain. There should be enough adults in proportion to the number of children to insure proper care and prevent undue strain on the part of all concerned. The trip should be discussed beforehand, and the points to be observed agreed upon by the children. Some sort of check-up in the way of expressional activity should follow the excursion, but this must be carefully handled, else the children resent it or are bored by it.

At the present time much effort is being directed toward effecting a better understanding between home and school and working out ways of co-operation between parents and teachers. In some private progressive schools the parents are even encouraged to participate in classroom activities as voluntary assistants. Whether or not it is wise to go to this length in welcoming parents to the school's precincts is an open question; at any rate, it is impossible in the majority of situations for the school to permit it or the parents to acquiesce in it. But parents, on the whole, are interested in the education of their children. They offer tutoring (frequently quite upsetting what the child learns in school by using a different method of working an arithmetic problem or of attacking difficult words in reading) and are often a nuisance from the school's point of view because of misdirected efforts to be helpful. One way in which parents can help effectively, and as often as not would be glad to help, is in this very matter of excursions. Help can be of various sorts: providing motor-car transportation, acting as extra assistants in trips involving the use of trolleys or trains, or merely accompanying the school group on long walks. Best of all, perhaps, they can take their own children, over the week-end, during vacation, or after school, to see the zoo or the wharves or the open markets, or whatever the teacher may decide. When little children go on excursions in large groups they get overtired, overstrained, confused, and cross. They do not get the most out of all the effort put forth to make the trips a success. If they make the same trips with their own parents, there is not the overstimulation of a crowd, presumably the parents have time to listen to individual questions and comments as a teacher cannot if she be shepherding forty children, and in general the youngsters carry away clearer impressions and a greater sense of enjoyment. Trips planned by parents and teacher in co-operation offer a good point of contact between home and school and a good chance for helpful and stimulating interchange of ideas, instead of the usual criticisms, complaints, or stupid questions which parents and teachers bandy about.

Of course in some underprivileged groups the parents can give the teacher little help, if any; but it is amazing how much overworked and meagerly paid parents will try to do for the education of their children if they are properly appealed to, and how much satisfaction they get out of teaching them about places of interest.

HEALTH EDUCATION

The connection between nature study, science, and the health education of children is often overlooked; but actually these aspects of a child's training should have great bearing one upon another. Through some of his experiences in the physical sciences the child should learn how to assure his own safety; through nature study he should learn facts which bear upon his own health and vigor.

From the point of view of the adult, health education has two main divisions, concerned, respectively, with physical and mental well-being. No intelligent reader needs to be reminded how inseparably these two phases are related, or told that they are stated thus separately only for convenience in discussion. Habits, attitudes. and appreciations developed with reference to either have a bearing upon both.

The physical aspects of health-teaching in the lower school may be considered under the following main headings: proper food habits, personal cleanliness, the hygiene of sleep, the hygiene of play, the proper choice of clothing, and the avoidance of infection.

In the nursery school parents are frequently seeking advice and assistance in solving problems of the child's eating. The two-year-old is just starting out on a regular solid diet, and in the next two or three years his food habits, his likes and dislikes, are well toward being permanently established. Nursery-school attendance, especially if the group takes luncheon at school, often helps a great deal in teaching the child to eat with enjoyment all the foods necessary for a balanced diet.

When children four, five, six, and seven years old present difficulties, the problem is rather more difficult, for their likes and dislikes are fairly well ingrained. Nevertheless the school may be helpful in stressing proper diet, and school reports and conferences can furnish incentives to eat properly. Also, comparatively few children go to nursery school, and many homes are quite remiss in teaching proper dietary habits. In some communities the school itself has to take the main responsibility for teaching children the basic principles of food selection. Pictures, charts, and the making of dietary lists are well-established methods, and in some progressive schools the children are taught some basic facts about food through experiments in feeding pets. A guinea pig left without cabbage or lettuce will soon pine, and will as rapidly recover if these important foods are restored to his diet before too much damage is done.

In an average preschool or lower-grade situation the teacher has some opportunity to help instill right food habits in connection with the midmorning lunch. If milk or orange juice and crackers are served by the school, emphasis can be laid upon proper service, upon tidiness and cleanliness, and upon the right social atmosphere for mealtime. With four-year-olds and five-year-olds considerable ceremony is worth while because they are just learning to eat in a group. In some communities the careful serving of a midmorning lunch is well worth school time for the health training and social training it gives even with children six and seven years old.

In some schools children bring their own midmorning lunches from home. If this be the case, the teacher can do health teaching in connection with the lunch period by stressing good selections and good ways of wrapping up a lunch. But this is a situation which takes great tact in the handling, and one should probably try to convince the parents that a few cents a week for milk and crackers to be nicely served at school is a worthy investment. When children bring their lunches, whether midmorning or midday, it is hard to prevent them from swapping them. Mrs. Smith's nicely prepared cream cheese and lettuce sandwiches are cheerfully exchanged for Mrs. Jones's pastry and dill pickle. The teacher has to have eyes in the back of her head to prevent such exchanges, and much tact to forbid them without hurting feelings.

The matter of eating breakfast before going to school is very important for the young child's health and frequently presents a problem. The child who dashes off to school without eating breakfast is not uncommon. Parents, of course, are responsible for seeing that children have a proper breakfast and eat it, but the school should co-operate with them. Keeping the child at home when breakfast is not eaten is sometimes effective, and naturally requires school supervision.

Describing to the teacher of the group what is eaten for breakfast is sometimes an incentive to eating properly. This method requires tact, for it is very easy to romance; but if the truth is encouraged and not too much praise and blame are lavished, respectively, on good or poor breakfast records, such reports and discussions present good opportunities for health teaching.

On the negative side the lower-school teacher can help the breakfast situation by being reasonable on the subject of punctuality. Of course punctuality is the concern of the school; but with the younger pupils a good breakfast eaten slowly, and followed by adequate elimination, is much more important than arriving on the dot of 8.45 at the school gate.

The teaching of personal hygiene presents different problems in different communities. In some situations the very rudiments of bathing, washing heads, and cleaning teeth have to be taught; in others the children are so well cared for at home that such teaching is uncalled for or is a positive insult to their parents. In all these personal, intimate aspects of teaching a great deal of tact is required, and teachers are not a notoriously tactful group. Great care should be taken not to embarrass children and parents, even in groups where standards appear very low. In mixed groups, in which some children are well cared for and others neglected and unclean, special care should be taken never to make issues of personal cleanliness which injure the feelings of individuals.

In the regular school routine children should be taught to wash their hands before eating and after going to the bathroom, and to take reasonable care of their clothing by wearing aprons when doing some of their work. The lavatories should be well supervised by the teachers themselves, and any difficulties which arise should be carefully handled. In the old days a teacher of young children thought herself abused if she were not assigned a maid to take children to the bathroom. Nowadays no intelligent teacher relegates this important part of her work to anyone else, with the possible exception of a trained assistant. Students in training should be carefully supervised when they first take over the management of the lavatory.

Rest and relaxation are as important for growing children as food. It is hard to provide them in sufficient amounts in these days of noise and haste and crowded living. Data on the proper amount of sleep for children of different ages are being gathered, although no absolute rules can as yet be laid down. The nursery child two to four years of age should have twelve or thirteen hours of rest in twenty-four, the child four to six needs eleven or twelve hours, and the child seven or eight a good ten hours and a half. With the younger child one to two hours of this sleeping time is taken up by the midday nap. Probably the midday nap should be continued much later in children's lives than it is in present practice.

The teacher in the school run on a country-day-school plan is responsible for the midday rest, and needs to work out a technique for managing it so that children will really relax. Her own manner is an important factor: if the adult is quietly certain that the children will relax, they usually do; if she wonders whether they will or not, they very generally don't. The arrangements for resting should be adequate: proper cots, proper covering, and plenty of ventilation, or a good sleeping porch. A good point in technique is to have the room dark and suggesting quiet when the children come into it. It is often a help to read quietly to children of six and seven during the first few minutes.

Schools which provide for midday rest as a part of their regular program are likely to be fairly well equipped to carry it out. But the teacher in the average preschool and primary classroom faces real difficulties in her attempt to provide a period of relaxation for her children in the middle of the morning. Such relaxation is really needed; for no matter how well managed the home and school regime may be, working and playing in a group is tiring to the young child, and the whole intense pressure of modern life has its general effect upon the adjustment of children as well as upon the nerves of adults.

The custom once in vogue of darkening the room and having the children rest their heads upon desks or tables is not desirable because of the bad posture which results. Therefore various schemes have been tried out to enable the children to rest lying down on a flat surface, a scheme desirable from the standpoint of posture. In some schools the children rest on tables, covering themselves with blankets. In by far the greater number, however, they rest on the floor. Neither of these methods seems really good. Lying on a table must keep the child in a certain state of tension, lest he roll off. Lying on the floor exposes him to cold and draft and is anything but sanitary. Of course the custom of having children lie on the floor is never followed without giving them something to rest themselves upon other than the actual surface of the floor. In some very meagerly equipped preschool and primary groups, the writer has seen the children resting upon several thicknesses of newspaper; in others they bring blankets from home and roll up in them; in still others the teachers laboriously make paper mats of heavy brown paper, lining them with newspapers. These homemade mats are then marked by a cross or label to identify the place where the child always puts his head, so that, presumably, this spot is never in direct contact with the floor and is not rubbed by the child's shoes. Often the mats are perforated with two holes at each end, and raffia handles are run through. When stored, they are hung up, double, with the side upon which the child is supposed to rest folded in.

If one must let children rest on floors, these homemade mats are probably the best arrangement yet devised; but they leave much to be desired. Teachers and supervisors who encourage children to lie fifteen or twenty minutes on such contrivances, especially in winter, when floors are always very drafty places, should try the scheme out themselves a few times and study its limitations!

Canvas cots can be provided at relatively little cost and shared by more than one group. The canvas can be taken off the frame periodically and sent to the laundry. Blankets may be used for covering. But cots create a problem because they must be stored somewhere while the regular classroom activities are going on.

Admittedly, a really good resting situation is hard to provide in a typical school. If, however, rests are necessary for children, and all seem to agree that they are, schools must work out better plans for them, even at the cost of extra rooms for resting. Classroom floors indeed should be clean and of proper surface quality, and well-built buildings should not have very drafty floors. However, it is impossible to keep floors immaculate, because we do walk on them; and a certain amount of draft must always be reckoned with. Therefore resting on floors can scarcely be counted an ideal arrangement, even when mats or blankets are provided. Blankets, especially, need care to keep them in a sanitary condition, even in private homes; they need more care when they are dragged over floors, and in most schools they certainly do not and cannot get it.

Normal children do not require much encouragement to play vigorously, and, when properly dressed, they enjoy playing in the open air unless there is something they greatly want to do indoors. (Little girls, especially, sometimes seem to get absorbed in indoor projects.) The school should make every effort to arrange as much outdoor play as possible and to add to its appeal by providing good play equipment. Home and school should co-operate in selecting and caring for warm, comfortable, and serviceable outdoor garments. The modern zipper suits are excellent. The knitted suits of the Teddy-bear variety are warm, cozy, and most attractive in moderately cold weather; but soft knitted fabrics are not good windbreaks and are poor protection against wet. For prolonged play in winter weather a hard-surfaced cloth is the most satisfactory for outer garments. A light knitted sweater inside adds to warmth and comfort.

Parents often think, and sometimes with justice, that teachers are lax in their supervision of the child's physical welfare in connection with this matter of wraps. No one wants teachers to fuss over children; but it is a definite part of their responsibility, especially in the modern school regime, to see that their charges are properly clothed while under their care. Zipper suits should be worn when needed, even if some child is lazy about putting his suit on or if some of the zippers have rusted and have to be manipulated by the teacher. Rubbers must be worn in wet weather; in well-regulated groups this is the law of the Medes and Persians. Beginning teachers find all this detail very exacting, and need some help and supervision at first. The capable soon reduce it to routine and learn a few simple methods to determine whether or not children are warm and comfortable. One such method is to feel under the child's chin. If the flesh is warm and very slightly moist, he is comfortable; if it is dry and cold, he is not warmly enough dressed, even if he (and often his mother) protests that he is. When he is actively perspiring, the child is too warmly dressed.

The expression "routine" was not intended to imply that individual differences among children can be ignored. Parents and pediatricians have many fads and fancies. In infancy individual children are reared according to these fancies, and accordingly become accustomed to much or little clothing. These individual peculiarities have to be regarded. The tactful teacher keeps in mind certain general rules of clothing: that it should be clean, loose, easily put on and off, and, if possible, attractive and becoming; that rubbers are needed for wet; and that leather or hard-surfaced fabric are needed for breaking the wind. Within these general rules she tries to see that individual children are comfortable and happy.

When nursery schools were new, some conservative pediatricians raised their eyebrows because of the supposed danger of infection which results from bringing small children into groups. In the ten years of its growing popularity in this country the nursery school has demonstrated rather conclusively that this fear was unwarranted. But it must be considered that most nursery-school teachers exert strenuous and intelligent effort in the prevention of infectious diseases. In a well-regulated group any child with the slightest sniffle is immediately segregated and sent home, and all the children are very carefully supervised by the teachers themselves and by nurses and medical officers. This care must be continued, and should be extended more adequately than at present to children in all the primary grades.

As a part of the prevention of infectious diseases, children themselves need to be taught some rudimentary precautions: to cover their faces when they are coughing and sneezing, not to put in their mouths things which have been on the floor, to keep food clean, and to avoid the use of the common drinking cup. In the upper primary grades they may be taught in a very elementary way about the action of microorganisms. But such teaching must be given with due regard for mental as well as physical hygiene. It is possible, even easy, to give sensitive children real phobias about germs. The records of child-guidance clinics prove this; for they provide numerous instances of children who were afraid to drink anything out of a glass lest they "get sick and die," and who were very badly scared of mysterious creatures called "germs." Good and wholesome teaching about the origin and prevention of infectious diseases furnishes a nice problem for the person who is interested in lower-school science work.

The responsibilities of the lower-school teacher for the health education of children may be summarized in the following way:

1. She should co-operate with the home in seeing that the children eat properly at breakfast and at the midmorning or noon luncheon at school. The teacher's knowledge of simple nutritional principles and of the psychology of difficulties about food should be sufficient to enable her to discuss these problems intelligently with parents, although an

exhaustive study of this field cannot fairly be expected of her. Classroom discussions of foods and eating and the management of luncheon periods in school should be well planned and so designed as to give the children as much information about food values as they can comprehend.

2. Little children should be encouraged to take as much responsibility as they can for their personal cleanliness in school, and inspection of their condition when they arrive at school should be thorough. Discussions with parents on this topic must be conducted with tact and discretion; even in dealing with very little children, one must be careful not to offend or give the less well-cared-for child a sense of inferiority.

3. With sleep, as with diet, home and school should cooperate closely. Adequate rest under hygienic conditions should be provided at school.

4. Healthful play should be amply provided for, and over-fatigue intelligently guarded against.

5. Within reasonable limits clothing should be handled with due regard for the prejudices of individual parents and the kind of clothing to which individual children are accustomed. Mass regulation constitutes rudeness to careful parents and may endanger children's health.

6. Infection should be carefully guarded against through adequate morning inspection, the teaching of health habits, such as covering the mouth when sneezing, and the provision of a clean schoolroom, well ventilated and adequately heated.

The development of healthful mental attitudes in young children is receiving a great deal of attention in current literature. Mental hygiene is one of the prime concerns of the nursery school; in fact, as we have seen, the American nursery school is largely the outcome of the mental-hygiene movement. In the lower school the child is making his first adjustments to the wider world which the community represents; he is transferring his interests and affections to new objects outside the close associations of the home. The personal relationships between young children and their teachers are very significant: to the little child the teacher stands as a mother substitute, and he looks to her for guidance, security, and affection. Good teachers learn how to assume this role of mother substitute without exploiting the child's confidence and affection, gradually developing the intensely personal reactions of the child into less personal and more mature attitudes. To rebuff a child's friendly and trustful advances is never wise; to exploit them, and develop the sort of relationship which makes it hard for him to go on to another teacher at the end of the year, is selfish and unintelligent. The small child needs a constant, satisfying relationship with an adult in whom he has confidence, and this relationship the successful teacher helps him to create. In some schools, because of the importance of constancy and continuity in the child's relationships, preschool, first-grade, and second-grade teachers are occasionally asked to carry their groups on through two or even three years. This seems a wise procedure only if the teacher is especially skillful in creating and maintaining really wholesome relationships. If she gets to the point of regarding the group as *her* children, who will never be adequately understood by anyone else, the arrangement is unfortunate for all concerned.

Very important for the mental health of the child is that he shall be successful in establishing good work and play relationships with the other children in his class; that he shall find his place as an accepted member of the group. Some of the most delicate and difficult tasks of the lower-school teacher lie here, for the guidance of the child in his relations with other children calls for a great deal of intelligence, patience, and tact. It is imperative also that the child achieve success in his school work; for attitudes of confidence or fear, expectations of failure or success, are often fixed in the earliest school years and are of the greatest significance for the child's future.

The responsibility of the lower school for mental-health education might be briefly summed up in the following manner: (1) Adequate and satisfying relationships with his teachers and his fellows should be regarded by the school as one of the most important outcomes of the child's attendance. (2) Control of self and environment through adequate knowledge and skill, caution rather than fear, should be stressed in all physical-health and safety education. (3) Children should be treated with the same courtesy and consideration with which teachers treat their adult friends. (4) The teacher should see to it that every child achieves feelings of success commensurate with his efforts. (5) The atmosphere of the classroom should be happy and full of merriment; strain and pressure should be constantly avoided. (6) Adequate contact should be maintained between home and school, so that parents and school authorities may co-operate intelligently in assuring the welfare and happiness of the individual child.

Each of these points will be developed further in the next chapter, which deals with character education in early years.

BIBLIOGRAPHY

BRUECKNER, S. J. "Certain Arithmetic Abilities of Second-Grade Pupils," *Elementary School Journal* (February, 1927), Vol. XXVII, pp. 433–443.

This article recommends pretests to avoid waste of time in the teaching of second-grade number.

California State Department of Education. Suggested Course of Study in Science for the Elementary Grades. California State Department of Education, *Bulletin No. 13*, Part I. Sacramento, California, 1932.

CALMERTON, GAIL. Practical Projects, Plays and Games for Primary Teachers. Beckley-Cardy, Chicago, 1924.

Contains some rather good suggestions for number games.

CRAIG, GERALD S. "The Program of Science in the Elementary School," in the Thirty-first Yearbook of the National Society for the Scientific Study of Education, Part I, "A Program for Teaching Science," pp. 133–191. Public School Publishing Company, Bloomington, Illinois, 1932.

CRAIG, GERALD S. A Tentative Course of Study in Elementary Science. Teachers College, Columbia University, 1927.

A syllabus in three parts. Part I deals with the first and second grades and will be helpful also to preschool teachers.

DE SCHWEINITZ, KARL. Growing Up: the Story of How We Become Alive, Are Born, and Grow Up. Macmillan, New York, 1928.

> An excellent book for teachers of young children.

Lincoln School Staff. Curriculum Making in an Elementary School. Ginn, Boston, 1927.

> See index and page 288.

LOSH, ROSAMUND, and WEEKS, RUTH M. Primary Number Projects. Houghton Mifflin, Boston, 1923.

> Some good material for classroom use.

MORTON, R. L. "Developing Number Ideas," *The Grade Teacher* (June, 1932), Vol. XLIX, pp. 770–813.

> The importance of meaningful, concrete experiences as a background for instruction in symbols.

National Education Association, Addresses and Proceedings, Vol. LXV, pp. 585–597. Department of Science Instruction, Washington, 1927.

> Good discussions of objectives.

National Education Association, Fourth Yearbook of the Department of Superintendence, Chapter IV, "Elementary Science and Nature Study." Washington, 1926.

REEDER, EDWIN H. Lessons in Our Schools, No. 3, "A Lesson in Science," *Teachers College Record* (February, 1929), Vol XXX, No. 5, pp. 425–431.

THORNDIKE, EDWARD L. The New Methods in Arithmetic. Rand McNally, New York, 1921.

> A classic in educational psychology. A book on method which should be read by every teacher.

UPTON, C. B. "Changing the Curriculum in Arithmetic," *Teachers College Record* (December, 1926), Vol. XXVIII, pp. 341–359.

WASHBURNE, CARLETON. "Social Practice in Arithmetic Fundamentals," *Elementary School Journal*, Vol. XXVII (1926–1927), pp. 60–66.

WOOD, THOMAS D. (Chairman). The School Program. Report of the Committee on the School Child, White House Conference on Child Health and Protection. Appleton-Century, New York, 1932.

WYLER, ROSE. "Studying Rocks in the First Grade," *Science Education*, (April, 1933), Vol. XVII, pp. 106–111.

ZYVE, CLAIRE. "An Experimental Study of the Teaching of Arithmetic Combinations," *Educational Method* (October, 1932), Vol. XII, pp. 16–18.

> Controlled experiment carried on with seventy-six second-grade and third-grade children. Blackboard and lantern-slides presentation of combinations compared.

CHAPTER XIII

CHARACTER EDUCATION IN THE LOWER SCHOOL

The responsibility of the school for character education has been the subject of much discussion during the last few decades. Fifty years ago, when the school was thought to exist solely for the purpose of teaching the three R's, and good character within the schoolroom was interpreted to mean submissiveness and industry in learning, the whole question of the school's role in moral training was taken for granted. Teachers, by methods persuasive or repressive, upheld law and order in the classroom; for the rest parents and the institution of the home were supposed to be responsible.

In the typical community at the time that the kindergarten found its way into the American educational scene, parents and teachers had little traffic with one another unless some very serious issue was at stake. This was partly owing to the unfortunate belief that the school was an institution set apart, with its own particular strength to do in isolation; and a tendency toward an association ened in the less intelligent communities to do in of the public-school authority with the power of the state. This power could be invoked to enforce attendance and to impose health regulations, the parents especially entertained considerable hatred for the school because of its repressive forces of the state.

From the very beginning teacher worked for a close rapport had an advantage over her fellow grades because kindergarten atten-y and also because her room was attractive, colorful, and inviting in comparison with any ordinary classroom. Among the parents of kindergarten children, too, there would naturally be a large proportion of young people more ready to co-operate and less set in their ways than many parents of older children. In the first chapter of this book, there was a discussion of the limitations of the old Froebelian kindergarten when it came to questions of health and physical care. It should be remembered, however, that although physical care was thought to be outside the kindergartner's province, her very contact with the home and her interest in the children were real factors in child welfare. Limited though her training and interest in hygiene may have been, she knew her children and their mothers, and just by means of her interest and their friendly response she was a powerful influence in raising their standards of cleanliness, habit-training, and general home management.

[In] school the Froebelian kindergartner accustomed her chil[dre]n to order, cleanliness, and beauty in their surroundings. [S]he taught them the mother-play series and pointed out [its et]hical significance. She encouraged them to be kind, cour[teous] and obedient. But for initiative, and for the [s]olution of their own social problems, she gave them [tr]aining.

[The progres]sive kindergarten, it will be remembered, as it dev[eloped und]er the leadership of Miss Alice Temple and Miss [Hill?] ... stressed character education of a different variety ... h prevailed in the older, more sentimental [sort. The conser]vative kindergarten teacher was on the whole [verge of trou]ble. If she saw two children on the she init[iate?] separated them. If the group as a attentio[n] ... or threatened to get out of hand, kinderga[rtner?] game or a finger play to distract squabble[r]. In contrast, the progressive toward [ch]ildren a freedom which made ... teacher directed her attention ... [t]o settle quarrels rather than toward preventing them. Instead of creating a situation in which no difficulties were likely to become overt, she deliberately allowed a degree of liberty which revealed children in their natural state of mischief, quarrelsomeness, and rough-and-tumble play. Fairly early in the development of the progressive kindergarten movement the leaders began to say that it was better to know about a case of "moral measles" than to keep such good order in the classroom that it never became evident.

Of course the progressive kindergarten group — or the "radicals," as they were then called — had as their authority for this position the philosophy of Dr. Dewey, with its emphasis on the identity of education with life itself, and its corresponding insistence that the school should approximate as completely as possible a real life situation. The prevailing educational psychology pressed the point that *learning is essentially reacting*. There followed from these theories the conclusion that the classroom should be a place where things happened as in life outside the school, and that social behavior of a desirable sort could eventuate only if the child had actual practice in social living,—if, under intelligent guidance, he had the chance to react as a member of a group.

In her introduction to *A Conduct Curriculum for the Kindergarten and First Grade*, Dr. Patty S. Hill gives an excellent summary of the way in which the modern point of view in character education developed at the Speyer School and later at the Horace Mann School. According to Professor Hill an experiment at the former school conducted in 1905 "was one of the earliest attempts in any field of education to apply the principles of democracy to school organization. To provide conditions suitable for training in the beginnings of self-government, wide opportunities were offered the children for learning from one another through their own experience, emphasis being laid upon the initiation and execution of their own purposes and plans."

For various reasons the 1905 venture described by Miss

Hill had to be discontinued, and a really permanent laboratory for the carrying out of these progressive theories was not provided until 1915, when the Horace Mann Kindergarten was reorganized. At this time, too, the freer sort of classroom organization was extended to the first grade. But, using Professor Hill's words, "this form of social organization impressed the more conservative pedagogical minds as radical and wasteful." In order to prove their case and to convince the unbelieving that something was being accomplished, the progressive group therefore attempted to work out, with the help of intelligent observers, some way of recording progress. These records were supposed to show the outcomes of the newer procedure in terms of individual and social behavior. They were planned to show the development of such qualities as "initiative," "ability to lead," "ability to follow," "ability to initiate plans," "perseverance in work." At first the captions used were awkward, and the methods of recording unwieldy, but a great deal of progress was made in perfecting these records in the ensuing six years. When it became apparent that expert guidance was needed in defining the specific habits and attitudes making up such traits as "initiative" or "perseverance," the services of Dr. Agnes Rogers, now professor of education and psychology in Bryn Mawr College, were enlisted. With the co-operation of a large number of mature workers in the field of kindergarten-primary education, Dr. Rogers published the tentative "Habit Inventory" mentioned in an earlier chapter.

In the process of using and testing this habit inventory, teachers and supervisors, Professor Hill writes, "began to think of all instruction in terms of desirable changes in thought, feeling, and conduct; in other words, in terms of changed behavior due to a changed nervous system." And then gradually the concept of "behavior" became enlarged to include not only moral and social reactions but all the child's reactions — physical, mental, emotional, *and* social-moral. Again Dr. Thorndike supplied authoritative background, and his psychological theory encouraged the re-creators of the early curriculum to apply the principles of habit-formation to all the school's activities. Once more quoting Professor Hill:

. . . Instead of making our Habit Inventory an appendix to the curriculum then in use with its subject matter, knowledge and technique, we found ourselves gradually transforming the curriculum, as a whole, by applying the principles of habit formation to all of the school subjects.

Accordingly, two procedures were followed in developing a new conduct curriculum: one group of research workers started with an inventory of desirable habits and attitudes and surveyed the possibilities of developing these through school activities; another group began with the school situation and considered what desirable character changes each subject might help to bring about. Thus character education in its narrower sense of improved moral conduct became completely fused with general education, and formal education was critically surveyed to determine its possibilities for desirably modifying behavior.

When the American nursery schools were first organized, in many cases they took over from the kindergarten and first grade, along with many other things, this general theory of character education. Dr. Ruth Andrus published *A Tentative Inventory of Habits of Children Two to Four Years of Age.* Desirable attitudes and habits were generally described as the goals of nursery-school training. The "habit psychology" was carried over into certain popular discussions for parents; and, based upon its theories, many suggestions were made for dealing with habits, good and bad.

John B. Watson, author of *Psychology from the Standpoint of a Behaviorist* (1924), *Behaviorism* (1925), and *The Psychological Care of Infant and Child* (1928), brought a new emphasis into popular discussions of habit formation. His contributions explained the practical significance of that process which he called "conditioning," a phenomenon long known to the laboratory psychologist.

Learning, according to Dr. Watson's behavioristic theory, consists in effecting a vast number of substitutions among original stimuli and unlearned responses from the child's organism. Light causes a closing of the eye-pupils, a turning of the head. Acid in the mouth causes salivary secretions. These stimuli, then, are unconditioned, and the reactions to them are unlearned. However, through education the original stimuli become potent in calling forth other reactions than those they first elicited; conversely, original, unlearned, *reactions* or responses, through a process of substitution, *begin to follow stimuli which in the first place were not biologically adequate to produce them.* When a red light, flashed for the first time just at the moment when an electric shock causes a subject to withdraw his hand, becomes sufficient to bring about the withdrawal of the hand *without* any accompanying shock, the red light has become a *conditioned stimulus.* When a two-year-old who yesterday played happily with a dog screams at the sight of the same puppy because last evening the puppy bit him too hard, the child is making a *conditioned* reaction. According to the behavioristic theory all our habits and characteristic attitudes are built through this conditioning process; nearly all emotional reactions are learned rather than inherited, and the emotional factor becomes of great significance in learning. Because of a strong emotional tone the first time a certain response is made, some little part of the situation which originally called forth the response may become powerful enough to produce the whole reaction forever after; it may be an efficient substitute. A child frightened by a loud gong the first time he stroked a rabbit may be conditioned against rabbits and eventually may react with fear to all furry animals, even though they are not encountered in connection with a sounding gong.

Many of the astonishing successes and inexplicable failures among school pupils which puzzle and annoy teachers can be explained in terms of conditioning, desirable and undesirable. A stable, well-balanced child, who in his preschool years has learned confidence rather than fear, outgoing friendliness rather than suspicion and anger, is conditioned to success. Throughout his school career he may outstrip a much more brilliant classmate who has been conditioned to fear and is haunted by shyness and self-consciousness learned through the experiences of his nursery life. Watson's terminology has rather wide use in books on child psychology, and many of his suggestions have proved practical and helpful, if at times a trifle extreme.

Another most powerful influence upon the trend of character education has been the mental-hygiene movement and its theoretical background — psychoanalytic psychology. The many ramifications of this way of looking upon life and character are beyond the scope of this chapter, but for our purposes certain of its basic practical conclusions are very important. Studies of children undertaken from the analytic point of view have demonstrated the need for a *sense of security*, for confidence in the stability and affection of the people closest to them. These studies have shown also that no event in behavior is accidental, but that everything we do can be explained in terms of our past experiences, remembered and forgotten. The analyst or the psychiatrist always wants to know *why* an individual child reacts in such and such a way, and he searches for his answer in his subject's past history. Analytic studies also stress the danger of repressions, because repressed thoughts and feelings may be forgotten by the conscious mind and yet retain their force as *unconscious* motives of conduct. The integrated self, in which no inharmonious unconscious motives are causing queer or erratic behavior, is the character the mental hygienist considers good. The divided self, the person who is swayed by various unconscious drives and presents a different face to the public with every different situation in which he finds himself, is, from this point of view, the undesirable character, the one who deteriorates under strain.

These concepts and some of their variations have been very helpful indeed in changing the attitude of the intelligent public toward the child's difficulties in development and toward the adult who is mentally ill. Sometimes, however, they are misunderstood and misapplied. One should read the theories of mental hygiene carefully and critically before applying them to one's pupils or one's friends.

The various influences just described as important in the development of our present-day theories of character education have resulted in a variety of principles and maxims which sometimes seem mutually contradictory and often are seriously misinterpreted. The most important of these principles of working beliefs are perhaps the following: (1) The development of desirable habits and attitudes is the aim of education. These desirable habits and attitudes can be studied, described, and tabulated. (2) A child must have emotional security if he is to play happily, work effectively, and adjust to the demands of social life. (3) One must try to condition a child to wholesome behavior and, conversely, try to prevent unwholesome conditioning, like the building up of fears. (4) Repressions are dangerous. (5) Ability to get on with grown people and playmates, to work happily and effectively as a member of a group, is symptomatic of a wholesome, well-integrated personality.

Each of these theories is of practical value and significance to the lower-school teacher; each is subject to misunderstanding and abuse. Worthy habits and attitudes *are* the desired outcomes of education. But our earlier conceptions of how these are developed were inadequate because they were oversimplified, and made too little of the emotional factors involved. Human reactions are much more complicated than some of the early practical discussions lead one to think. Overzealous emphasis on one desirable habit may incidentally inhibit the growth of other habits and attitudes equally desirable. For instance, Miss Harriet Johnson once cited a case of a small child, the youngest in a nursery school, who was entered in the school with a proud assurance from his mother that he never had "accidents," had not had any for a long time, although he was only fifteen months old.

This seemed true enough. For months there was not the slightest mishap; toilet-training, it appeared, had been completely successful. But he seemed listless and not normally playful. Then one day he became really excited about building a tower of blocks. His perfect record for dryness was forthwith ruined. The mother was horrified until it was explained to her by the school psychologist that her assiduous training had certainly taught him to inhibit excretory processes, but it had also resulted in a generally overinhibited, repressed child. During the period of readjustment, while the baby learned to play like others, there were many "accidents."

The need for emotional security is often overlooked by schools and overworked teachers. It is a very real need, one without which no child (for that matter no adult, either) can be happy and successful. The small child needs personal security — direct, personal confidence in the adult most responsible for his welfare. The mother normally fills this need in the home; the teacher must take over the responsibility in the lower school. Seeing to it that each child has confidence in the adults about him is an important part of character education. But as the child grows older he should find this security less and less through direct dependence upon mother or teacher, more and more through his own success as a member of a group.

The explanation of behavior in terms of conditioning has resulted in many good practical suggestions for teachers and parents both. Whether or not Dr. Watson's theory is really adequate to explain all human behavior is beyond our province to decide. But in concrete situations children do learn fears; they do learn to be annoyed at situations which would not originally bother them; they do learn to transfer affection and love beyond their immediate families, and sometimes even learn to "love" stimuli originally neutral or unpleasant. The mere reminder that most of our feelings are acquired, that feelings are easy to acquire, and that, once acquired, they determine conduct in both desirable and undesirable ways, is excellent for those of us who work with young children. Most fears are destructive rather than helpful; it is far better to cultivate caution than fearfulness. Intense anger is not a serviceable emotion for modern social life. Since love or pleasure, like anger, may become attached, through learning, to more and more people and situations, we want it attached in wholesome ways. We do not wish to cultivate the boy who is tied to his mother's apron strings, nor the girl who never has developed any liking for her other primary-school teachers because she was so strongly attached to the kindergartner and never outgrew the attachment. These simple facts about the emotional life are important for teachers to know, and they have been most simply and clearly expressed in terms of conditioning. Sometimes, however, even these are misunderstood, and are used in such a way that they are contrary to common sense or to some of the other beliefs which have been mentioned. Some ardent followers of Dr. Watson, for instance, were so afraid that a small child might become too attached to his mother, too strongly conditioned to her presence, that they advised mothers to absent themselves from their children frequently and, so far as possible, to avoid displays of affection. For the same reason certain nursery-school supervisors are disposed to criticize any teacher who permits the least expression of affection from her small charges. According to these enthusiasts children must be conditioned to independence; they must not develop absorbing attachments to individuals.

Carried to this extreme, and misinterpreted in this manner, Dr. Watson's theory is contrary to common sense and, above all, violates the principle that young children need a sense of permanence, warmth, and confidence with respect to the adults who care for them.

The danger of repression has been stressed in many of the books on the mental hygiene of childhood, particularly the books written eight and ten years ago. No one who has read many case histories of difficult children doubts that too much repression is harmful and that certain repressions (for example, in connection with sexual curiosity) are definitely dangerous. But repression, *as such*, is necessary, inevitable, and altogether wholesome: growing up amounts to exercising this power over childish, crude, and undesirable impulses, in the interest of cultivating a desirable adult personality. Schools which permit absolute, unrestrained liberty of action for every individual proceed upon a mistaken notion about the place of repression in human growth. No one can live in civilized society without learning to inhibit and control any number of strong impulses.

The child who adjusts well to the demands of group living at home and at school, who initiates plans and carries them through to successful conclusions, who can exert leadership upon occasion and follow with enthusiasm, is the successful child, the product of successful character education. Such a general adjustment, rather than a faultless check-up against a list of habits and attitudes, is the present aim of character-training. On the other hand, a person who has achieved a working adjustment to his environment would incidentally score well on a list of desirable isolated habits. The classroom teacher does well to use both standards in estimating her results. Do these children, as a group or as individuals, give evidence of possessing many desirable habits and attitudes in connection with their work and play, their response to adults, and their social relationships with their peers? And, again, without reference to particular habits, do these children seem to be happy, successful personalities?

In American education, then, theories of character-training have evolved somewhat in this way. First, the school undertook little or no responsibility for the child as a human individual whose whole attitude toward life was being shaped during school years. The home was held responsible for all the fundamental, more intimate sorts of teaching; the classroom was a place in which one learned lessons, not a place in which one learned to live. Then, with the coming of so-called modern education, the school gradually came to see its responsibilities in a new light, and to realize its obligation for the development of intelligent citizens with worthy social ideals. At the lower end the kindergarten made an entering wedge, as it were, into the home, greatly facilitating the achievement of a better understanding between home and school. In the beginning this contact was perhaps not very effective, and the old-fashioned kindergarten itself left much to be desired as an institution for character education. As time went on, the progressive group of kindergartners, with their keen interest in the possible contributions of psychology to education, began to see character as the outcome of conduct and to think of personality as the sum total of habits and attitudes. This excellent although not sufficiently dynamic analysis of the aims and methods of character training has undergone considerable translation and modification because of what we have learned from mental hygiene and psychoanalysis. The *motives* of conduct; the origin, or, to use a more technical term, the *etiology*, of conduct disorders; the processes whereby an entirely egocentric baby, with his strong desires for primitive, personal satisfactions, develops into a social individual, — these are now the prime considerations. Habits and attitudes, good and bad, are but the by-products of the process of adjustment. The end of character training is the well-adjusted personality.

The method of character education as it is now understood is entirely in line with Dr. Dewey's theories, especially in the form in which Dr. Kilpatrick has explained them. It is the method of activity, happily engaged in,— the method of purposing, planning, and carrying out one's plans in a social situation, of judging one's results in terms of personal satisfaction and social value. In the language of mental hygiene the requirements for successful living are freedom, a task, and a plan; how closely this language parallels that of a democratic philosophy of education the reader may see for himself.

From time to time the general public launches its criticisms against the schools for their supposed failure in character education. The critics offer various suggestions: restoring the use of corporal punishment, offering rewards and medals for good conduct, giving direct, systematic moral instruction. The answer of the progressive school, to quote from Dr. Kilpatrick, is that these forced measures should be regarded much as we regard drugs: they may be used in emergencies, when things have gone awry; they have no place in the ordinary, wholesome regime, and in and of themselves they may damage character, just as drugs used in too large quantity hurt physical health. It is interest in satisfying activity, effort to perfect one's own plans as against strain to compete with others, which make for the wholesome character. Ethical discussions in the abstract have little or no effect; the only time when discussion really works is when the children themselves see the need for it and themselves contribute to it. Morals can only be learned through the leading of a moral life, a life of joyful although earnest activity as a responsible member of a social group. This theory holds at four, at fourteen, and at forty, and at all the ages between.

BIBLIOGRAPHY

CHALLMAN, ROBERT C. "Factors Influencing Friendships among Pre-school Children," *Child Development* (June, 1932), Vol. III, pp. 146–158.

7248 spontaneous groupings of 33 nursery-school children were studied with reference to the relation between similarity (in age, sex, and personality traits) and friendship.

CHARTERS, W. W. The Teaching of Ideals. Macmillan, New York, 1927.

A detailed description of character-education methods and an exposition of the author's point of view on the subject.

CHASE, LUCILE. Motivation of Young Children: An Experimental Study of the Influence of Certain Types of External Incentives upon the Performance of a Task. University of Iowa Studies in Child Welfare, Vol V, No. 3. University of Iowa, 1932.

DEWEY, JOHN. Moral Principles in Education. Houghton Mifflin, Boston, 1909.

A very valuable monograph stating clearly Dr. Dewey's position.

HARTSHORNE, H., and MAY, M. Studies in the Nature of Character. Teachers College, Columbia University, in Co-operation with the Institute of Social and Religious Research. Macmillan, New York, 1928–1930.

> Vol. I, Studies in Deceit; Vol. II, Studies in Service and Self-control; Vol. III, Studies in the Organization of Character. A detailed account of a comprehensive research project.

HEATON, KENNETH L. The Character Emphasis in Education. University of Chicago Press, Chicago, 1933.

> An interesting study of character education.

HILL, PATTY S. (Ed.). A Conduct Curriculum for the Kindergarten and First Grade. Introduction. Scribner, New York, 1924.

"How Children Learn the Truth," *Child Study* (October, 1932), Vol. X, pp. 3–21.

> A series of six articles on telling the truth.

ISAACS, SUSAN. The Children We Teach. University of London Press, London, 1932.

> This book deals with children from seven to eleven years of age. However, it is a valuable reference for lower-school teachers, for it explains clearly and simply the principles of education which follow from a dynamic psychology.

KILPATRICK, WILLIAM H. Foundations of Method. Macmillan, New York, 1925.

> A practical discussion of character education from the standpoint of a democratic philosophy of education.

LEE, MARY A. M. "A Study of Emotional Instability in Nursery School Children," *Child Development* (June, 1932), Vol. III, pp. 142–145.

> According to this observational study, moods seem to be closely related to situations in which they occur.

McDONOUGH, SISTER MARY ROSA. The Empirical Study of Character. Williams and Wilkins, Baltimore, 1929.

McGRATH, SISTER MARIE CECELIA. Research Findings in the Moral Development of Children. Catholic Education Press, Washington, D.C., 1925.

McLESTER, AMELIA. The Development of Character Traits in Young Children. Scribner, New York, 1931.

> This book is "a faithful record of free discussion." It will be very helpful to many readers.

MAY, MARK A. "What Science Offers on Character Education," *Religious Education* (June, 1928), Vol. XXIII, No. 6, pp. 566–584.

RICHARDS, ESTHER L. Behavior Aspects of Child Conduct. Macmillan, New York, 1932.

> A discussion of the nature, causes, and treatment of conduct disorders.

SLAGHT, W. E. A. "Untruthfulness in Children: Its Conditioning Factors, and its Setting in Child Nature," in Studies in Character, Vol. I, No. 4. Institute of Character Research, Iowa University, Iowa City, 1928.

STRANG, RUTH. Introduction to Child Study. Macmillan, New York, 1927.

    Dr. Strang's book is very helpful on the whole subject of character education, for it brings out very clearly what are the capabilities of the child at the early age levels, the concepts he may form, and the control which may be expected of him.

WATSON, J. B. Psychological Care of Infant and Child. W. W. Norton, New York, 1928.

    The character-education theories of a behaviorist.

WICKES, FRANCES G. The Inner World of Childhood. Appleton, New York, 1927.

    A nontechnical discussion of the psychoanalytic point of view in character education.

CHAPTER XIV

TESTS AND MEASUREMENTS IN THE LOWER SCHOOL

The movement for objective measurement has gradually effected changes in both the content and the method of early education. Many books have been written on measurement; indeed, the subject is now such a vast one that long and serious study is required to get only an adequate idea of its uses in the lower school. The object of this chapter is merely to inform the reader of the varieties of tests which are applicable to young children, and to state briefly, from the point of view of lower-school teaching, the underlying theories of the testing movement.

Objective tests, as their name implies, include all those methods and techniques which have been devised to help psychologists, teachers, and other specialists to estimate the ability and achievement of pupils with the least possible reference to biased personal judgment. As used in lower schools they are of two principal varieties: intelligence tests and tests of achievement. For older children and adults there have been devised a large number of tests designed to measure special ability,— for instance, mechanical ability, or artistic ability, or musical sensitivity. These testing instruments play a large part in the educational and vocational guidance of older pupils; in the lower school their use is only occasional, and therefore they will not be included in this brief discussion.

Intelligence tests may be subdivided into individual and group tests. The individual test is the most accurate single measure of an individual pupil's ability. Such tests should be used only by trained examiners who, by reason of training and experience, are able to use these instruments with a high degree of precision. Their indiscriminate use by semi-trained or untrained persons is not legitimate. If teachers (or, worse yet, ambitious parents) try out intelligence tests on their children, those tests become valueless for use with those same children by an expert. A practice effect following upon their first use invalidates the expert's results.

In 1927 Gambrill and Farwell published *An Analytical List of Kindergarten-Primary Tests of Intelligence and Achievement.* The list of one hundred included twenty-one intelligence tests, sixteen of which had norms, or standards, for children of second-grade age and younger. Of the achievement tests there were sixteen tests of reading which could be used for first and second grades, two of handwriting, three of drawing, and two of citizenship. If this analytical list were brought up to date, the number of tests for children younger than six years would be far greater, for much progress has been made in preschool testing in the seven years since this list was published.

Intelligence tests purport to measure native intelligence, plus those learned reactions which all children have had the same chance to acquire. The most reliable individual test is the Stanford Revision of the Binet-Simon. Most teachers are familiar at least with the name of this test. It is an "age scale" consisting of a series of questions and tasks which are expected of children at different age levels. At three a child is expected to give his name; point to parts of his body; enumerate at least three objects in one of three simple pictures; repeat simple sentences, such as "I have a little dog"; name familiar objects, such as a key, a watch, a penny; and tell whether he is a little boy or a little girl. There is a group of tests for each year of age up to ten years, and a group each for the twelve-year-old level, the fourteen-year-old level, the sixteen-year-old, or average adult level, and the eighteen-year-old, or superior adult level. The results of the test are expressed in terms of mental age. That year level at which a child passes all the tests and beyond which he has one or more failures is taken as his "basal age." He is given credit in terms of mental-age months for each test passed in the groups above this basal-age group. For instance, if Mary Smith passes all the tests at the four-year level, two tests at the five-year level, and one at the six-year level, she is given a mental age of four years six months, or fifty-four months. Her intelligence quotient, or I. Q., is the quotient which expresses the relationship between her chronological age and her mental age. Should Mary have been four years and two months, or fifty months, old when tested, her I. Q. would have equaled $\frac{54}{50}$, or 108 (the decimal point is omitted in expressing I. Q.). Had she been exactly four years six months old, her I. Q. would have equaled 100. Again, had she been four years eight months of age when tested, her quotient would have equaled $\frac{54}{56}$, or 92. All this is probably well known even to the beginning student of education. However, it seems again and again necessary to point out that the I. Q. is not a fixed *quantity*, but a *measure of relationship*.

The giving of individual tests, such as the Stanford-Binet, which we have been considering, is time-consuming. Even a shorter form of the Binet test, such as the Herring Revision, is at present more than can be assured for every child. For the younger children, too, these tests may present considerable difficulty in the giving. Little children are not especially interested in answering questions or in looking at black-and-white pictures. They are socially too immature to care what the result of the test is, and it is often impossible to get any response from them on a test item which bores them. The Binet tests make no provision for refusals; if a child won't, the examiner must assume he can't. It does not take much imagination to realize what "won'ts" can do to an intelligence rating if the child loses two months of mental age for each refusal.

Again, these tests are at best not very broad or very varied. The child has relatively few chances to show what he knows, approximately only six at each age level. Since the lowest level for the Stanford Revision is three years, children of three and four have little opportunity indeed to reveal themselves. So the various adaptations of the Binet scale were soon seen to have very limited usefulness for young children. Accordingly, various steps have been taken to improve upon them, not all of which could possibly be enumerated here, but the most significant of which were the following: first, efforts were made to extend the scale downward, so that it would test infants, instead of beginning at three years. The Kuhlmann Revision accomplished this feat, providing for tests from the three-months-old level up. The uninitiated reader may say, "*How* can you test the intelligence of a three-months-old baby, who can't utter a word?" The answer is, by testing those responses we know he *should* be able to make to his environment, such as raising his head, spitting out a bitter substance, noticing a bright light. Responses such as these are tested by the Kuhlmann technique from the three-months-old level on.

The uninitiated might again inquire, "*Why* test young babies?" To this the answer is that in some situations it is imperative to know as accurately as possible what a baby's endowment is. Perhaps he is being considered for adoption; perhaps he is such a gifted, healthy baby that a special attempt might well be made to give him a fine chance in life or to study his growth in a psychological laboratory. Again, if the baby is slow, if he shows signs of feeble-mindedness, it is helpful to get an estimate of his possibilities as early as possible so that his regime may be planned wisely.

In his laboratory at the Yale psychoclinic, Dr. Gesell has elaborated a method of diagnosing the intelligence of babies and very young children which he calls a "developmental diagnosis." This diagnosis is not expressed in intelligence quotients, but is descriptive. At one month, two months, and all the other months and years thereafter, there are certain behavior responses which are typical. A normal child makes them; a subnormal child makes relatively few of them; a supernormal child makes responses which are normal or typical for a child older than himself. In studying children's behavior responses Dr. Gesell divides them into motor responses, language, adaptive behavior, personal-social behavior. He has drawn up his normative schedules after making an infinite number of observations in which he *compared* children of different age levels to get the typical reactions of each. A simplified normative schedule or description of behavior for a thirty-months-old child is the following:[1]

Normative Summary for Thirty-Months Level

Motor development: (1) Goes up and down stairs alone; (2) piles seven or eight blocks with co-ordination; (3) tries to stand on one foot; (4) copies vertical or horizontal line.

Language. (1) Points to seven pictures; (2) names five pictures.

Adaptive behavior. (1) Attempts to build bridge from model; (2) adapts to form-board with corrected initial error; (3) places one completion form; (4) marks twice for cross.

Personal-social behavior. (1) Gives full name; (2) helps mother to put away things.

Such, at two and a half years, is the child who at six will learn to read with reasonable ease, and, with wise guidance, at thirteen will graduate from the eighth grade. For Dr. Gesell's work and the observations of other psychologists indicate that as development begins, so will it in general proceed: the child who grows rapidly in his responses and adjustments in infancy will on the whole keep his accelerated pace throughout childhood; the one who develops slowly will tend to lag behind; the "average" child will be average still when he enters high school, that is, as far as *capacity* goes. Industry or laziness, poise or nervousness, success or failure in his social relationships, will of course affect the child's actual *achievement*.

Dr. Gesell's normative schedules give a more rounded and adequate measure of the ability of the child under six than

[1] Arnold Gesell, *Infancy and Human Growth*, pp. 134–135.

can be obtained from the few items on the Binet test. It is a painstaking piece of work to make a real developmental diagnosis, but because of its descriptive character the result is much more satisfying than a mere I. Q.

Young children delight in motor expression, and, as we have mentioned, are often negativistic about making verbal responses. Recognizing this and wishing to create a testing situation in which the child would express himself more fully and freely than he would or could through language alone, the late Dr. Baldwin at Iowa and his staff, Stutsman at Merrill-Palmer, and Anderson at the University of Minnesota, as well as other psychologists, have worked at the standardization of *performance tests*, or testing situations which require the manipulation of material. These performance tests employ picture puzzles, various "games" of inserting blocks of different shapes and sizes into form-boards, "matching games," blocks, and other devices. At each half year or so the child is expected to succeed in a given number of these performances. The results are usually expressed in terms of *percentile rank*, that is, the position of the individual child among any theoretical group of one hundred children his own age. If Mary is given a percentile rank of 98, this implies that her score would be equaled or excelled by only two out of every hundred children. This *percentile rank* of 98, which, as one can see, is a very superior rank, must on no account be confused with an I. Q. of 98. An I. Q. of 98, of course, is only an average intelligence rating. Again the scores are expressed in terms of "standard deviation," another statistical device for expressing a child's ability not in terms of I. Q., but in terms of his position in a group of children his own age. This method of expressing results is becoming more popular than the quotient method, because it is more meaningful for use in guidance.

Performance tests are interesting and appealing to children. They give examiners a chance to see the child when he is playing naturally and unselfconsciously, when his mind is off himself and on his task. This the question-and-answer test naturally did not do. Performance tests are in process of development; much more work is yet to be done before they will be really satisfactory instruments. Yet on the whole the correlation of their results with those of the Stanford-Binet is high enough to be significant, and because of their intrinsic interest they are much less difficult to use with small children. Whether the abilities the various performance items test always indicate *abstract intelligence* is not certain, and much remains to be done in trying out the real validity, as an indication of mental ability, of each game or puzzle used. But because of their interest and variety the examiner is able to get a much better picture of the child's whole personality than was possible in the Stanford-Binet test situation. What a child's attitude toward work is,— whether he is self-critical to a normal or an exaggerated degree, whether his interest span is characteristically long or short, how he reacts toward failure,— all these observations may be made in connection with performance tests.

If the giving of the Stanford-Binet test is time-consuming, the giving of a series of performance tests is much more so. The practicability of these instruments is much limited by the time factor involved. The lower school has a number of uses for intelligence tests: first, they are needed for diagnosing cases of individual difficulty; then they are needed for deciding what to do with gifted children, whether they are really so highly endowed that some special provision must be made for them or whether the school is already giving them all they need; again, intelligence tests are needed in the general grouping and classification of large numbers of children. Among the first-grade entrants in any town or city there are each year very bright children, average children, slow children, subnormal children. Especially when teachers must deal with large numbers in first-grade classes, an early, if tentative, classification into slow groups, average groups, and superior groups is probably helpful. Waiting for a child to demonstrate his ability through school achievement is not a very efficient method, since in large groups little help can be given him in overcoming his first difficulties of adjustment.

To meet this mass situation, there have been devised group tests of intelligence for use with children from four years of age up. Ingeniously devised so that the child need not read but merely follows verbal directions by marking in a booklet,— putting a tail on a cat, drawing a line around the hat the little girl lost, and so forth,— these tests are helpful as a sort of rough sieve to separate the very intelligent from the average and the subnormal. For individuals they are often very unreliable in their results; for groups of children these instruments are precise enough to be useful in rough, tentative classifications.

One of the first attempts at a nonreading mental test for young children was the Pintner-Cunningham test for kindergarten and first grade. However, when it is used with children of four and five years, only a small number should be tested at a time, and the examiner should be supplied with assistants who make sure that each child knows what he is expected to do: draw with his pencil, turn over his page, and so on. The Detroit Kindergarten Test is another example of a nonreading group examination. The Kuhlmann-Anderson and Metropolitan Readiness tests have been developed more recently and are very useful instruments. For slightly older children in the primary school there are a number of interesting group intelligence tests.

While most psychologists would positively enjoin teachers not to use individual intelligence tests without first taking long and arduous training in the theory and practice of testing, in the administration of mental examinations and in their interpretation, group tests may be used to advantage by capable teachers. They are not fine, precise instruments, and their administration requires good technique of group management rather than the establishment of rapport between child and adult. However, such tests when given by teachers should be supervised and interpreted by experts, and they should be carefully scored and checked, for the least carelessness invalidates the results. In situations where there is no school psychologist or public-school psychological bureau within call, other ways of securing expert psychological advice may still be available. Departments of psychology or education in colleges and universities can often supply such service. There are recognized consulting psychologists in private practice, and the facilities of the Educational Records Bureau in New York City or those of the Psychological Corporation may be engaged.

In the lower school, with the child up to the age of seven or eight, achievement tests in any subject but reading have no place. The value of reading tests was mentioned in an earlier chapter. Here we may simply restate the functions of the achievement test. To begin with, the test may be given simply as a survey, or it may be used for diagnosing individual and group difficulties. When a school or a teacher is selecting the instrument for an achievement test, thought should be taken as to the purpose of the examination. Whenever possible an experienced psychologist should guide the selection. There are excellent tests on the market which are interesting only for purposes of comparing classes and ages and different grades in the country at large. There are other tests which also make interschool comparisons possible, but which are especially valuable in showing just where a class or an individual excels or falls short, and what remedial teaching is needed. Dr. Gates's reading tests, before cited, are a splendid example of diagnostic testing; properly studied, the results of these will show whether a child's weakness in reading is due to faulty word recognition, or to failure in getting the thought of a sentence, or to inability to read with reasonable speed, or what not.

Like other achievement tests, the scores on reading tests may be translated into subject ages. A child who makes a reading score equal to that of the average seven-year-old has a *reading age* of seven. Perhaps a comparison of his score with general age standards may show that he falls somewhere between seven and eight, say at seven years seven months. These measures are valuable data for child guidance, especially when studied in relation to the child's mental-test rating.

Because tests and testing programs are so much discussed in schools today, it is necessary for every teacher, even a beginning teacher, to think through for herself where the real values of objective measurement lie and how the results of testing should be used. As a start, it will help to consider what educational leaders who are very much interested in objective measurement claim for it. There is, first of all, the undoubted advantage of getting an estimate of the ability and achievement of one's pupils which is untinged by personal prejudice. There is, in the second place, the advantage of having norms, or standards, which represent the distribution of intelligence and the average work being done throughout the country with which to compare the intelligence and achievement of the pupils in a certain school or grade. There is, in the third place, a great satisfaction in placing child management and education on a more scientific basis by assembling, classifying, and generalizing from a survey of definite facts instead of a conglomeration of feelings, enthusiasms, prejudices, and sentimentalities. There is the great satisfaction of definiteness. Again, the results of using both mental and achievement tests yield interesting comparative data: not merely may the achievement of Grade 4 in School X be compared with the achievement of fourth grades throughout the country, but also what Miss Jones did with this group can be considered in the light of the intelligence with which nature endowed its members. The guidance of individual children, remedial teaching in certain grades, the supervision of teachers in service, and the training of student teachers, all can proceed much more intelligently than formerly because of all we have learned and are learning through the accumulation and study of objective evidence.

Yet no thoughtful student of education can deem the testing movement, as it has developed in some schools and systems, an unmixed blessing. Certain dangers and difficulties are very apparent. These have been discussed elsewhere by many other writers, but a reminder of them is in place here. The desire for tangible, measurable results may lead to an emphasis on the sort of teaching which lends itself to testing: overemphasis on drill, the cramming of facts. Such overemphasis may result in neglect of certain less tangible but more important educational values. If it can be proved that a teacher gets as good results in reading, writing, and arithmetic when she teaches forty-five children as when she teaches thirty-five, the demonstration should not be used as an argument for classes of forty-five or fifty. One would need to know, first, what was sacrificed in the way of desirable social attitudes and the finer appreciations in the scramble to teach forty-five children to read and write and cipher. This seems especially important with the classes in the lower school, although it is not to be ignored anywhere in the school.

Again, the results of a testing program may be badly misunderstood unless a qualified person explains them clearly to supervisors and teachers. Group tests, it must always be remembered, can be very unreliable for individuals when they are used to estimate general intelligence. Achievement tests may be quite unfair to some really fine teaching if they are not well chosen. Factors other than intelligence make for success in school: a bright child whose achievement seems unworthy of his mental endowment is not necessarily loafing, nor is his teacher to be judged incompetent without further evidence. The personal equation can never be left out in judging people.

It must not be thought that the leaders in the mental-testing movement today are unaware of the limitations of objective measurement. Indeed, they are well cognizant of them, and are endeavoring to decrease them by greater and greater care in the selection and validation of test material, by more and more accurate and simple directions for administering tests, and by the provision of every possible help in the way of explanation and interpretation. Above all, attention is being centered upon the development of more objective methods of judging the more intangible results of teaching and of rating personality traits. The number of good rating scales for use by teachers or supervisors or psychologists is constantly increasing; they are designed to bring out in individuals the qualities other than intelligence which make for success or failure in life. There are great difficulties in the making of these new instruments, and any one of them may leave a critic with a sense of great incompleteness; but the fact that there are difficulties should not discourage the use of the various methods, formal and informal, suggested for the measurement of personal qualities. If these efforts did no more than constantly remind teachers, administrators, and parents that character development *is* the final aim of education, and that the more subtle traits of aggressiveness and shyness, perseverance and flightiness, honesty, and ability to face reality are of paramount importance, they would still be exceedingly valuable.

The uses to which the results of mental and educational testing should be put may well be given thought. The first and most obvious use is for the school office files. A cumulative record of achievement-test scores and a periodic record of intelligence-test results over a period of years afford valuable information to be used in the guidance of individuals. Records of this sort should be available for teachers when needed, provided the teachers have studied educational measurement enough to understand something of their significance, and provided they are so professionally minded that the records of individual children will not be discussed • carelessly.

Again, the substance of test results gives a good background for discussions between parents and school principals or psychologists or visiting teachers. Classroom teachers should not quote such records in their contacts with parents without the approval and permission of the principal or psychologist. The chances of misunderstanding are too great, and much damage can be done to children by careless discussion of their intelligence-test ratings. Parents are frequently resentful of low ratings and sometimes boastful about high ones. Psychologists themselves frequently find difficulty in this connection; but they should be allowed to work out their difficulties with the co-operation of the school office and without the interference of the classroom teacher, who is herself not trained for fine interpretation of tests. Individual experts follow their own best judgments in what they do about telling parents results of tests. A general rule which many follow is to tell the parent the general classification into which the child falls, that is, very intelligent, above average, average, slightly below average, or "developing slowly." This is a safe procedure if for no other reason than because the results of an intelligence test are far from completely reliable. The Stanford Revision of the Binet-Simon in the hands of a qualified examiner, for instance, is theoretically reliable only within five points and, on a retest, often varies much more than five points. That is to say, if Mary, who tested I. Q. 116 at five, tests only 111 upon re-examination at seven years of age, there is no criticism upon the accuracy of the examiner in either case. If she tests 121, it does not reflect upon the previous examination either. The best-trained of psychologists may even get two test results varying by more than five points.

In the lower school especially it is most unfortunate for teachers or supervisors to accept an I. Q. as a final picture of a child's ability. To begin with, preschool children do not take examinations seriously and often are too immature socially to co-operate in a mental test. Again, preschool children come from widely different home environments. The public school is a powerful factor in leveling differences in home environment, but the young child has been subjected to this equalizing influence for a very short time, if at all.

Tests and retests of nursery-school children made at the Merrill-Palmer School and elsewhere show how great may be the changes in results of tests during a year of nursery-school attendance. Many children gain from ten to fifteen points in intelligence quotient after a year in the nursery group. This probably means that because of the child's age and social experience he was unable to cope with the testing situation properly in the first instance. It may also mean that nursery-school experiences have given him indirect training for the tests. Through being at school, seeing many strange adults, and playing with a group of children, he gained the social poise to respond to his second test in a way in which he could not respond to his first. The opinion of most competent psychologists is that the theoretical I. Q. is constant; that is, that the relationship between mental development and chronological age is a continuing ratio that does not shift and change. However, unless one can guarantee a perfect examination situation, an omniscient examiner, and a perfect testing instrument, one must expect the I. Q., as estimated by intelligence tests, to vary sometimes with the child's physical condition, his moods, and with his rapport or antipathy toward a particular examiner.

In progressive schools, where the procedure is informal and the curriculum requirements are flexible, wisely interpreted objective tests serve as a valuable means of checking achievement. They give teachers and administrators the chance to compare the achievement of their groups with averages for grade children throughout the country. But the progressive school using tests as a check differs a great deal from the test-ridden school in which such examinations are regarded as all-important. To the progressive lower school the results of tests would always be a means to an end, rather than ends in themselves. The fact that the children in the first grade of a progressive school are not up to standard in reading need not necessarily concern the school head at all; perhaps ends other than reading seem more important for that group. But it is well to have some means of knowing where they are in comparison with other groups, rather than guessing it, even if one does not think it necessary or wise to try to force the group up to standard. Sometimes, too, the test result comes as a wholesome reminder that reading is being neglected, or, on the other hand, that children and teacher are putting much more time on it than is necessary, since the scores are far above first-grade norms.

In reading current discussions of education, one is at times conscious of a wide gulf between the strong trend toward measurement and rigid classification on the basis of results of tests on the one hand and individual freedom and the flexible classification of many of the laboratory schools on the other. Much improved practice in lower-school classrooms would come of a real effort to bring the two aims into mutually helpful relationships. Testing and placement would then be regarded as a means toward individual growth rather than administrative devices for teaching-efficiency in the narrow sense of the word, and as methods of classification in accordance with what is found concerning their results in individual cases.

The gradual development and perfection of means for estimating the finer outcomes of teaching — social adjustment, appreciation, growth in interest and in the technique of creative work — will in all probability result in the correction of the greatest weakness in the original testing movement, namely, its tendency to focus attention upon the less important elements in teaching to the neglect of the more fundamental. As these develop and, above all, as teachers and specialists achieve better insight into the application of tests and ratings in individual guidance, objective measurement will be more and more directed toward the gathering of data which give real insight into the nature of the development of personality.

BIBLIOGRAPHY

ARTHUR, MARY GRACE. A Point Scale of Performance Tests. Commonwealth Fund, New York Division of Publications, 1930.

   Employs a number of the same tests used in the Pintner-Paterson scale. Main purpose: to supplement the Binet rating. Usable for children five to sixteen.

ATKINS, R. E. [Measurements of the Intelligence of Young Children by an Object-Fitting Test. University of Minnesota Press, Minneapolis, 1931.

CUNNINGHAM, K. S. Measurements of Early Levels of Intelligence. Teachers College, Columbia University, New York, 1927.

DRISCOLL, GERTRUDE P. The Developmental Status of the Preschool Child as a Prognosis of Future Development. Teachers College, Columbia University, New York, 1933.

> The predictive value of the preschool test is limited. Prognosis on the basis of a composite rating better than a mere I. Q.

GAMBRILL,'B. L. Analytical List of Kindergarten-Primary Tests of Intelligence and Achievement. Whitlock's Bookstore, New Haven, Conn., 1927.

> A complete inventory up to 1927.

GESELL, ARNOLD. Mental Growth of the Preschool Child. Macmillan, New York, 1925.

> Dr. Gesell's first book about his developmental study of children. Includes many interesting and instructive photographs.

HALLOWELL, D. K. Mental Tests for Preschool Children. University of Pennsylvania, 1928.

HILDRETH, GERTRUDE H. A Bibliography of Mental Tests and Rating Scales, pp. 28–31. The Psychological Corporation, New York, 1933.

> Lists tests of mental capacity for children of preschool and kindergarten levels.

HILGARD, JOSEPHINE R. "Learning and Maturation in Preschool Children," *Pedagogical Seminary and Journal of Genetic Psychology* (September, 1932), Vol. XLI, pp. 36–56.

> Seems to show that specific training has only a small effect upon such skills as climbing stairs, buttoning buttons, and cutting with scissors in the third year.

KUHLMANN, FREDERICK. A Handbook of Mental Tests. Warwick and York, Baltimore, 1922.

> A complete account of Kuhlmann's revision of the Stanford-Binet test. Tests described begin at the three-months level.

KUHLMANN, F., and ANDERSON, R. G. Intelligence Tests for Grade I to Maturity. Educational Test Bureau, Minneapolis, Minn., 1927.

National College of Education. Curriculum Records of the Children's School, by members of the staff, pp. 504–547, "The Functions of the Psychology Department." Bureau of Publications, National College of Education, Evanston, Ill., 1932.

PINTNER, R. Intelligence Testing (rev. ed.). Henry Holt, New York, 1931.

PINTNER, R., and PATERSON D. A Scale of Performance Tests. Appleton, New York, 1917.

> Describes the Pintner-Paterson scale of performance tests. This scale is usable for children five years of age and older.

RUST, M. M. Effect of Resistance on the Intelligence-Test Scores of Young Children. Teachers College, Columbia University, New York, 1931.

An interesting statistical study.

STUTSMAN, R. Mental Measurement of Preschool Children. World Book Company, Yonkers, N. Y., 1931.

A comprehensive account of the standardization and use of the Merrill-Palmer performance tests for preschool children. Excellent illustrations from the clinical notes made by the psychologist in using these tests.

UPDEGRAFF, RUTH. "The Determination of a Reliable Intelligence Quotient for the Young Child," *Pedagogical Seminary and Journal of Genetic Psychology* (September, 1932), Vol. XLI, pp. 152–166.

Shows the advisability of waiting until a child is accustomed to the new group situation before giving tests.

VAN ALSTYNE, D. Environment of Three-Year-Old Children. Teachers College, Columbia University, New York, 1929.

A study of the relationship between environment and individual growth. Interesting and suggestive for any student of child development.

WEBB, L. W., and SHOTWELL, ANNA M. Standard Tests in the Elementary School: Nursery School to Sixth Grade. Ray Long and Richard R. Smith, New York, 1932.

Chapter V, "Intelligence Tests for Nursery School and Kindergarten Children"; Chapter VI, "Intelligence Tests for Grades I, II, and III."

WELLMAN, BETH L. "Some New Bases for the Interpretation of the I. Q.," *Pedagogical Seminary and Journal of Genetic Psychology* (September, 1932), Vol. XLI, pp. 116–126.

Seems to show that I.Q. ratings jump on an average of 7.8 from autumn to spring and decrease on an average of 0.9 during summer in the case of nursery-school children.

CHAPTER XV

RECORDS AND RECORD KEEPING

When schools were concerned merely with providing a literary education, records were not difficult to keep. Enrollment and attendance were recorded in the teacher's roll book, which, once compulsory attendance was in force, became a legal document. Progress was recorded in terms of passes and failures, expressed in the form of per cent or some arbitrary system of letter classification; promotion or non-promotion was justified by marks; and the teacher's arbitrary judgment or the principal's ultimatum was delivered to the pupil and his parents without benefit of explanation. The reports sent home in the course of the school term were the briefest and most succinct, showing nothing beyond the fact that children were passing, failing, or distinguished in their work, and that individual conduct was good, bad, or indifferent.

Gradually the progress of health legislation and the growing interest in the physical hygiene of school children made necessary the recording of vaccination, physical examinations, and the recommendations of school physicians and nurses; and these data were collected and preserved in the form of a cumulative record passed on from grade to grade or, in cases of transfer, from school to school. Often the material as recorded was intelligible only to the person writing it upon the child's card, and the whole process of entering and preserving information on health was perfunctory in the extreme.

Significant changes in the whole character of school records followed naturally and inevitably upon the acceptance by the school of broader responsibilities for child training and child welfare. When character education — the growth of the whole child as a member of society — became a recognized aim of education, many things other than attendance and absence and promotion and failure became of interest to the administrator, and the need for more descriptive data about individuals and groups was acutely felt. The increasing use of standardized tests of intelligence and achievement demanded some sort of cumulative recording; and where curriculum revision was undertaken, the need for more minute description of classroom activities became increasingly apparent.

At the outset it must be admitted that not all schools have kept pace with the times in the matter of keeping records, just as not all of them have kept abreast of the changing curriculum. But in the more progressive systems teachers and administrators are alike experimenting in the attempt to develop records which shall be significant, accurate, and practical from the point of view of the time and effort involved in the keeping of them. In certain progressive schools most elaborate descriptive material is collected; in the fully staffed schools the school psychologist and, indeed, the parents assist in the accumulation of data. The National College of Education at Evanston, Illinois, in a publication called *Curriculum Records of the Children's School*, publishes a minute account of the records kept from the nursery school up through the sixth grade, which will repay careful reading by anyone deeply interested in the subject of keeping records. Such elaborate recording is beyond the resources of the average good school; but the material which it brings together is valuable for purposes of research, and the record plan itself is suggestive and helpful for study, even if only a small part of it can be generally adopted.

For purposes of discussion the records of the lower school may be classified according to the following general plan: (1) cumulative records for the school office; (2) records of classroom activities; (3) records to be used as bases for reports to parents and for recommendations to adults other than the child's teacher who may be interested in his welfare; (4) records representing data for educational research. The relative importance of these varies with the age of the child and the general character and purpose of the individual school.

Cumulative records in the school office should be adequate to serve as data for the solution of any problems relating to the transfer of children to other schools, for dealing with cases of truancy, and for furnishing the minimum information required in cases of commitment to institutions. Needless to say, the school office must keep on file any information which might be required by the board of education in the discharge of its duties to the community. This minimum of legal recording is equivalent to "child accounting," as the term is used in school surveys. Such accounting has been vastly improved in efficiency in the last fifteen or twenty years. The Cleveland Survey, the report of which was published in 1915, mentions the fact that at that time child-accounting systems were inadequate and unsatisfactory. Of late, owing to the increasing study of education at the universities, the practice of encouraging school surveys, and the general interest in accumulating significant educational data, methods of recording have been greatly refined. In addition to information on attendance and promotion, good office records at the present time usually show the results of standard achievement tests given annually and of group intelligence tests given biennially or at longer intervals. In schools which include a psychologist or a visiting teacher on their staffs more elaborate records of individual progress are kept in special files.

There is some discussion at the present time as to who shall have access to the material accumulated on office cards. Some think that such information should be reserved for the use of school administrators; others believe that teachers, who, in these enlightened days, are supposed to understand the general principles of objective measurement, also should have access to official information. Still others hold that teachers should have all the information available, but with the following provisos: classroom teachers should receive complete information on previously accumulated records only after they have had time and opportunity to form their own independent judgment of their pupil's ability; they should be permitted to consult records only after they have given evidence of the knowledge about objective measurements which the understanding of such records requires; they should be put in possession of confidential data only after they have demonstrated a high standard of professional ethics. Satisfactory professional ethics preclude gossiping about pupils to other teachers, or discussing school records without the advice and approval of the school administration, or talking carelessly or maliciously about pupils in the community after school hours. Teachers need all the available information about their pupils that there is; but it is necessary to use this information with intelligence and discretion.

Records of classroom activities have been mentioned before in the course of this book. They can be exceedingly valuable; indeed, many people believe that they are the most important factor in the intelligent reorganization of curricula. They can also be quite valueless, as well as prodigal of the teacher's time and effort. In every individual situation teachers and supervisors together need to decide what records of classroom activities can be kept effectively, always bearing in mind that such records are a means to an end and should eventually result in better teaching. If they distract the teacher's attention from her teaching or take the time and energy which should go into preparation for the next day's work, the keeping of records is a mistake. On the other hand, no teacher should be so overworked that a minimum of descriptive recording becomes the last straw. Such a minimum in a well-staffed school with classes of thirty-five to forty children would be the following:

1. A description of the units of work covered, telling how

the unit originated, the direction followed by the work, the references and community resources utilized, the time involved in carrying the unit out, the results of the work from the point of view of the whole group, and a few significant comments on results in individual cases.

2. Every teacher who is attempting anything like "progressive" teaching should keep rough, running notes of unusual happenings — the sort of notes which can be jotted down in the course of a hasty trip to one's desk or some other convenient spot. The habit of keeping such notes can be acquired, like any other habit, and the data accumulated are very significant, provided they are periodically organized and digested. The material comes to be a good check upon the progress of individual children, a significant indication of how the group is progressing as a whole, and also serves to give the teacher a little insight into how her own mind is working. The kind of happening she notices and records is an indication of her real aims, as well as of difficulties which cause her distress.

In the last chapter the development of habit inventories as a step toward a better definition of the goals of teaching was mentioned. During the era of inventories the "diary record" was perfected as a technique. These records were mostly made by trained graduate students who were not burdened with the work of classroom teaching. Diary records, at the zenith of their prestige, purported to give a complete and accurate picture of everything a certain child did during a given period of time. No interpretation was permitted to the recorder. For instance, "Mary seemed very happy when she came to kindergarten this morning and appeared glad to see the children" was not acceptable. An approved record would read, "Mary came in smiling, hung her coat and hat on the hook, arranged her hair with her right hand, went over to the sand table, and began to build a tunnel, shouting to Charles, 'See what I do!'" On the basis of protracted recording such as this, Mary was finally rated on a habit inventory.

Such meticulous note taking is beyond the capabilities of a hard-working teacher. Nor is the amount of detail amassed truly valuable unless someone is at hand to organize and interpret it. Too elaborate records defeat their own purpose : the mass of detail obscures the important points, and one fails to see the woods, on account of all the trees. The informal jotting down of significant happenings is, for most teachers, the best approximation to a good diary record possible ; such selective note taking is simultaneously a way of organizing, in the sense that important items alone are recorded. One might ask, "How is importance to be estimated ?" To this the reply is that the very fact that a certain happening *seemed* important to a teacher *makes* it important for her in that situation. The taking of such notes in the first busy days of the school year frequently more than repays the effort, in the valuable comparisons with later happenings which these early comments make possible.

When difficulty is encountered with an individual child, it is sometimes well to confine one's note taking for a week or two to the activities of that child. Looking back over the notes often changes one's original judgment. "Jimmy is *very* quarrelsome," says Miss Smith to herself. After a week or so of recording Jimmy's quarrels she may conclude that, after all, he doesn't start the quarrels : he is just the sort of child who always gets himself into the middle of the picture and gets the blame. Recording the doings of Jimmy may well give Miss Smith a new insight into the personality traits of Sammy and Susie and Mary as well.

The collecting and recording of data helpful in making reports to parents is receiving much attention in progressive schools, because these schools are making a strenuous effort to devise report forms which shall be meaningful and which shall challenge the home to co-operate intelligently with the school. Such reports stress the character traits which the child shows in the course of his work and play at school — traits which are apparently responsible for his success or failure. Usually the descriptive material is collected by asking teachers to make out long reports two or three times a year, rating the children on various items of behavior and commenting on progress. A simple method of rating is the following:

Does this child (1) sometimes   (2) often   (3) never
    attack his work with energy?
    carry out his plans persistently?
    criticize his own performance?
    keep his hands away from his face?
    refrain from chewing on his pencil?
    stand with ease and poise?
    sit quietly?

Provided the list of items to be noted is well selected, significant, and not too long, a rating such as this has great value. First, it forces the teacher to think carefully about the individual child; second, it focuses attention on important matters; third, it makes it possible to interview parents on the basis of full, objective descriptions of their children as they appear in the school environment. No one would wish to prevent the teacher from making her own running comments on a report like this; or perhaps one should say, no one would be willing to keep her from making comments. But the list of traits which she has before her and the suggested method of recording her judgments add to the objectivity of her report.

Reports such as this seem particularly important for children in the preschool and early grades. For one thing, they help the parent who wonders why he sends his child to school at three and four and five, to see that the school is vitally interested in teaching things very different from the three R's. Again, they help parents see their children objectively. When there is disagreement between school and home as to a child's standing on a certain trait, say, the ability to work by himself, very interesting discussions can be motivated. The disagreement may be entirely justified. Perhaps this child does behave in one way at school and in another way at home. The interesting question is, Why?

In one progressive school, before a report system such as the one just described was put into operation, the parents were invited to meet with the teachers and the head of the school and to suggest the traits upon which they would like to have reports about their children. All the suggestions offered at the meeting were considered before a final selection was made. As a sort of preliminary exercise in the use of such report forms, the parents themselves were asked to fill out the forms, on the basis of home observation, and submit them to the school.

To repeat, the use of such report forms is successful when the list of behavior items is not too long. Parents become almost as impatient about reading overlong reports as teachers do about writing them.

When records are being kept for purposes of research, the nature of the research determines the character of the records. Sometimes the purpose is to evaluate play materials; again, many studies have been made on curriculum content; and another large group of studies is directed toward the understanding of children's personalities. So the material gathered may be concerned with children's use of equipment, with the description of group and individual activities, with the success which groups or individuals achieve in the tool subjects, or with data about social and emotional reactions. In any case the matter must be accurately recorded and clearly and legibly preserved in either descriptive or tabular form. All such accumulation of material for research requires an enormous amount of clerical work, work that must be carried out with conscientious precision. How much of this work should be expected of teachers and how much should be done by research assistants or trained clerical workers must be considered carefully in any school before the gathering of data is undertaken.

Curriculum Records of the Children's School, previously mentioned as published by the National College of Education, includes material for practically every sort of educational research. A large part of the book is devoted to records of units of work, another large part to program arrangements and sketches of various school days, and still another part to the recording of "progress in terms of school subjects." In the last part of the book, "Individual Records and their Use," there are described reports from teachers in nursery school, kindergarten, and grades, reports from special teachers, and reports from parents to the schools. The school physician's records and reports to the home are included also, as well as various reports on personality and achievement kept by the school psychologist. All the forms have been worked over with great care and are probably as complete and adequate as any records now in use. Very interesting, too, are the uses to which individual profile graphs accompanied by explanatory letters are put in reporting to parents.

Such elaborate records are neither feasible nor really necessary in typical school situations, but their development in the National College of Education and in other progressive schools is nevertheless a service to the schools of the country. They demonstrate what can be done in a system of complete reporting, and from this demonstration individual schools can select those elements appropriate to their particular situations.

In a summary of the important points about record keeping in the lower school the following suggestions may be offered: (1) Those reports which are absolutely essential for the child's welfare and health, such as the interchange of records between nursery-school teachers and parents, must be taken care of first of all. (2) Cumulative records for adequate "child accounting" in the school system must be well worked out and scrupulously kept. (3) Enough must be achieved in the way of descriptive reports of class activities to assure progress in curriculum revision. (4) Reports about individual children should stress important character traits rather than bare school achievement and should be sufficiently descriptive in character to be meaningful. (5) Reports to parents should be so framed that they are a means of parent education as well as a form of "child accounting." (6) Teachers and school administrators should think of records as means toward ends, rather than as ends in themselves. Their real purpose is to help teachers to do better teaching and to create a finer understanding and co-operation between the home, the school, and the community in the interest of children. (7) The recording of data for the specific purpose of educational research should be undertaken only when it can be done without prejudice to the regular work of the school staff.

In the long run all records, no matter how slight, if they are conscientiously taken, may prove valuable both for research and for the immediate welfare of children, parents, and teachers.

CHAPTER XVI

THE PROFESSION OF LOWER-SCHOOL TEACHING

Lower-school teaching was once considered a ladylike occupation for the girl of good family, limited intelligence, and motherly instincts. Today it is a profession offering to the gifted abundant opportunity for original work and, in many progressive school systems, affording recognition and remuneration on a par with those enjoyed by upper-school teachers. There is no longer a dearth of candidates for lower-school positions who shall have the equivalent of normal-school training; on the contrary, in filling most lower-grade vacancies school boards and their representatives may pick and choose among several well-trained applicants. For this reason a discussion of the personal qualifications which seem to make for success in this field of work may not be out of place.

The teacher of young children should be physically vigorous. For nursery-school work the physical endurance needed by a hospital nurse is actually demanded, and even in the primary grades no one can make a satisfactory adjustment who is not inured to being on her feet a good part of the day or who is not able to stand the biting wind which often sweeps across the school playground. Children in their active play are warm and comfortable out of doors on many days when the cold puts a real strain upon their teachers, who, by reason of preference and convention, do not romp. Attempting to do lower-school work without actually possessing the requisite physique to survive such inconveniences easily places an undue strain upon one's endurance. Such strain frequently shows itself in emotional difficulties.

Today, and even more distinctly tomorrow, the teacher

of the lower grades must be sufficiently gifted and well trained intellectually to grasp the underlying significance of modern studies of growth. Less and less is the work of a teacher thought to be summed up in teaching skills and content ; more and more is she expected to be an expert in the guidance of growing children. In addition, the very teaching of skills and content is becoming increasingly scientific. The well-equipped teacher is expected to evaluate the various suggestions which psychologists make for drill and for testing and to assist supervisory and administrative officers in their use of standard test material. She stands in a position with regard to the individual child which is very different from that of the school administrator or the expert psychologist who occasionally visits the grade : she knows, or should know, the child as he reacts day after day in the varied activities of work and play. The modern teacher should understand how to use her knowledge ; just as she should be able to evaluate tests and textbooks, she should be able to gauge the objectivity and value of her own observations. Further, the modern teacher of even the youngest children requires an academic training both broad and thorough in order to carry out adequately an activity curriculum. She must know what to teach as well as how to teach, and, above all, she must know where to look for what she does not know ; that is, she must have an elementary knowledge of how to do research.

In the early days of kindergarten and freer primary work the ability to sing and play and the ability to draw cleverly were considered prime requisites. Now, though these abilities are still much appreciated as very helpful in working with the small child, they are certainly held subordinate to general intelligence, academic training, and the rudiments of psychological insight. The victrola and the radio can compensate for lack of musical ability. Taste and musical appreciation are needed for the intelligent use of these substitutes, but these depend upon general education and cultural background rather than upon specific talent. Teachers who have very little ability with plastic materials can encourage and direct astonishingly good work on the part of their pupils, provided, of course, their artistic standards are good and their appreciation of the process of creative work is keen. A feeling for the general qualities of plastic materials through having played with them oneself, a discernment which recognizes honest effort, and an appreciation of art which recognizes the creative spark are much to be preferred to the mere ability to do clever things oneself, useful as this may be as an added qualification. Parenthetically one might add that the person who is very skillful herself has harder work to resist the temptation of changing a child's product by a deft poke or one stroke of the brush than the person who is not.

However, the more decidedly emotional traits of a candidate for lower-school teaching influence her success in most radical fashion. The old-fashioned idea was that it takes endless patience to work with little children. Probably it does; but we have learned to discriminate between a make-believe patience which the quick-tempered person laboriously "keeps" and the patience which is born of such a real interest in growth that it hardly amounts to patience at all. The latter sort of patience is the distinguishing quality of the first-rate nursery-school worker and, to a lesser degree, of the lower-grade teacher. The forced sort of patience probably accounts for not a few nervous breakdowns among teachers and for very many unhappy children. A child feels when you "keep your patience." Perhaps if one has to keep it, it is actually better to lose it. Children react in a rather wholesome way to an occasional loss of temper on the part of a usually pleasant and helpful adult.

There is a good deal of discussion nowadays about how much adults should try to keep any expressions of annoyance out of their dealings with the young. Some people say that it is much better to be cross, express annoyance, and be done with it, as was suggested above; others think that a neutral, quiet emotional atmosphere is so necessary for small children that adults who cannot maintain such an atmosphere had better not try to deal with them. A sensible middle ground seems to be this: any "regular" person has some temper, and occasionally shows it. Small children can be exceedingly irritating, especially if they choose to be annoying at a time when, because of some other reason, the adult's temper is particularly short. A headache, an argument at the family breakfast table, a sleepless night, do something to a teacher's nerves, as well as to children. When truly irritating situations arise, it is probably better to give vent to one's annoyance; but if they arise very often, then the teacher herself needs attention. Maybe she is in the wrong job; maybe she is overworked; maybe her irritation with the children is just a reflection of her own dissatisfaction with life. In any case she should look into the matter intelligently; for children should not be subjected to frequent outbursts of temper, just as teachers should not be expected to repress natural irritation all the time.

According to the older idea of a successful teacher, the children should be very fond of her, perhaps also a little afraid of her. In any case, what we now call a strong emotional rapport was expected between the successful lower-school teacher and her children. In the discussion on mental health in the lower school it was mentioned that expert opinion at present holds such rapport to be an important factor in the child's development, and very necessary at one stage of his growth; but according to the modern theory it should not be so intense that the child cannot go on happily to another teacher. From the teacher's angle of the matter, if she tends to call forth from her children an affection so strong that they are miserable about leaving her, one suspects that her own emotional adjustment is not a very satisfactory one. She is seeking and getting from her pupils an emotional gratification which she is failing to find in her other human relationships. It is easy to see how and why some very good teachers find themselves in this sort of difficulty: their work is an absorbing one; their energy, time, and funds for out-of-school diversions are distinctly limited.

Often, too, they have been unable during their training to have as much enjoyment as young people need. Accordingly, they look to their profession for all their satisfactions. This is not the wisest way of planning one's professional life. Other interests — social, intellectual, and emotional — must be sought if one is to be enough of an all-round person to be a really good lower-school teacher.

Indifference, the "I put on my hat and walk out with the children" attitude, is truly deplorable and altogether incompatible with a really professional attitude. On the other hand, staying at school till all hours of the day, getting so identified with one's pupils that one feels intensely their every joy and sorrow, or blaming oneself for every pupil's failure, are almost equally disastrous. The teacher must realize at the outset her limitations in remaking the characters of her pupils. They are in school for only a part of their waking time — only five days a week; at the most, ten months of the year. The rest of their time they are living with their families and subjected to all sorts of community influences — good, bad, and indifferent. The teacher cannot work against all these outside influences and achieve miracles; she has to work with those influences which are good, do her best while the children are in school, try to understand their home conditions, and leave the rest to destiny while she herself goes on to work out her own personal problems.

The training of teachers in service has received much attention in the last ten or fifteen years, and it has been a great boon to the teacher of young children. When one's whole job amounted to dropping down to the level of a five-year-old or six-year-old for several hours a day and teaching him the rudiments of learning, lower-school teaching was a dismal calling; but once teachers in service were encouraged to study psychology and were urged to undertake research in curriculum reconstruction, the whole outlook changed. Certainly, too, the classrooms of our country have been quite remade as a result of the new techniques of teaching which teachers in service have been able to acquire through extramural courses, summer school, and well-planned teachers' meetings. Nothing enhances one's enjoyment of one's life work more than the determination to find out all one can about it. But this study, like tests and measurements, record keeping, and several other modern additions to school work must remain a means to an end — the better teaching of children. Perhaps one should add the better teaching of children because the teacher herself has acquired a larger personality through achieving a broader outlook. When courses and classes are engaged in to such an extent that teachers turn up in their classrooms at eight thirty too tired to do good teaching, or when they must dash away on the minute of three so that they can arrive at a lecture at three thirty (probably too breathless to gain anything from it), the fact that such further education is not an end in itself seems to have been forgotten. Real good for the schools and real professional advancement for teachers are not acquired through the mere accumulation of credits. Courses should be organized and engaged in in the hope and belief that they will help alert, growing teachers to do creative work in their classrooms. This is the one sound *raison d'être* for plans to educate teachers in service.

Studies in mental hygiene have demonstrated on the whole that in dealing with their children those parents are the most successful whose own lives are full and satisfying; that the parent with many worth-while interests of his very own is the one who holds the affection and respect of growing boys and girls. The martyr type of parent, even when martyrdom seems justified by poverty, seldom succeeds well in the all-important job of child guidance. The same thing is surely true of teachers.

A successful lower-school teacher has a life of her own outside of school. This balancing out-of-school life enables her to take the inevitable jars and rubs of her professional existence sanely and objectively. Being objective, she realizes that the troublesome children in her grade are not aiming their misdemeanors at her, but are troublesome because of maladjustments in which she plays a very small part, if any part at all.

In summary, the profession of lower-school teaching to-day requires adequate preliminary training and well-planned graduate study. Professional study carried on while in service as a teacher should lead to a better understanding of general educational problems and probably to increased proficiency in some one phase of lower-school work: child guidance, educational testing, the techniques of remedial teaching, or methods of curriculum construction. For some teachers special professional study should be undertaken in the arts — music or painting or modeling — or, perhaps, in the industrial arts. Some part of the time given to study for professional advancement should go in every case toward an enrichment of the content of one's own knowledge: of history or literature or languages or mathematics, as individual tastes may dictate. In addition, the lower-school teacher should cultivate hobbies and other activities with no direct relation to her profession, and within the limits of her time and strength she should have an interesting and varied social existence, taking an active part in community life.

This is very far from the old idea of the drab and devoted "little-read schoolma'am" — as far as the warm, cheerful, modern school building is from the little red schoolhouse. But this new lower-school teacher is indispensable for the development of the new school: it is on her intelligence, her leadership, and her professional enthusiasm that progressive education ultimately depends.

INDEX